MORAL ENCOUNTERS IN TOURISM

This first full length treatment of the role of morality in tourism examines how the tourism encounter is also fundamentally a moral encounter. Drawing upon interdisciplinary perspectives, leading and new authors in the field address topics that range from volunteer tourism to fertility tourism to reveal new insights into the ways tourism encounters are implicated in, and contribute to, broader moral reconfigurations in Western and non-Western contexts.

Illustrating the role of power and power relations in tourism encounters within different political, economic, environmental and cultural contexts, the authors in this anthology analyse, theoretically and empirically, the implications of the privileging of some moralities at the expense of others. Key themes include the moral consumption of tourism experiences, embodiment in tourism encounters, environmental moralities as well as methodological aspects of morality in tourism research. Crossing disciplinary and chronological boundaries, *Moral Encounters in Tourism* provides a much-anticipated overview of this new interdisciplinary terrain and offers possible routes for new research on the intersection of morality and tourism studies.

Current Developments in the Geographies of Leisure and Tourism

Series Editors:

Jan Mosedale, University of Applied Sciences HTW Chur, Switzerland and **Caroline Scarles**, University of Surrey, UK and in association with the Geographies of Leisure and Tourism Research Group of the Royal Geographical Society (with the Institute of British Geographers)

Tourism and leisure exist within an inherently dynamic, fluid and complex world and are therefore inherently interdisciplinary. Recognizing the role of tourism and leisure in advancing debates within the social sciences, this book series is open to contributions from cognate social science disciplines that inform geographical thought about tourism and leisure. Produced in association with the Geographies of Leisure and Tourism Research Group of the Royal Geographical Society (with the Institute of British Geographers), this series highlights and promotes cutting-edge developments and research in this field. Contributions are of a high international standard and provide theoretically-informed empirical content to facilitate the development of new research agendas in the field of tourism and leisure research. In general, the series seeks to promote academic contributions that advance contemporary debates that challenge and stimulate further discussion and research both within the fields of tourism and leisure and the wider realms of the social sciences.

Other titles in the series:

Travel and Transformation
Edited by Garth Lean, Russell Staiff and Emma Waterton

Travel and Imagination
Edited by Garth Lean, Russell Staiff and Emma Waterton

Lifestyle Mobilities
Intersections of Travel, Leisure and Migration
Edited by Tara Duncan, Scott A. Cohen and Maria Thulemark

Mediating the Tourist Experience
From Brochures to Virtual Encounters
Edited by Jo-Anne Lester and Caroline Scarles

Moral Encounters in Tourism

Edited by

MARY MOSTAFANEZHAD
University of Hawai'i at Mānoa, USA

KEVIN HANNAM
Leeds Metropolitan University, UK

ASHGATE

Published by
Ashgate Publishing Limited
Wey Court East
Union Road
Farnham
Surrey, GU9 7PT
England

Ashgate Publishing Company
110 Cherry Street
Suite 3-1
Burlington, VT 05401-3818
USA

www.ashgate.com

British Library Cataloguing in Publication Data
A catalogue record for this book is available from the British Library

The Library of Congress has cataloged the printed edition as follows:
Moral encounters in tourism / edited by Mary Mostafanezhad and Kevin Hannam.
    pages cm. -- (Current developments in the geographies of leisure and tourism)
    Includes bibliographical references and index.
    ISBN 978-1-4724-1844-9 (hardback : alk. paper) -- ISBN 978-1-4724-1845-6 (ebook)
    -- ISBN 978-1-4724-1846-3 (epub)
    1. Tourism--Moral and ethical aspects. 2. Tourism--Social aspects.
  I. Mostafanezhad, Mary. II. Hannam, Kevin, author, editor of compilation.

G155.A1M628 2014
174'.991--dc23

2014000194

ISBN 9781472418449 (hbk)
ISBN 9781472418456 (ebk)
ISBN 9781472418463 (epub)

MIX
Paper from
responsible sources
FSC
www.fsc.org
FSC® C013985

Printed in the United Kingdom by Henry Ling Limited, at the Dorset Press, Dorchester, DT1 1HD

Contents

Figures

Contributors

Jim Butcher lectures at Canterbury Christ Church University. His interests are in the sociology of tourism. He has looked critically at the labelling of mass tourism as problem, and the transformation of green niches such as ecotourism into "ethical" alternatives. The former was a theme in *The Moralisation of Tourism* (Routledge, 2003) and the latter examined in *Ecotourism, NGOs and Development: a Critical Analysis* (Routledge, 2007). His forthcoming book, *Volunteer Tourism, Politics and Development*, co-written with Peter Smith, focuses on how and why holidays are today viewed as vehicles for people's political and social aspirations (Routledge, 2014).

Kellee Caton is an Assistant Professor and Chair of Graduate Studies in Tourism at Thompson Rivers University. She received her PhD from the University of Illinois Urbana–Champaign in 2008. Her research interests include morality and ethics, consumer culture, the role of tourism in ideological production, the lived experience of tourism and its role in human development, and epistemological and pedagogical issues in tourism. She sits on the editorial board of *Annals of Tourism Research* and the executive committee of the Tourism Educational Futures Initiative, as well as the scientific committee of the Critical Tourism Studies conference series. She also serves as chair of the university-wide curriculum committee of Thompson Rivers University.

Matilde Córdoba Azcárate is a Lecturer in the Department of Communication, University of California, San Diego. Her research explores the socio-cultural, spatial and political dimensions of tourism when used as a development tool. She has extensive experience in Southern México where she is conducting a multi-sited ethnography on the reproduction of uneven landscapes through tourism production and consumption practices. She is currently participating in two interdisciplinary research projects, *Tourism imaginaries and mobilities in times of crisis* (Ministry of Science and Innovation, Spain), and *Understanding the Dynamics of Urban Flexibility and Reconstruction* (University of Oxford, UK).

Anne-Marie d'Hauteserre is a Tourism Studies Convenor in the Faculty of Arts and Social Sciences at the University of Waikato, New Zealand. Her research interests are in critical issues raised by tourism development or by development based on tourism projects such as the indigenization of tourism development in the French Pacific and the Walt Disney and French state partnership in the urbanization of the Eastern Paris Basin. She has published numerous articles and book chapters on these topics in both French and English.

Tara Duncan is a Lecturer in the Department of Tourism at the University of Otago, New Zealand. With a background in geography, her research interests focus on lifestyle mobilities, the complexities of young budget travel and more recently, academic mobility, specifically framed within the climate change, transport and mobilities literature.

Robert Melchior Figueroa is an Associate Professor of Philosophy in the Department of Philosophy and Religion Studies at the University of North Texas, Director of the Environmental Justice Project for the Center for Environmental Philosophy, and has served as a graduate faculty for the Masters of Science in International Sustainable Tourism. Figueroa works extensively in environmental justice studies and has published on critical tourism studies as a single-author and a number of writings with co-author Gordon Waitt. He is the co-editor of *Science and Other Cultures* (Routledge, 2003) and currently writing *Environmental Justice as Environmental Ethics* slated for 2015 with Routledge.

Lindsey A. Freeman is a cultural sociologist, atomic historian, and critical tourist. Her work concerns collective memory, nostalgia, utopia, space/place, atomic history, and sometimes art. Lindsey is currently working on a manuscript about the rise and fall of the Atomic Age, centring on Oak Ridge, Tennessee, a secret atomic city created in the 1940s for the Manhattan Project (The University of North Carolina Press, forthcoming). Away from the keyboard, she currently teaches in the Sociology Department at SUNY Buffalo State.

Shelley K. Grant PhD (Queen Mary, University of London) is a legal and political geographer who possesses a longstanding interest in assessing the construction of family political economies and in comparing the evolution of civil identities in European and American cultural contexts. Her critical engagement with interdisciplinary theorists and mixed methods of analysis informs her progressive study of democratic participation, transnational consumptions and the constitution of populations across the human life course. Her approach to policy analyses is grounded in a career background in positions of legal research, civil rights advocacy and corporate business management.

Kevin Hannam is Professor of Tourism Mobilities at Leeds Metropolitan University, UK and Visiting Senior Research Fellow at the University of Johannesburg, South Africa. With John Urry and Mimi Sheller he is a founding co-editor of the journal *Mobilities*. He is the co-author of the books *Understanding Tourism* (Sage, 2010) and *Tourism and India* (Routledge, 2010). He is currently collaborating on an EU funded research project on entitled *Mobility and Employability Research for Generation Erasmus* (MERGE).

Heather Hindman PhD is an Assistant Professor of Anthropology and Asian Studies at the University of Texas at Austin. Her recently published book, *Mediating the Global: Expatria's Forms and Consequences in Kathmandu* explores the bureaucratic constrictures of employment policy on elite transnational labourers in Nepal, as well as their everyday perpetuation of similar forms of "best practices" regulation. She has recently published work on Nepal's labour and governmental links with South Korea, as well as parts of a more extended project on young Nepalis' engagement with entrepreneurship and rejections of politics during the recent period of long-term provisionality in the country.

Cori Jakubiak is an Assistant Professor of Education at Grinnell College in Grinnell, Iowa, USA. Her research focuses on English language voluntourism, or short-term, volunteer English language teaching in the Global South. She teaches courses in teacher education, place-based education, and world language methods.

Brent Lovelock is an Associate Professor in the Department of Tourism at the University of Otago, New Zealand. His research falls under the umbrella of sustainable tourism, with particular interests in tourism and the natural world, governance, ethics and human rights. He has recently co-authored a text entitled *The Ethics of Tourism*. Being located on the edge of the world has given him much valuable time sitting in aircraft to reflect upon tourism, climate change and the morality of flying.

Mary Mostafanezhad is an Assistant Professor in the Department of Geography at the University of Hawai'i at Mānoa. Mary's research interests lie at the intersection of geopolitics with mobilities such as travel, displacement and humanitarianism. Her current research examines humanitarian travel and the geopolitics of hope in the Thai–Burma border zone. Mary is the author of *Volunteer Tourism: Popular Humanitarianism in Neoliberal Times* (Ashgate, 2014) and a co-editor of *Cultural Encounters: Ethnographic Updates from Asia and the Pacific Islands* (University of Hawai'i Press). She is also a board member of the American Anthropological Association Anthropology of Tourism Interest Group, an acting board member for the Association of American Geographers Recreation, Tourism and Sport Specialty Group and the co-founder of the Critical Tourism Studies Asia-Pacific Consortium.

Tom Nagle is a Training Coordinator for the Kimberley Land Council, Broome, Western Australia. After stumbling onto an Honours degree in Land and Heritage Management at the University of Wollongong he became fascinated by the various intersections of western science and indigenous knowledge, particularly how they operate in modern day conservation practise. His working life to date has included leading teams of troubled youth in bush regeneration projects along the South Coast of NSW, working with the United Nations World Tourism Organization (UNWTO) in West Java, Indonesia to build local capacities to respond to unsustainable tourism by adapting to current threats and working to mitigate future challenges by developing sustainable tourism products. His current role sees him travel across the Kimberley region working with federally funded Indigenous ranger groups charged with the task of looking after their country and culture with a mix of traditional and western scientific methods.

Elissa J. Sampson is a PhD candidate in urban geography at the University of North Carolina, Chapel Hill. She studies the active use of the past in the creation of new geographies of migration, memory and heritage. Her research interests include Lower East Side migration; American Jewish culture; Triangle Fire commemoration; historic preservation; gentrification; memory studies; the history of geography; and the practice of genealogy. She has lived most of her life in New York's Lower East Side and has spent over twenty years as a part-time tour guide, sharing the neighbourhood's past and present with visitors and residents.

Peter Smith is the Director of Tourism at St. Mary's University College, Twickenham, London. He is currently researching volunteer tourism and perceptions of development. Prior to working at St. Mary's, Peter was the UK customer relations manager for a leading global student/youth travel company and worked in the independent travel sector for many years.

Hazel Tucker is an Associate Professor in Tourism (Department of Tourism, University of Otago). She has a PhD in Social Anthropology from Durham University, UK. She is author of *Living with Tourism* (Routledge, 2003) and co-editor of *Tourism and Postcolonialism* (Routledge, 2004) and *Commercial Homes in Tourism* (Routledge, 2009). Other areas of research interest include gender and also tour guiding and interpretation.

Gordon Waitt is a Professor of Human Geography at The University of Wollongong, Australia. Over the past twenty years Gordon's research has focussed on people in relationship to place. Drawing on geographical perspectives, Gordon's research interests over the years have included nature tourism, festivals, mobility, creative industries and rurality. His recent work draws on geographical perspectives that takes seriously the "materiality" of the body, while remaining alert to the importance of sets of ideas that frame ideas about race, gender, sexuality, places, nature and the environment. These ideas provide a helpful tool for rethinking how to critically engage with patterns of economic, political, social and environmental change.

Michael Wearing is a Senior Lecturer in The School of Social Sciences, Faculty of Arts and Social Sciences, University of New South Wales (UNSW) Sydney, Australia. He completed a PhD in sociology from UNSW whilst a scholar at The Social Policy Research Centre UNSW in the 1980s and has gone on to teach and publish in the areas of social policy, sociology and political sociology while an academic at Sydney University and then UNSW. He is the author of several books and over 50 refereed publications. These include the research areas of socio-cultural aspects of tourism, community services, social welfare and social policy. His current research interests are in the environment and ecotourism, the politics of welfare rhetoric, change in human service organizations, and comparative social policy.

Stephen Wearing is an Associate Professor at the University of Technology, Sydney (UTS). His research is in the area of leisure and tourism studies, with a PhD focused on sustainable forms of tourism. Stephen has taught at a variety of universities in his career, including Wageningen University, The Netherlands and Newcastle and Macquarie Universities, Australia. In 2008 he received an Australian National Teaching Award. In 2013 he published two books: Wearing, S. L. and McGehee, N. 2013. *International Volunteer Tourism: Integrating Travellers and Communities*, Oxon, CABI, and McDonald, M. and Wearing, S. L. 2013. *Social Psychology and Theories of Consumer Culture: A Political Economy Perspective*, London, Routledge.

Sharon Wilson is a Programme Leader for Events Management at the University of Sunderland, UK and is currently undertaking a doctorate about VW Campervan Subcultures and Tourism Mobilities. With a background in artistic practices, she recently collaborated with Pau Obrador-Pons on a publication about communal creativity and political subversion in temporary settlements.

Chapter 1
Introducing Moral Encounters in Tourism

Mary Mostafanezhad and Kevin Hannam

Tourists are travellers in hypermorality ... (MacCannell, 2011, pp. 216–217).

Introduction

Concerns over the ethical production and consumption of tourism experiences have become frequent topics of consideration among scholars, practitioners and advocates over the last two decades. Numerous non-governmental organizations (NGOs) (such as *Tourism Concern*) and academic advocacy networks (such as the *Responsible Tourism Network*) focused on ethical tourism agendas reflect the contemporary institutionalization as well as a growing consensus regarding the need for ethical tourism programs (Duffy and Smith, 2003; Hultsman, 1995; Lea, 1993; Lovelock, 2008; MacCannell, 2011). Academic research on ethical tourism is well represented in the literature including numerous publications which examine the ethics of travel, tourism experiences as well as research on tourism (Bergmann and Sager, 2012; Castañeda, 2012; Duffy and Smith, 2003; Fennell and Malloy, 1999; Molz and Gibson, 2012).

While increased attention has focused on the intersection of ethics and tourism, with a few notable exceptions surprisingly little has been said about the role of morality in tourism (see Butcher, 2003; Phillimore, 2004). The inattention to morality by tourism scholars is curious given the obvious centrality of morality to tourism as both a practice and object of study. Indeed, it is noted how "The paucity of formal discussion about this issue is particularly unfortunate in tourism studies, given that those of us working here operate on loaded moral territory, confronting a phenomenon that at once speaks of light hearted pleasure and heavy social consequences" (Caton, 2012, p. 1906).

While there has been little discussion about the role of morality in tourism encounters, tourism itself has been heavily moralized. As Castaneda notes, tourism is widely viewed as an inherently moral activity. From the 1960s to the 1980s tourism was viewed as either inherently good or inherently bad: "Those who considered it a positive force saw it not simply a 'passport to development' (e.g., de Kadt 1979), and thus a solution to problems of endemic poverty and cultural 'backwardness' based in Third World under development, but also a 'force for world peace' (D'Amore, 1988; Castenada and Burtner 2010)," while other studies explicitly moralized tourism, as an 'evil' force derived from European colonialism, capitalism, and modern nation-state building projects (see Brown 2000; Turner and Ash 1976)" (Castañeda, 2012, p. 47).

In the early days of tourism studies, tourism scholars contributed to a widespread moralizing of tourism as a frivolous, inauthentic, consumerist experience. Daniel Boorstin (1961) and Dean MacCannell's (1976) seminal publications outlined the tourism studies agenda for at least the following two decades with their theories on tourists' acceptance of pseudo-events and their apparent "search for authenticity," respectively. Among scholars who moralized tourism as inherently "bad," there was, and still is, a notable focus on tourism's impact on local communities. As Castañeda (2012, p. 47) notes,

> The very idea of impact is inherently associated with this morality because it is an ideological concept that was used to argue single, one-way cause-effect relationships without taking into account long term socio-historical processes or considering the multiple and different consequences and effects that tourism could have on the diverse stakeholders, communities, classes, businesses, policy-makers, governments, and social groups that are involved in tourism and tourism development projects.

These blanket assessments of tourism worked well to overshadow the varied ways that tourism affects a diverse range of actors.

By the 1990s, "we started to define how to make tourism ethical instead of asserting that it was morally good or bad in all social contexts" (Castañeda, 2012, p. 48). Thus, tourism scholars began thinking beyond moralizing commentary on a homogenized "industry" and began focusing on the role of ethics in diverse tourism experiences. It was during this period that a widespread panic in tourism studies emerged over the ethics of tourism. Numerous publications emerged to caution us about the potentially unethical nature of tourism, generally. Butcher notes how this panic led some to ask: "wouldn't you be better off at home?" (Butcher, 2003, p. 2). And indeed, some did arrive at such a conclusion. The effectiveness of this concern has been effective to some extent as today ethical issues are now part of mainstream conversations regarding tourism practice and policy.

We begin this anthology with our main argument that the tourism encounter is also a moral encounter, the implications of which have yet to be fully worked in popular or academic circles. We focus on encounter as it "enables closer dissection of the moments and spaces in which power is exercised, and relations of care extended" (Gibson, 2010, p. 521). Whether engaging with explicitly moral tourism or tourism where engagements with morality is less obvious, tourism is mediated by a range of moral issues that are often more implicit than clearly expressed. Like mobility, we argue that tourism "is not a neutral term, not even if we frame a technical definition. It will always have moral implications" (Zeitler, 2012, p. 233). In this anthology we seek to develop an argument about the relationship between tourism and morality. We see tourism as a moral field of experience that is ripe for theoretical and empirical investigation (MacCannell, 2011, p. 3). Thus, along with Caton (2012, p. 1906), we seek to bring tourism studies into the moral turn, yet caution that "the road before us is long. We have only just taken up the journey in earnest, and we have far to go."

Defining Morality

Morality is perhaps one of the most contested concepts in philosophy. Like the culture concept for anthropologists, there may be as many definitions of morality as there are philosophers. Smith (1997, p. 585) has noted that:

> we are told that engaging in moral practice presupposes moral facts, and that this presupposition is an error, and that moral commitment involves no such error; we are told that moral facts exist, and that these facts are no different from those that are the subject-matter of science, and we are told that moral facts exist but they are of a special kind; we are told that moral facts exist and are part of the causal explanatory network, and we are told not just that moral facts play no causal role but that there are no moral facts at all; we are told that there is an internal and necessary connection between moral judgment and the will, and we are told that this connection is altogether external and contingent; we are told that moral requirements are requirements of reason, and we are told that it is not necessarily irrational to act immorally, that moral evaluation is different in kind from the evaluation of people as rational or irrational; we are told that morality is objective, that there is a single true morality, and we are told that morality is not objective, that there is no single true morality. Numerous distinguished philosophers are associated with these various conflicting positions ... The scene is so diverse that we must wonder at the assumption that these theorists are all talking about the same thing.

In this anthology we understand morality is a socially constructed set of values that are agreed upon by individuals and societies (Pennycook, 1994). This perspective departs from moral philosophy in that we understand morality in Foucauldian terms to refer to the mediation of personal conduct through socially constructed or learned ways of being (Foucault, 1976, 1990) rather than ascribing to a universal moral code. As a social—and by implication—cultural system, morality differs within and between cultures and is embedded in particular relations of power and spatial contexts. The spatiality of morality is mapped on to an uneven terrain of political, economic and cultural relations. As Caton (2012, p. 1906) suggests, morality refers to the "human imaginative and discursive capacity for considering how things should be, as opposed to describing how things are—what is sometimes referred to as the "is" versus "ought" distinction." This distinction regarding what "is" and "ought" to be is part of broader, historical and political discursive project that extends to one's personal character as well as belief systems about how one "ought to be." In this way, morality is distinguished from ethics which addresses the philosophy behind one's beliefs within social system. Ethics tends to refer to individual behaviour or codes of behaviour for a social group (professional ethics, family ethics, etc.) while morality refers more broadly to beliefs regarding how things ought to be across the range of human experience (Smith, 2000; Duffy and Smith, 2003; Williams, 2012).

Critical Tourism Studies

The chapters in this anthology thus highlight various ways in which the tourism encounter is also a moral encounter. This is particularly so because tourism is also a highly mediatized encounter where issues of history, race, class, ethnicity, gender and sexuality, among others, play central roles. Diekmann and Hannam's (2010) discussion of the influence of the film *Slumdog Millionaire* on practices of slum tourism in India provides a case study of such mediatized moral tourism encounters. Indeed, attention to issues of social, economic and political inequality as well as social and environmental justice is what brings this anthology into conversation with emerging work in critical turn in tourism studies (Ateljevic, Harris, Wilson, and Leo Collins, 2005; Ateljevic, Pritchard, and Morgan, 2007; Bianchi, 2009). Following Gibson, for us, "research is critical because of its opposition to systems of domination, orthodoxies, injustices and oppressions," and like Gibson, we "report on recent research organized via critical 'threads'— which are admittedly neither complete nor perfectly linear" (Gibson, 2009, p. 527). As a social practice, tourism is therefore mediated by a range of moral and therefore political issues as in our view, morals have both political foundations as well as effects (Castañeda, 2006, p. 132). This is in part because morals are spatially organized and situated within particular relations of power that makes a "morality before politics" position theoretically suspect. For example, Smith (1997, p. 588) points out how "the original position, under which people decide on institutions behind a veil of ignorance as to their actual position in society, as an imaginary moral landscape ... a particular geography of morality ... the ultimate colorblind, non-sexist, non-racial community ... a utopia with a moral order we can only dream about."

While we situate this anthology within the growing field of critical tourism studies, we want to distinguish between our positioning and that of scholars who adopt an overtly "critical-of-tourism" stance (as was common in scholarship between the 1960s–1980s [Castañeda, 2006]). Critical tourism studies, we observe, is frequently misinterpreted as disgruntled, pessimists who moralize tourism as "all bad." On the contrary, we understand critical tourism studies in the sense of critical theory and its revolutionary possibilities for denaturalizing what are sometimes, but not always taken-for-granted experiences of injustice and marginalization as they exist in relation to tourism. Thus, while the chapters in this anthology contribute to emerging conversations in critical tourism studies, we also want to make the point that critical tourism studies need not seek refuge in critique alone. We argue with Caton (2012, p. 1915) that "anti-foundationalism represents a great step forward in terms of forcing us to come face to face with the inherently situated nature of human knowing, but it leaves us no less impotent than does traditional positivism when comes to the ability to produce value-engaged research." All human experiences, according to this perspective, can be critiqued in terms of its hegemonic or anti-hegemonic persuasion. Thus, we concur with Gibson (2010, p. 525) who argues that "[w]ithout tourism, the world would be dull—and, more pointedly, tourism's only alternative, immobility, is an invitation to xenophobia. For this reason tourism encounters warrant further analysis and reflection."

The Moral Turn in the Social Sciences

While it is argued that "[m]orality tends to receive little direct consideration in the realm of mainstream social science" (Caton, 2012, p. 1906), we suggest that this paucity is particularly problematic in tourism studies. Indeed, other social science disciplines have engaged with issues of morality in explicit ways.

Historical geographers such as Felix Driver (1988) showed how moral concerns in the nineteenth century gave rise to new spatial regimes of disciplinary power that sought to shape the conduct of certain populations. David Matless (1997), meanwhile, has shown how in the 1930s and 1940s, leisure practices in the English countryside were presented in terms of moral citizenship, with intellectual, spiritual and physical cultures of landscape being combined as a means to 'improve' the citizen. The important point here is that moral concerns can signal the emergence of new notions of space and society which are not neutral.

Since the 1990s geography's "moral turn" has also led to new studies of contemporary geographies of responsibility, of understanding regimes of caring at a distance (Holloway, 1998; Conradson, 2003; Valentine, 2005; Lawson, 2007). Indeed, it has been noted that, "All geographies are, in the last analysis, moral geographies" (Clive Barnett and Land, 2007, p. 499). Additionally, the intersection of race, class, ethnicity, gender with morality, is a frequent topic of geographical inquiry (Barnett and Land, 2007; Freidberg, 2003; Goodman, 2004; McEwan and Goodman, 2010; Smith, 1998, 2000).

Anthropology has a long history of addressing moral issues from a subjective as well as cross-cultural perspective. Marcel Mauss's seminal publication *The Gift: The Form and Reason for Exchange in Archaic Societies* (1954) influenced generations of anthropologists to examine morality cross-culturally. There has also been a renewed interest among anthropologists who address the phenomenology of morality as well as the role of morality in anthropological fieldwork and ethnographic methods (Castaneda, 2006; Clifford, 1988; Clifford, 1998; Mattingly, 2012; Munzel, 1998; Zigon, 2009). More recently, interdisciplinary fields such as cultural and visual studies have also experienced similar "moral turns" since the early 2000s (Chen, 1996; Durham, 2001; Jancovich, 2002; Wood, 2003).

The chapters in this anthology complement emerging trends such as those in geography and anthropology as well as integrate social science research on morality within tourism studies. Building on current research such as embodied encounters in tourism, the political economy and political ecology of tourism, moral economies of production and consumption as well as moral issues in tourism research, this anthology provides ethnographic and theoretical illustrations of moral issues in tourism and tourism research.

Moral Tourism Encounters

As an anthology on moral tourism *encounters*, we feel the need to emphasize the centrality of the role of *encounter* in tourism. As Gibson (2010, p. 521) notes, "beyond its industrial and labour market structure, at the heart of tourism is encounter—perhaps its defining, distinguishing feature." It is within these borderlands of encounter that "hosts" and "guests" find themselves with a range of moral decisions that extend well beyond the potential of their individual experience and cultural knowledge. Additionally, encounter or contact involves the uneven merging of varied flows of cultures that are not wholly distinct but always, already in the process of recreating themselves. As such, "[c]ontact approaches presupposed not sociocultural wholes subsequently brought into relationship, but rather systems already constituted relationally, entering new relations through historical processes of displacement" (Clifford, 1997, p. 7). It is for this reason that MacCannell (2011, p. 28) notes how "Fantasy is the only thing that easily and naturally occupies the moral no-man's –land between tourists and the people who live in the places they visit." Yet, these fantasies emerge not within a distinct set of boundaries between inside and outside, but instead, "travel, or displacement, can involve forces that pass powerfully through—television, radio, tourists, commodities, armies" (Clifford, 1997, p. 28). It is through what Gibson (2010) describes as the "micro-analysis of encounters" that we can begin to understand the varied ways that morality mediates the tourism encounter. MacCannell (2011, p. 228) argues that "[t]he defining characteristic of tourists is that they purposefully cross lines of moral difference in order to experience that difference." Thus, he outlines a range of tourists' reactions to moral difference including 1) the relativist position (i.e. they accept the moral differences without trying to 'go native'); 2) the assimilationist position (i.e. they assimilate to local morals); 3) the missionary position (i.e. their way is morally superior and the 'natives' should be converted); 4) transgressive entitlements (i.e. they disregard moral differences altogether); and 5) cool indifference (MacCannell, 2011, pp. 221–222). These modes of encounter provide a range of possibilities for the tourist. Yet, they also emphasize a theoretical and empirical gap around the role of morality for tourism producers and host community members (a topic that we believe demands further analysis).

It is clear that there is a new generation of tourists who align themselves with the relativist and, or assimilationist position and these positions are highlighted in what has become known as moral tourism experiences. Numerous networks and organizations have developed to engage with the morality of tourism encounters. Examples include the UNWTO World Committee on Tourism Ethics, Tourism Concern and the International Centre for Peace through Tourism Research, among others. Indeed, by the late 1990s, the UNWTO Global Code of Ethics put an institutional face to ethical tourism agendas (Castañeda, 2012, p. 48). The UNWTO and related institutions and organizations play an important role in codifying ethics in the tourism industry.

These emergences parallel fair and ethical trade movements which brand themselves as such based on their environmental sustainability, cultural understanding and labour practices (Gibson, 2010, p. 522). It is widely observed that the emergence of ethical tourism programs and institutions reflect broader trends in alternative consumerism in the Global North where tourism has taken on a "kaleidoscopic character" in its proliferation of niche tourism markets (Gibson, 2009). Key characteristics of these markets include sustainability, fair trade and ethical production practices (Butcher, 2003, 2008; Mowforth and Munt, 2009; Wearing, 2010). These characteristics are echoed in sustainable tourism, responsible tourism, fair trade tourism and ethical tourism.

Over the last decade these practices have become increasingly mainstream, while new niche markets have emerged such as volunteer tourism, dark tourism, slum tourism, food tourism and medical tourism: all now significant players in the tourism industry. This is perhaps unsurprising given that "The moral issues raised by consumption therefore have a dual nature (at least); they are both grounded in common human experience, in 'practical reason', and at the same time they are part of public discourse about morality, a discourse that has a broader cultural, symbolic, and political context" (Wilk, 2001, p. 255). Theories of consumption, we observe, are especially pertinent to tourism theory.

Yet, within tourism studies, there are numerous critiques of the so-called ethical tourism industry. As Gibson notes, "branding masks the possibility of more or less ethical practices under the 'ethical tourism' banner (Duffy, 2000); it codifies ethical tourism (against all other tourism, which is unethical by implication); and it introduces a moralizing element that merely endorses one type of tourism against an amoral 'other' (Butcher, 2003)" (Gibson, 2010, p. 523). Key players in this industry are non-governmental organizations, community based development entrepreneurs and non-profit organizations that seek to circumvent unethical capitalistic practices. The primary consumer for these kinds of experiences are broadly referred to as "new moral tourists" (Butcher, 2003, p. 2). This target market is "characterized by its advocacy of more 'sensitive' behaviour with regard to environments and culture" and as Butcher notes, the "New Moral Tourism ... is presented as ethical consumption—an attempt to make a difference to issues held dear through what and where one buys" (Butcher, 2003, p. 3). This new school of tourism has acquired a certain sense of moral superiority in relation to its packaged counterpart" (Butcher, 2003, p. 2). Critics call for caution of this approach that favours small-scale, locally owned and operated tourism providers at the expense of mass tourism. Thus, the emergence of critiques launched against ethical tourism highlights how "[L] imitations and contradictions are apparent even for the most well-meaning or best-designed ethical tourism enterprises" (Gibson, 2010, p. 523).

Yet, like the "critical-of-tourism" stance, we argue that these critiques fail to recognize the plurality of experiences associated with what falls under the banner of ethical tourism experiences. In a similar respect, ethical tourism, like "the singular 'tourism industry' is now redundant: 'the contestation that tourism is supported by one giant industry has no robust theoretical foundation'" (Gibson, 2009, p. 529). Rather, tourism is a hodgepodge of diverse industries, the state, natural environments, formal and informal economies, technologies and numerous other 'actors' (Castañeda, 2012; Gibson, 2009, p. 529). The emerging field of mobilities studies recognizes the blurring of boundaries between tourism and other forms of travel such as international volunteering, temporary business relocations and diasporic travel experiences (Duncan, 2008, 2013; Gibson, 2009, p. 529). Moreover, mobilities research has become concerned with the moral implications of the freedoms afforded by car and air travel such as climate change (Freudendal-Petersen, 2009; Urry, 2011).

Moral Dilemmas in Tourism Research

Our main argument is based on the observation that tourism, like all social practices, is embedded within myriad questions of morality and moral being. Like other forms of consumption, tourism tends to fall outside traditional Marxian political economic rationalities, and as Gibson (2009, p. 2) notes, "use and exchange value become complicated by intangible, commodified culture and producers and consumers are brought into direct contact." This becomes especially true in the context of ethical consumption, where morality and consumption are deeply intertwined. It is noted how "a basic contradiction between the means and ends of ethical consumption, in so far as the practical devices through which an ostensibly universalistic responsibility is made possible are also a means of socially and cultural differentiating certain classes of persons from others" (Barnett, Cloke, Clarke, and Malpass, 2005, p. 41).

It is worth noting the continued marginalization of tourism studies within academia. This positioning is arguably at least in part the result of some who perceive tourism as a superficial the topic of study. But it may also be a result of the incongruence of theories and object of study. Caton's (2012, p. 1906) work conceptualizes "the fraught space that is tourism practice, as being a site of both individual fulfilment ... and social consequence." This distinction between individual fulfilment and social consequence helps explain the noticeable lack of attention to morality in tourism studies. Caton

(2012, p. 1906) further argues that "tourism must be recognized as a space that awkwardly houses both of these realities."

In an attempt to reconcile these divergences, we argue for a foregrounding of morality in the tourism encounter. And like the tourism encounter, the research encounter, we suggest, is also a moral encounter. The research encounter may include both physical encounters between researchers and research collaborators or "hosts" as well as the re-presentation of research texts (oral, visual or written). The re-presentation of research is a site of moral consideration in that it is ultimately a co-construction of the story that one tells of their "data" and all re-presentations, we surmise, are indeed political (Hall, 1997; Rabinow, 1986). It with this in mind that we concur with Clifford when he asks, "Is it possible to locate oneself historically, to tell a coherent global story, when historical reality is understood to be an unfinished series of encounters?" (Clifford, 1997, p. 13). Like the tourist encounter, the research encounter is a highly moralized physical and ideological territory. Additionally, as MacCannell (2011) notes, as tourism researchers, our methodological toolkit will never allow us to accurately detail touristic desire or host attitude in any all-encompassing way. Rather, "the closest we will ever get to discovering what tourists want will be via detailed descriptions of what they do, from which we might deduce their desire" (MacCannell, 2011, p. 211). We argue that these challenges also open up many opportunities for tourism scholars, practitioners and participants to create new forms of tourism encounters that foreground the morality of the encounter. Thus, in the re-presentation of the peoples that we claim to represent in our stories about tourism encounters, we need to remember that "Every focus excludes; there is no politically innocent methodology for intercultural interpretation" (Clifford, 1997, p. 19).

The spatiality of tourism research begs for introspection. How is that we come to consider the "culture" of the other? For example, Clifford (1997, p. 21) writes: "Of course, one is always a participant-observer some*where*. How is this place of work bounded in space and time? The question brings into view a more persistent localization: 'the field'." Additionally, it is notable that tourism scholars have tended to homogenize the culture of the other as if it were bounded in space and time. It seems that there may be a methodological failing in the suggestion of cultural wholes (such as American vs. European tourists). This is especially evident in simplistic notions of so- called "cross-cultural" tourism research which parades around as culturally sensitive research on groups of people perceptively locating in a particular time and place. These kinds of studies can be identified by their description of their research that attempts to classify entire countries or regions. Discussion of the "Chinese tourist," the "Middle Eastern host," or the "African culture"—for example—are all causes for moral concern as through their classificatory scheme, they homogenize entire countries regions and continents while also denying the fluid and dynamic human experience. Additionally, there is a certain immorality in the ahistoricity of tourism studies. The lack of historical depth to tourism research essentially displaces the peoples and conditions that make the sight/site, experience or "gaze" possible. Clifford (1997, p. 9) notes that by thinking historically, location becomes "an itinerary rather than abounded site—a series of encounters and translations." Morality, we suggest, mediates both the encounter and translation of tourism and tourism research.

Structure of the Book

Moral Encounters situates morality in tourism encounters through empirical, ethnographic and theoretical chapters that bridge the "morality gap" in tourism studies. This anthology is organized into four main sections.

The first section, *Moral Consumption in Tourism* examines a range of issues from lifestyle politics to consuming development. In his chapter, Jim Butcher discusses tourism, development and politics and concludes that, "[c]ontrary to the claims that ethical tourism is progressive politics, it diminishes politics in two senses. First, politics is diminished as personal qualities replace political categories in public development discourse. This reflects and reinforces the emptying of the public sphere and hence narrows both political and moral agency. Second, ethical tourism is a particular outlook masquerading, via terms such as care and responsibility, as a universal ethics for all. As such, it narrows discussion of different development options." Peter Smith then picks up on this in his critical review of the volunteer tourism industry and argues that it may be better to view volunteer tourism as a reversal of the 'politics of care' and of hosts as providers of moral encounters for paying tourists from the North. Heather Hindman, then unpicks in detail the moral dilemmas of volunteer tourism in her analysis of Nepal. The final chapter in this section by Matilde Córdoba Azcárate reflects on the how both old and new tourism developments in Yucatán have proven to reproduce a moral economy of mutual dissociation. This moral economy, she argues, is entangled in different imaginaries of tourist escape— from the ordinary, into the past—that have created asymmetrical entitlements to land and resources.

Section 2, *Embodied Tourism Encounters*, engages with morality from the perspective of embodiment in tourism encounters and addresses topics ranging from fertility tourism to heritage tourism. In her chapter, Shelley Grant argues that "[r]ather than dismissing the exercise of parental interests within reproductive tourism, I instead wish to emphasize the distinction between governance by law and the moral circumscription of intimate activities through the interpretation of legal standards." Anne-Marie d'Hauteserre then examines whether tourists can behave morally in the course of encounters in remote destinations when facing oppressive political practices that also maintain gendered cultural practices through a case study of Kayan women in Myanmar. Cori Jakubiak focuses critical attention on the moral dimemmas embodied in English Language volunteer tourism based upon research in Costa Rica. Finally, Elissa Sampson reflects on the moral economy of heritage tourism as it is embodied through museum practices in New York's Lower East Side.

Section 3, *Environmental Tourism Moralities*, examines how the environment is heavily moralized in tourism studies where perspectives range from proponents of ecotourism development to activists for a depopulated landscape. This section addresses topics such as climate change, ecotourism and environmental justice. In their critical discussion of neoliberalism, Stephen and Michael Wearing attempt to map cultural alternatives to ecotourism, while Brent Lovelock reflects on moral issues of climate change and the growth of 'aeromobilities'. Lindsey Freeman then examines morality in the case of the Cold War plutonium tourism, and Gordon Waitt, Robert Melchior Figueroa and Tom Nagle focus on human-animal moral encounters in Australia.

The concluding section, *Moral Methodologies* offers empirical examples of morality in tourism research and methodological approaches. Ethnography, emotional reflexivity and power in tourism encounters are among the topics covered. Kellee Caton begins this section by reflecting on the theoretical relations between humanism and tourism. Hazel Tucker reflects on her own ethnography in Turkey in terms of the multiple moralities encountered. Tara Duncan examines the moralities surrounding her research with young budget travellers and, finally, Sharon Wilson experiments with how she has approached her ethnography with VW campervan owners from a mobilities perspective.

We conclude with an overview of the new interdisciplinary terrain that is carved out by the preceding chapters as well as possible routes for new research on the intersection of morality and tourism studies by focussing on the moral politics of funding tourism research.

The empirical and theoretical contributions of this anthology advance our understanding of the role of morality in tourism encounters in new and multiple contexts. Additionally, the chapters in this anthology offer critical and ethnographically grounded understandings of the contemporary relevance of morality in tourism encounters to larger issues such as power, uneven development, international humanitarianism, globalization and political economy. It highlights how race, class and gender are embodied aspects of tourism encounters as well as the power relations that mediate these subjective positions. It also ethnographically illustrate how morality mediates and is re-constituted through tourism encounters as well as how particular types of tourism encounters work to normalize and stabilize existing structures of power and privilege. The overall aim of *Moral Encounters* is to highlight the role of morality in tourism and tourism research. In this way, *Moral Encounters* expands tourism studies into new interdisciplinary terrain through its approach of these themes from historical, contemporary and methodological perspectives to advance theoretical knowledge and empirical understanding of this emergent and increasingly important topic of tourism research. Rather than moralizing tourism, we argue for a re-examination of how morality mediates the tourism experience. As tourism scholars we believe that a focus on morality in tourism sheds light on the multiple commitments we have to our research collaborators, students, businesses, organizations, communities and the broader public. These commitments—we believe—begin with an acknowledgement of the ways in which the tourism encounter is also a moral encounter.

References

Ateljevic, I., Harris, C., Wilson, E., and Leo Collins, F. (2005). Getting 'Entangled': Reflexivity and the 'Critical Turn' in Tourism Studies. *Tourism Recreation Research*, 30(2), 9–21.

Ateljevic, I., Pritchard, A., and Morgan, N. (2007). *The Critical Turn in Tourism Studies: Innovative Research Methodologies*. Oxford: Elsevier.

Barnett, C., Cloke, P., Clarke, N., and Malpass, A. (2005). Consuming Ethics: Articulating the Subjects and Spaces of Ethical Consumption. *Antipode*, 23–45.

Barnett, C., and Land, D. (2007). Geographies of Generosity: Beyond the 'Moral Turn'. *Geoforum*, 38, 1065–1075.

Bergmann, S., and Sager, T. (2012). *The Ethics of Mobilities: Rethinking Place Exclusion Freedom and Environment*. Farnham: Ashgate Publishing.

Bianchi, R. V. (2009). The 'Critical Turn' in Tourism Studies: A Radical Critique. *Tourism Geographies*, 11(4), 484–504.

Butcher, J. (2003). *The Moralization of Tourism: Sun, Sand ... and Saving the World?* New York: Routledge.

Butcher, J. (2008). Ecotourism as Life Politics. *Journal of Sustainable Tourism*, 16(3), 315–326.

Castañeda, Q. (2006). Ethnography in the Forest: An Analysis of Ethics in the Morals of Anthropology. *Cultural Anthropology*, 21(1), 121–145.

Castañeda, Q. (2012). The Neoliberal Imperative of Tourism: Rights and Legitization in the UNWTO Global Code of Ethics for Tourism. *Practicing Anthropology*, 34(3), 47–51.

Caton, K. (2012). Taking the Moral Turn in Tourism Studies. *Annals of Tourism Research*, 39(4), 1906–1928.

Chen, K.-H. (1996). Post-Marxism: Between/Beyond Critical Postmodernism and Cultural Studies. In D. Morley and Kuan-Hsing Chen (eds.), *Stuart Hall: Critical Dialogues in Cultural Studies*. New York: Routledge.

Clifford, J. (1997). *Routes: Travel and Translation in the Late Twentieth Century*. Cambridge, MA: Harvard University Press.

Duffy, R., and Smith, M. (2003). *The Ethics of Tourism Development*. London: Routledge.

Duncan, T. (2008). The Internationalisation of Tourism Labour Markets: Working and Playing in a Ski Resort. *International Business and Tourism: Global Issues, Contemporary Interactions*. London: Routledge, 181–194.

Duncan, T. (2013). The Mobilities of Hospitality Work: An Exploration of Issues and Debates. *Annals of Tourism Research*, 41, 1–19.

Durham, M. G., and Douglas, K. (eds.). (2001). *Media and Cultural Studies: Key Works*. Malden: Blackwell Publishers Inc.

Fennell, D. A., and Malloy, D. C. (1999). Measuring the Ethical Nature of Tourism Operators. *Annals of Tourism Research*, 26(4), 928–943.

Foucault, M. (1976). *The Birth of the Clinic*. London: Tavistock.

Foucault, M. (1990). *The History of Sexuality: The Use of Pleasure* (Vol. 2). London: Random House.

Gibson, C. (2009). Geographies of Tourism: Critical Research on Capitalism and Local Livelihoods. *Progress in Human Geography*, 33(4), 527–534.

Gibson, C. (2010). Geographies of Tourism: (Un)ethical Encounters. *Progress in Human Geography*, 34(4), 521–527.

Hall, S. (1997). *Representation: Cultural Representations and Signifying Practices*. New York: Sage.

Jancovich, M. (2002). Cult Fictions: Cult Movies, Subcultural Capital and the Production of Cultural Distinctions. *Cultural Studies*, 16(2), 306–322.

MacCannell, D. (2011). *The Ethics of Sightseeing*. Berkeley: University of California Press.

Molz, J. G., and Gibson, S. (2012). *Mobilizing Hospitality: The Ethics of Social Relations in a Mobile World*. Farnham: Ashgate Publishing.

Mowforth, M., and Munt, I. (2009). *Tourism and Sustainability: Development and New Tourism in the Third World*. New York: Routledge.

Pennycook, A. (1994). *The Cultural Politics of English as an International Language*. Harlow, Essex, UK: Longman Group Limited.

Phillimore, J., and Goodson, L. (eds.) (2004). *Qualitative Research in Tourism: Ontologies, Epistemologies, Methodologies*. New York: Routledge.

Rabinow, P. (1986). Representations are Social Facts: Modernity and Postmodernity in Anthropology. In J. Clifford and G. Marcus (eds.), *Writing Culture: The Poetics and Politics of Ethnography*. Berkeley: University of California Press.

Smith, D. M. (1997). Geography and Ethics: A Moral Turn? *Progress in Human Geography*, 21(4), 583–590.

Wearing, S. (2010). A Response to Jim Butcher and Peter Smith's Paper 'making a difference': Volunteer Tourism and Development. *Tourism Recreation Research*, 35(2), 213–215.

Wilk, R. (2001). Consuming Morality. *Journal of Consumer Culture*, 1(2), 245–260.

Wood, H. (2003). Cultural Studies for Oceania. *The Contemporary Pacific*, 15(2), 340–374.

Zeitler, U. (2012). The Ontology of Mobility, Morality and Transport Planning. In S. Bergmann and T. Sager (eds.), *The Ethics of Mobilities: Rethinking Place Exclusion Freedom and Environment*. Farnham: Ashgate.

SECTION 1
Moral Consumption in Tourism

Chapter 2

Moralizing Tourism: Personal Qualities, Political Issues

Jim Butcher

Introduction

Discussing tourism, and indeed consumption generally, as part of a moral strategy for making a positive difference to the world, is a relatively recent phenomenon. The 1980s witnessed the rise of ethical consumption (Nichols and Opal, 2005), and it is doubtful anyone seriously considered their holidays a moral intervention into the world's problems until the 1990s (Butcher, 2003). Today ethical consumption and ethical tourism are prominent. Gap years are no longer about dropping out, but instead about signing up to global citizenship and contributing to wellbeing through caring for children or assisting community development projects as a volunteer tourist (Lyons et al., 2012). Niches such as ecotourism have morphed into markers of moral intent (Butcher, 2003, 2005). A range of tourisms—responsible, green, ethical, community etc.—proclaim their moral stance in relation to the environment and also development issues (Butcher, 2005). They do this typically through a discourse that draws heavily on personal qualities such as care, awareness of others and responsibility.

Care, awareness of others and responsibility are admirable personal qualities. However, up until fairly recently they did not feature prominently in development or politics at all. Instead, development politics was informed by competing visions of social transformation through growth backed up by macro-economic theories and critiques (Chang, 2010). The politics of Left and Right, albeit encompassing a diverse set of positions, framed development politics and animated distinctly social movements and beliefs (Chouliaraki, 2013). This chapter considers what the prevalence of the language of 'responsibility', 'caring' and 'awareness'—all laudable personal qualities pushed into the public realm of political debate on development through the advocacy of ethical tourism—tell us about development and politics today.

Care, Responsibility and Politics

With the rise of ethical lifestyle strategies such as Fair Trade, ethical tourism, advocacy of organic food and localism, *personal attributes* have become the stuff of politics and are directly linked to desirable development outcomes. Questions such as are you 'responsible'? do you 'care'? or maybe you lack 'awareness'? are implicit in much of this. Such questions are also evident, and often explicit, in much of the advocacy of a self consciously moral approach to tourism consumption. The way development is presented to the public through the media and in everyday life, a process sometimes referred to as the 'public face of development' (Smith and Yanacopulos, 2004), emphasizes these personal traits. High profile telethons, charity challenges, Fair Trade and ethical consumption generally are examples of this trend. Arguably, the personalized approach to development was first brought to the fore through Bob Geldof's 1985 'Live Aid' concerts, although as Chouliaraki shows, since then the humanitarian impulse has increasingly come to be shaped by personal morality as opposed to finding expression in politics (Chouliaraki, 2013).

An early and notable example of the focus on ethical lifestyle in leisure travel is Krippendorf's (1987) often quoted book *The holiday makers: understanding the impact of leisure and travel*. Krippendorf (1987) focuses on personal behaviour, awareness and attitudes as key to the role of tourism in development. For Krippendorf (1987, p. xiv) our personal freedoms 'threaten to engulf us' unless we engage in a pre-travel education to 'learn how to travel'. He writes that tourism is a 'new and devious form of colonialism' (1987, p. 56) and a 'kind of friendly conquest' (1987, p. 55)—personal freedom has profound negative consequences in this view. Since Krippendorf placed personal ethics at the heart of tourism's development impact, 'care', 'awareness' and 'responsibility' have loomed ever larger. Charities such as *Tourism Concern* in the UK see their role as raising awareness of injustices (see www.tourismconcern.org.uk). The assumption here is that if people are 'aware', then they might consider moral questions relating to their impact on other cultures and the natural environment, leading to more 'responsible' and 'caring' social outcomes. Laudable goals, such as the livelihoods of Nepalese porters, and more debatable ones, such as codes of conduct for travellers, are frequently discussed in terms of care, awareness and responsibility on the part of private consumers.

'Responsible Tourism' has become a well known brand courtesy of academic and ecotourism promoter Harold Goodwin and former Body Shop marketing executive Justin Francis, through their *ResponsibleTravel.com* web site (www.responsibletravel.com) (the late Anita Roddick, formerly prime mover in ethical consumption with her Body Shop stores, was part of originating the brand). For these advocates of ethical holidays, responsible tourism 'simply means holidays that *care* about local communities and culture as well as wildlife conservation and the environment.' (italics added) (www.responsibletravel.com).

The laudable personal qualities of care and responsibility are explicitly linked to the social project of development in the campaigning and academic literature. *Responsibletravel.com* and *Tourism Concern* (tourismconcern.org.uk) are examples of the former, and the academic volume 'Responsible Travel' edited by rural development expert Anna Spenceley (2012) is indicative of the latter.

Indeed, the adjective 'responsible' has been widely adopted, including early on by the world's biggest conservation body the World Wide Fund for Nature, as a label for their attempts at utilizing tourism to link conservation and development in economically poor, biodiversity rich destinations (Woolford, 2002).

The link between personal qualities and social outcomes is clearest with volunteer tourism, a recent addition to the lengthy list of moral tourism labels. Here the impulse to act upon the world privileges personal experience and reflection over any political framing of the issues being addressed (Butcher and Smith, 2014, forthcoming). Attempts to assist others are mediated through a self conscious process of identity formation, a process focused on personal rather than political identities and morality (Chouliraki, 2013). The very term 'volunteer tourism' would have seemed odd a generation ago precisely because of its conflation of private behaviour and political agency.

It is worth noting that what is taken to be 'responsible' in tourism consumption and development is generally discussed and decided amongst a milieu of non-governmental organizations (NGOs), academics and campaigners and codified in statements ranging from the United Nations' 'Quebec Declaration on Ecotourism' (UN/WTO, 2002) through to numerous codes of conduct and declarations such as ResponsibleTravel.com's 2002 'Cape Town Declaration' (www.responsibletravel. com). What does and does not, or should and should not, qualify as responsible or ethical tourism is hotly debated. For example, the accusation of 'greenwashing' is commonly made against corporate attempts to develop ethical tourism (Robbins, 2008). Voluntourism in particular attracts praise for its development potential and enlightening role (Wearing, 2001) alongside criticism that it is a conduit for neoliberalism and neocolonial attitudes (Vrasti, 2013). Nonetheless, the tenor of all these discussions is very much how we can make our holidays truly moral pursuits, rather than a questioning of the efficacy of the lifestyle politics central to ethical travel.

The ethical sounding adjectives (responsible, caring, green, aware ...) that are commonplace in the above examples suggest personal qualities, not political categories. To describe oneself as 'caring' or 'ethical' gives nothing away as to your politics and beliefs about society and the people in it. Likewise, to say your policy is 'responsible' gives no indication of its position on any wider political spectrum. Neither does it even place it on a moral spectrum beyond what Chouliaraki refers to as a 'self-oriented morality' (Chouliaraki, 2013), one that is only capable of framing the attendant issues in terms of the identity and feelings of, in this case, the tourist. It does, however, serve to place the view on the moral high ground. This is especially case *vis a vis* mass package tourism, the consumers of which are implicitly less moral, less responsible (Butcher, 2003). Responsible tourism is a rhetorical orthodoxy amongst campaigners, lecturers and many commentators. The ethical lobby now colonize the moral high ground, which can on occasion have the effect of closing down political debate on contrasting development choices and visions. After all, who could be against care and responsibility?

The Public and Private Spheres

The issue is not at all whether people should care or act responsibly. Rather, it is the prominence of these code words for goodness in the public realm of political debate on development that is significant. The elevation of a discourse of 'responsibility' and 'care' into the realm of the politics of development is indicative of an important trend in politics: that of the diminution of public life and the consequent extension of private concerns and personal qualities into the centre of hitherto political debate. Therefore in order to situate the 'new moral tourism' (Butcher, 2003) it is worth considering the relationship between personal qualities and private reflection on the one hand, and debate in the public sphere as an expression of politics on the other.

Historically, the establishment of a public life outside of the private realm of home marked the rise of a sense of society, of a social order constructed out of and subject to the wishes of the people. Aristotle was probably the first to consider a distinctive public sphere beyond the individual citizen: the polis or political community. The Roman forum as an arena for trade and the discussion of public affairs is a further example of the public sphere. The Italian city states in the Renaissance, the development of parliamentary authority and political parties and subsequent demands to democratize, and the ideas of the Enlightenment that placed human beings at the heart of the social, are all indicative of the rise of an active public sphere and also of the widening and deepening of human agency beyond private feelings and interests.

Richard Sennett (2003) in his ground breaking book *The Fall of Public Man* provided an analysis of the changing character of the private and public spheres in modern times. The coffee houses of eighteenth century Britain are discussed by Sennett as indicative of the rise of the modern public sphere. The patrons drank coffee and talked about the public affairs of business and politics. France's salons served a similar purpose. The codes and institutions of public life, in the salons, the societies and in political institutions, separated it off from private, intimate life to the benefit of each—public involvement is dependent upon, but at the same time removed and different from, private life and reflection (see Sennett, 2003 and Arendt, 1958 on the private and public sphere).

Sennett argued that the blurring of boundaries between the two marked a diminution of public life, and of politics. The extension of personal qualities (awareness, care, responsibility), associated with private actions (individual purchases, lifestyle, behaviour) directly into the realm of politics, as is the case with the claims made for ethical tourism, is surely a case in point. That is not to suggest that these qualities are corrosive in any way, but that a healthy public, political scene involves a recognition of a world beyond the individual and the capacity of the individual to involve themselves in understanding, commenting upon and negotiating issues that cannot be explained or understood through a discourse focused on personal qualities and private interventions.

The process Sennett noted in the 1970s has gone further since. The dual crisis of both capitalism and any alternative to it has emptied politics of competing visions of social change—the very stuff of politics. Russell Jacoby (1999) was amongst the first to argue that the fall of the Berlin Wall and the collapse of Eastern European communism exposed the exhaustion of Left alternatives to capitalism and also, ironically, of capitalism itself. The latter had justified itself in relation to its communist opponent throughout the period of the Cold War, and hence the victory of the market in the Cold War was pyrrhic. For Jacoby (1999), the search for better forms of society, 'utopias', had been linked to the political projects of Right and Left. In the absence of these projects a dull managerialism generally pervades all manner of public institutions, from parliaments to Universities. The saying associated with British Conservative leader Margaret Thatcher in the 1980s, 'There Is No Alternative', accompanied by the failure of the market (the thing that it was claimed there is no alternative to), left a vacuum which has been filled by trends such as the politics of behaviour (e.g. Thaler and Sunstein's 'Nudge' (2009), lifestyle politics e.g. Giddens (1991) concept of 'Life Politics' and the politics of ethical consumption (Barnett et al., 2011)). All of these are associated with hitherto *private* aspects of life (shopping, personal behaviour, everyday life), now central to the public sphere, to the *political* scene. The rise of ethical holidays, and their association with development— really a sort of lifestyle politics (with the emphasis on lifestyle)—is indicative of these trends.

Some would view the developments Sennett describes in a positive light. For example, feminists have politicized the private sphere as a site of the oppression of women, and the slogan 'the personal is political', originating from feminist Carole Hanisch's (1970) often quoted essay, neatly sums up the desire to view the intimate and private world of relationships as a directly political issue for discussion in the public sphere. Similarly one could argue that the politicization of lifestyle opens up new avenues for a politics more relevant to everyday experience (Barnett et al., 2011). That just about everything is political has become a hallmark of post-structuralist political thought, drawing upon Foucauldian ideas of dispersed power.

But the efficacy of 'the personal is political' presupposes a clear recognition of the social roots of personal struggles. The defining difference today is a lack of social critiques—the public sphere has been emptied out by the apparent exhaustion of both mainstream and alternative political philosophies (Leys, 1996; Laidi, 1998; Furedi, 2005; Chouliaraki, 2013). Laidi (1998) argues that the end of the Cold War destroyed the principal framework through which political identities were defined. Chouliaraki (2013) concurs—the grand narratives of Left and Right, flawed as they were, mediated between on the one hand private experiences, emotions and reflections, and on the other a public realm of political contestation. Their decline has not been paralleled by new ideas that facilitate political reflection and judgement. We might meet in the coffee shop, but it is unlikely we will talk politics when politics seems devoid of principal and passion.

The nearest we might get to politics, if we accept the ethical consumption agenda, is to worry about what brand of coffee we are drinking, or whether next year's holiday is 'responsible'.

Care, Responsibility and Anti-Politics

The trend towards a politics that revolves around responsibility, awareness and care—indicative of a blurring of the private and the public as discussed by Sennett—is clearly reflected in human geography's 'moral turn'. 'Geographies of care' (Silk, 1998) and 'responsibility' (Popke, 2006, Massey 2004) hold that through an awareness of our place in global trade, which can be developed through a focus on the commodity chains that link consumer and distant producer, we may be able to extend a 'care' normally associated with those close to us (by family ties, geography or nationality) to distant others. We can buy ethically here to extend care globally. Giddens (1994: 5) for example, comments that:

> Our day to day activities are increasingly influenced by events happening on the other side of the world. Conversely, local lifestyle habits have become globally consequential. Thus my decision to buy a certain item of clothing has implications not only for the international division of labour, but for the Earth's ecosystem.

This argument has been developed quite extensively in relation to Fair Trade (e.g. Lyon, 2010; Nichols and Opal 2010). One recent intervention, 'Globalizing responsibility: the political rationalities of ethical consumption', sees a recognition of these links between everyday consumption and global, often distant, impacts as part of developing a new progressive politics (Barnett et al., 2011). However, aware of the charge that this is a 'consumer politics' with limited horizons, they further argue that such an approach can lead to wider 'political' recognition of how to change society (ibid.).

What is most notable about this view, though, is the way that politics is written out of the analysis precisely in the name of 'responsibility'. What is considered responsible (in this case organic agriculture, Fair Trade and green tourism) is a given in 'Globalizing Responsibility'. Political contestation of ideologies of development (the stuff of politics) is completely absent from the analysis. Those who don't act in the prescribed ethical manner are deemed to lack *awareness* and the opportunity to act *responsibly*. This is anti-political and also patronizing. A direct example of this trend from the advocacy of ethical tourism is Goodwin's casual equating of being responsible with the promotion of organic agriculture and localism: 'You just have to look at the growth in ethical consumption,' says Goodwin. 'People buy into Fair Trade, organics and local produce, so why would you not take that mindset with you when you go on holiday?' (cited in Rowe, undated). The political, contested question of agricultural production can be ignored as the 'responsible' side of the argument is for organic agriculture and localism. Politics is circumvented by a prescriptive discourse of responsibility.

There is hence an implicit assumption in the politics and geographies of care that buying non Fair Trade food—for example factory farmed, genetically modified (GM) food—means you don't care (or lack 'awareness', a slightly less pejorative characterization). That you may believe farming utilizing GM to be a better option for the future of the developing countries, or that you may not believe consumption can really address political issues of development, is outside of the framing of this debate. Similarly, buying a cheap package holiday is not failing to care. It could reflect the view that holidays are a poor vehicle for advancing social and political aspirations. It could legitimately reflect the opinion that the eco-options that go under the heading 'responsible' more often than not have nothing much to offer by way of development (Butcher, 2003, 2007). In this way the 'moralisation of tourism' leads away from a political framing of the issue of development (Butcher, 2003). 'Caring and uncaring', 'responsible and irresponsible', 'awareness and lacking awareness' not only reproduce a discourse of personal qualities as the key to acting on the world, but they close down debate on other development perspectives that don't conform to the characteristics favoured by the ethical lobby. In this sense the rise of personal ethics mirrors the decline of politics, and an attendant public discussion of political morality.

Academics and non-governmental organizations are the arbiters of what is 'responsible' or 'ethical'. Consumers who do not problematize their shopping or their holiday are assumed to be lacking 'awareness' or 'care', or simply to be 'irresponsible'. It is in this way that unappealing caricatures from the past of the masses on holiday are reproduced in a coded politically correct form. The 'unwashed' or 'unworthy' masses of the Victorian era are replaced by the 'unaware' or 'irresponsible' masses of today. Indeed, for ResponsibleTravel.com, responsible travel 'is a new way of travelling for those who've had enough of mass tourism'. Given the unflattering portrayal of package holidaymakers in their full page advertisement placed in British newspapers in 2004, it would be fair to assume they have had enough of mass tourists too (http://www.responsibletravel. com/copy/had-enough-advertisement). The advert carries the strapline 'Had Enough?' next to a picture of tourists crammed in to a small pool, followed by their alternative: 'Thousands of Holidays to hundreds of places that haven't been ravaged by mass tourism'. This is the nasty side of the responsible outlook—when private prejudice passes for a public campaign for 'sustainable development'.

Personalizing Politics—Is Closer Better?

Ethical consumption has been viewed as a progressive humanizing of politics (see Shah et al., 2012), although perhaps it could more accurately be characterized as a *personalizing* of politics. In contrast to abstract theories and grand narratives, it appears to bring political issues down to every day human relationships. This is attractive in anti-political times. Take Fair Trade for example, which is assumed absolutely central to ethical consumption (Barnett et al., 2011). Consumers are encouraged to consider the impact of their consumption upon the producer, and to pay more to support them, very often on the basis that they are small scale and organic producers. Fair Trade favours small scale production over large, and organic over modern methods such as the use of genetically modified organisms. The latter is barred from being certified 'Fair Trade'. Cafes and Fair Trade packaging and publicity carry pictures of the farmers, and their names—the connection is personal and empathy (or perhaps sympathy) is encouraged.

In similar vein, the clientele of 'ethical' holiday companies are also encouraged to make a difference to the individuals they meet. Through tourism, the care associated with ethical consumption is given and experienced personally (Meletis and Campbell, 2007). If care is seen as bonds associated with those close to us (family, friends, neighbours) then tourism is an exemplary case as tourists are both literally and metaphorically developing a closeness to the objects of their care. The clearest example of this is the new 'voluntourism', which links holidays directly to the active promotion of wellbeing of the people personally encountered. The personal element—names, acquaintances, friendships—is key, unsurprising given that the aim is to care. Consumers not only see and learn a little of the workers producing their product –their village, their names, their farms etc—but visit them and work with them on projects to assist their livelihoods. Hence attempts at moralizing consumption through tourism are an excellent case study of this personalization of agency and its corollary, the eschewal of political agency.

This personalized aspect of ethical tourism plays well at a time when government and business are often associated with being 'big', 'distant' or even 'dirty', and in the social sciences 'grand narratives' are not only not in evidence, but are regarded as untenable by many (see Minca and Oakes [eds.], 2012, with regard to tourism). Ethical tourism fits well with contemporary anti-politics and often adopts a populist rhetoric—'the local community' are often contrasted favourably to the perceived impersonality of governments and global trade (Butcher, 2007, 2013). But the closeness to the object of our care, in itself, provides no moral guidance. If we encounter a poor trader selling coral necklaces whilst on holiday, should we buy it to help the man and his family (but contribute to the destruction of the coral) or refuse to buy to discourage damage to the reef (but leave the man and his family poorer)? Holiday encounters, like all consumption based ethical strategies, seems to expand the possibilities for moral action, but in doing so narrows the scope for moral agency.

A similar argument has been made by Giles Mohan (2001) with regard to development volunteers. He points out that being over reliant upon personal contact for one's view of development tends to encourage a conception of development and inequalities based upon a fetishized view of culture, rather than through fundamental historical and material inequalities (Mohan, 2001). The personal touch—'being there'—is no substitute for politics. Likewise, the intimate and 'can do' approach of ethical tourism seems to encourage this fetishized view of the culture personally experienced, cut adrift from a wider political framing.

Whilst reducing literal distance between the subject and object of care doesn't lead to enlightenment, the same can be argued with regard to metaphorical distance. Elie Chouliaraki (2013) argues that the immediacy of emotional and personal responses to humanitarian issues—for example a response to a poster of a poor orphan, a half built village school or a film showing starving children—without the mediating influence of a healthy 'agonistic' public sphere, leave us with a 'post humanitarianism': an inability to think and act beyond a 'self oriented' moral framework in relation to the suffering of others. She argues, in effect, to re-establish some metaphorical distance between the humanitarian individual and the object of their humanitarian impulse. That distance makes possible a framing of the issues in social and political terms, and a contestation of the roots of the humanitarian matter at hand. It enables us to see other people as having agency within the context of their lives and society, rather than collapsing this into our own search for a moral lifestyle. Without this distance, Chouliaraki (2013) argues that solidarity will be fleeting, fitting around the lifestyle of the humanitarian, reacting to the surface rather than the substance of the issue. This is the limit of lifestyle, personalized politics informed by the language of responsibility, awareness and care. Ultimately, as Chouliaraki (2013) shows, the best intentions can feed in to a narcissism, where the issues we wish to act upon are a backdrop for a western search for selfhood and purpose—a self oriented moral project rather than an Other oriented one.

This argument is illustrated, albeit in an extreme way, by the controversies over volunteer tourism to orphanages in poor countries such as Cambodia (Pitrelli, 2012; Al Jazeera, 2008). The impulse to help a poor child motivates volunteer tourism, and this, alongside the personal benefit the tourist will get through the experience, is what is promised by volunteer tourism operators. Yet the political and economic roots of poverty, the social struggles of families to get by, the construction of childhood in different circumstances—issues in many ways for the public sphere and for Chouliaraki's (2013) metaphorical distance from the object of concern—appear beyond the individual. The social agents are the tourists alone, and the children, their families and societies are presented as victims and bystanders. Most children in the orphanages are reported as having at least one surviving parent, but in Cambodia tourist dollars and the emotions of well meaning volunteers can push desperate families apart (Pitrelli, 2012). Effectively, albeit unwittingly, help is available if you give up your child, but unavailable if you don't. Care from a western volunteer attracts money, care for your own children doesn't. Outcomes for the children in some orphanages are reported to be poor to the extent that some volunteer tourism companies have recently withdrawn from this area of work (Francis, 2013). Beyond the material outcomes, orphanage volunteer tourism reinforces damaging political assumptions of a dependent, vulnerable Third World in need of the benevolent, caring westerner (Guiney, 2013).

That is neither to neither condemn nor praise volunteering in foreign orphanages, but to point out the poverty of such actions *as social or political interventions in development*. Charity is always an admirable impulse. However, the good Samaritan who crosses the road to help someone in need is in a sense the opposite to the new moral tourist. One claims to be a player in development gathering valuable life experience, the other simply acts in a charitable manner. Private charity as a conspicuous lifestyle politics diminishes politics. It may also diminish charity as a selfless act for others.

Not only does ethical tourism and the claims made for it mark a diminished politics and public sphere, it also does not benefit our capacity to reflect and act in our private lives. Here we are constantly confronted with moral dilemmas— do we castigate the naughty child, do we give the beggar some money, do we tell our friend that they are in a bad relationship? Do we volunteer at the Cambodian orphanage, send a donation or redouble our attempt to understand and challenge the reasons why Cambodia is a poor country? We develop and exercise our own moral autonomy in these everyday encounters. There is no benefit in prescribing or proscribing private, lawful individual behaviour in the name of ethical conduct.

Specifically with regard to tourism, the thrill is to negotiate new people, new places, cultures and relationships. Travel may well provide opportunity for critical reflection of oneself and society. However, making the exciting private journey of the tourist subject to a set of ethical imperatives linked to a particular political outlook cuts down the potential for personal development—or in Sennett's (2003) terms, the development of moral autonomy through reflection in the private sphere.

Conclusions

Contrary to the claims that ethical tourism is progressive politics, it diminishes politics in two senses. First, politics is diminished as personal qualities replace political categories in public development discourse. This reflects and reinforces the emptying of the public sphere and hence narrows both political and moral agency. Second, ethical tourism is a particular outlook masquerading, via terms such as care and responsibility, as a universal ethics for all. As such, it narrows discussion of different development options. This is a stifling etiquette for anyone who wants to discuss real political and social choices. It is a problem for anyone wanting to widen political horizons and re-establish a public forum for development politics beyond the moralistic declarations about how individuals choose to spend their holidays.

References

Al Jazeera (2008). Cambodia's 'Fake' Orphans (video). 8th November. *Al Jazeera*. Accessed at http://www.youtube.com/watch?v=emYlQf-7piA accessed on 10 September 2013.

Arendt, H. (1958). *The Human Condition*. Chicago: University of Chicago Press.

Barnett, C., Clarke, N., Cloke, P., and Malpass, A. (2011). *Globalizing Responsibility: The Political Rationalities of Ethical Consumption*. Oxford: Blackwell.

Butcher, J. (2003). *The Moralization of Tourism: Sun, Sand ... and Saving the World?*. London: Routledge.

Butcher, J. (2005). The Moral Authority of Ecotourism: A Critical Review. *Current Issues in Tourism*, 8 (2/3), 114–124.

Butcher, J. and Smith, P. (2014). *Volunteer Tourism and Development*. London: Routledge.

Chang, H. (2010). Hamlet without the Prince of Denmark: How Development has Disappeared from Today's 'Development' Discourse. In S. Khan and J. Christiansen (eds.), *Towards New Developmentalism: Market as Means Rather than Master*. London: Routledge.

Chouliaraki, L. (2013). *The Ironic Spectator: Solidarity in the Age of Post Humanitarianism*. Cambridge: Polity.

Francis, J. (2013). 'Orphanage Volunteering Holidays Removed.' 25 July accessed at http://blog.responsibletravel.com/orphanage-tourism/ accessed on 4 September 2013.

Furedi, F. (2005). *Politics of Fear: Beyond Left and Right*. London: Continuum.

Giddens, A. (1991). *Modernity and Self-identity*. Cambridge: Polity.

Giddens, A. (1994). *Beyond Left and Right: The Future of Radical Politics*. Cambridge: Polity.

Guiney, T. (2013). 'Constructive Development or Commodification of Orphans? Orphanage Tourism Impacts in Cambodia'. Unpublished paper presented at the American Association of Geographers conference, Los Angeles, March 2013.

Hanisch, C. (1970). 'The Personal is Political'. Originally published in Firestone, S., and Koedt, A., *Notes from the Second Year: Women's Liberation in 1970*. New York: Radical Feminism.

Heath, S. (1997). Widening the Gap: Pre-university Gap Years and the 'Economy of Experience'. *British Journal of Sociology of Education*, 28(1), 89–103.

Jacoby, R. (1999). *The End of Utopia: Politics and Culture in an Age of Apathy*. New York: Basic Books.

Krippendorf, J. (1987). *The Holiday Makers: Understanding the Impact of Leisure and Travel*. London: Butterworth-Heinemann.

Laidi, Z. (1998). *A World without Meaning: The Crisis of Meaning in International Politics*. London: Routledge.

Leys, C. (1996). *The Rise and Fall of Development Theory*. London: James Currey.

Lyon, S. (2010). *Coffee and Community: Maya Farmers and Fair-Trade Markets*. Colorado: University Press of Colorado.

Lyons, K., Hanley, J., Wearing, S., and Neil, J. (2012). Gap Year Volunteer Tourism: Myths of Global Citizenship? *Annals of Tourism Research*, 39(1), 361–378.

Massey, D. (2004). Geographies of Responsibility. *Geografiska Annaler* 86B, pp. 5–18.

Meletis, Z. A., and Campbell, L. M. (2007). Call it Consumption! Reconceptualizing Ecotourism as Consumption and Consumptive. *Geography Compass* 1(4), 850–870.

Minca, C., and Oakes, T. (eds.) (2011). *Real Tourism: Practice, Care, and Politics in Contemporary Travel Culture*. London: Routledge.

Mohan, G. (2001). Beyond Participation: Strategies for Deeper Empowerment. In Cooke, B. and Kothari, U. (eds.), *Participation: The New Tyranny*. London: Zed Books, pp. 153–167.

Nichols, A., and Opal, C. (2005). *Fair Trade: Market-driven Ethical Consumption*. London: Sage.

Pitrelli, M. (2012). Orphanage Tourism: Help or Hindrance? *Daily Telegraph*. 3rd February. Accessed at http://www.telegraph.co.uk/expat/expatlife/9055213/Orphanage-tourism-help-or-hindrance.html accessed on 4 September 2013.

Popke, J. (2006). Geography and Ethics: Everyday Mediations through Care and Consumption. *Progress in Human Geography*, 30(4), 504–512.

ResponsibleTravel.com (2013). 'What is Responsible Tourism'. Accessed at http://www.responsibletravel.com/copy/responsible-tourism accessed on 4th September 2013.

Robbins, T. (2008). Are you being Greenwashed? *The Observer*. Sunday 6 July. Accessed at http://www.theguardian.com/travel/2008/jul/06/green.ethicalholidays accessed on 1/9/13.

Rowe, M. (n.d.). Future of Tourism Dossier. Accessed at http://www.responsibletravel.com/resources/future-of-tourism/dossier.htm accessed on 13th April 2013.

Sennett, R. (2003). *The Fall of Public Man*. London: Penguin.

Shah, D. V., Wells, C., Friedland, L. A., Kim, Y. M., and Rojas, H. (eds.). (2012). *Communication, Consumers, and Citizens: Revisiting the Politics of Consumption*. London: Sage.

Silk, J. (1998). Caring at a Distance. *Ethics, Place and Environment*, 1, 165–182.

Smith, M., and Yanacopulos, H. (2004). The Public Faces of Development. *Journal of International Development*, 16(5), 657–664.

Spenceley, A. (ed.) (2012). *Responsible Travel: Critical Issues for Conservation and Development*. London: Routledge.

Thaler, R. H., and Sunstein, C. R. (2009). *Nudge: Improving Decisions about Health, Wealth, and Happiness*. London: Penguin.

Tourism Concern, www.tourismconcern.org.uk.

UNEP/WTO (2002). *Quebec Declaration on Ecotourism*. Paris: UNEP/WTO.

Vrasti, W. (2012). *Volunteer Tourism in the Global South: Giving Back in Neoliberal Times*. London: Routledge.

Wearing, S. (2001). *Volunteer Tourism: Experiences that Make a Difference*. Oxford: CABI.

Woolford, J., pers. comm. (2002). Tourism Policy Officer in International Policy Unit of WWF-UK, on 30/5/02, telephone interview to WWF-UK offices in London.

Chapter 3

International Volunteer Tourism as (De)commodified Moral Consumption

Peter Smith

Introduction

The last two decades have witnessed a growing literature on 'moral' or alternative tourism that links the behaviour and purchasing habits of consumers to development outcomes in developing countries (see Krippendorf, 1987; Patullo, 1996; Scheyvens, 2002; Weaver, 2008; Buckley, 2008; Fennell, 2008; Patullo and Minelli, 2009; Wearing and Neil, 2009, among others). This emergence is in contrast to classical views of political economy which consider leisure as a discreet area lying outside of politics (Rojek, 2001). This transition in tourism has a strong affinity with moral consumer markets in that through our consumer habits we can make companies more moral, favour products that are deemed more sustainable or are fairer for the producers combined with concern for other issues such as the environment (Lury, 1996; Paterson, 2006). Volunteer tourism is now widely recognized as an important and growing segment of the alternative tourism sector. In the last decade a significant body of literature has emerged on volunteer tourism in tourism studies, human geography and related disciplines.

By way of a formal definition Wearing's (2001: 1) foundational study defines volunteer tourists as tourists who, 'undertake holidays that might involve aiding or alleviating the material poverty of some groups in society, the restoration of certain environments or research into aspects of society or environment'. Volunteer tourists, primarily young people from Western countries, devote a proportion of their leisure time to volunteer projects largely in developing countries. More prosaically McGehee and Santos (2005: 760) define volunteer tourism as 'utilizing discretionary time and income to travel out of the sphere of regular activity to assist others in need'. Volunteer tourism can, therefore, be characterized as a form of moral consumption, the aim of which is to assist conservation and community well-being goals in the global South.

Recent studies interrogate volunteer tourists' motivations and experiences (McGehee, 2002; Brown and Lehto, 2005; McGehee and Santos, 2005; Cousins, 2007; Coghlan, 2006, 2007 and 2008); focus on the attitudes of the host community to the volunteer projects (Broad, 2003; Clifton and Benson, 2006; McGehee and Andereck, 2009; Sin, 2010; Barbieri et al., 2012) or take a case-study approach to exploring volunteer tourism projects (see contributions to Lyons and Wearing,

2008a; Benson, 2011) to name a few. This literature, like much of the advocacy of moral tourism more broadly, tends to focus on small-scale, community oriented tourism that explicitly aims to promote both conservation and host community well-being (Mowforth and Munt 1998; Butcher, 2007). Despite this emerging body of literature, volunteer tourism is acknowledged as being under-theorized and critical studies are lacking (Sin, 2009; Vrasti, 2009; Wearing, 2010; Conran, 2011; McGehee, 2012). Indeed the benefits to the host communities from volunteer projects are often accepted without question and the views and opinions of host communities are largely absent from the literature (Guttentag, 2011). This chapter contributes to emerging research in critical tourism studies on the discourse of volunteer tourism.

It has been argued that volunteer tourists are 'alternative' tourists (Brown and Lehto, 2005; Novelli, 2005; Pearce and Coghlan, 2008); at the committed end of a spectrum of ethical tourism (Coghlan, 2006) and part of 'hard' rather than 'soft' ecotourism (Weaver, 2008). It has also been suggested that volunteers represent a significant force in the development of ecotourism in the global South (Duffy, 2002). Volunteer tourists are considered as committed moral tourists (Cousins, 2007); sharing many of the characteristics of ecotourism (Wearing, 2001) and 'new moral' tourism (Butcher, 2003). Indeed, Lyons and Wearing (2008c: 153) have argued that the ideological proposition of volunteer tourism is to provide a sustainable alternative to mass tourism.

Volunteer tourism is certainly motivated by altruism (Soderman and Snead, 2008; Matthews, 2008) in contrast to mass tourism, which is usually characterized as self-interested, carefree or pejoratively labelled hedonistic pleasure seeking (Singh, 2004). Volunteer tourists' desire to 'make a difference' contributes to expanding what has been discussed as the 'geographies of care' (Popke, 2006). Care is considered as the active interest of one person in the well-being of another (Silk, 2000). For Popke (2006) the desire to care for others is a moral and ethical issue that can be the basis for an alternative ethical outlook: through caring for others the moral position of the individual is acted out. Smith (2000: 93) suggests that in a more globalized world, with greater economic interdependence, there is an increased capacity to harm others in distant places through our consumption patterns. As such, the ethics of care can and should be extended beyond people we have existing contact or relationships with, such as friends and family members, towards 'different and distant others', who we have no personal connection with and who are dispersed in time and space (Smith, 1998; Silk, 1998). Fair trade is often cited as an example of this type of care for others through moral consumption (Barnett et al., 2005; Nicholls and Opel, 2005; Jackson, 2006). Here there is an overlap with the practice of volunteer tourism, where volunteers purchase products that aim to help and assist host communities in the global South.

Volunteer tourism could be seen as an exemplar of moral consumption that embodies a concept of the geographies of care; with volunteer tourists caring for 'distant others'. Silk (2004: 231) suggests that with normal acts of aid-giving the donor, or carer, never meets or hears from the intended beneficiary, yet in volunteer tourism they do: with NGOs or gap year companies acting as a bridge between the volunteers and the communities in need (Keese, 2011: 258). Further, through sharing a physical space with the host community the volunteer tourist experience is less charity from afar; commendable 'caring at a distance' for distant others but more active caring *in situ* (Sin, 2010: 984–985). Thus volunteer tourism is seen as having the potential to bridge the spatial distance between the giver and receiver of moral concern and altruistic intent associated with ethical consumption. Volunteer projects aim to alleviate poverty in the developing world and bring consumers—in this case the volunteers—face-to-face with the consequences of under-development to host communities, alongside the need to conserve natural habitat and capital. For these reasons, volunteer tourism has become the new 'poster-child' for alternative tourism (Lyons and Wearing, 2008b: 6).

One area where there is a developing critique is a discussion of the experience and practice of volunteer tourism. Whilst altruism may certainly be a key factor in volunteers' motivations, studies suggest participation in volunteer projects is not exclusively altruistic (Mustonen, 2005; Coghlan 2006; Broad and Jenkins, 2008; Sin, 2009). For example, it has been suggested the volunteer tourism experiences can express a desire to gain 'cultural capital', with curriculum vitae building and personal and professional development motivations playing an important role in the experience (Halpenny and Caissie, 2003; Cousins, 2007; Palacios, 2010). Jones (2011) argues that through volunteering young people gain preparatory experience and informal training in cultural sensitivity which benefits them in their careers in the corporate world. Drawing on fieldwork among volunteer tourists in Africa, Sin (2009) argues that volunteers' motivations are in part altruistic but are also heavily associated with personal or 'self' development. For example, she suggests that experiencing something 'exotic', or Other are key motivations for volunteering. Similarly, Barbieri et al. (2012) in their study of volunteer tourists in Rwanda conclude that self-development is a key motivation for project participants alongside bonding with the host community and experiencing the local lifestyle.

Butcher and Smith (2010) argue that this concern for volunteers' self-development and exploration, including the desire to experience host communities first hand, is aligned to personal 'life politics' and an individual approach to the politics of development. It has been suggested that it would be useful to develop a scale of commitment among volunteer tourists which would identify 'shallow' commitment on one side of the spectrum and 'deep' commitment on the other (Callanan and Thomas, 2005). It is predicted that those at the more committed end of the spectrum would cite ethical values as an important motivating factor informing their decision to volunteer.

Advocates of volunteer tourism suggest that it is an alternative form of consumption with the potential to challenge the dominant 'neoliberal paradigms of tourism' (Higgins-Desbiolles and Mundine, 2008: 182). Critics of volunteer tourism on the other hand argue that it embodies particular features of neoliberalism, where the 'guests' are objectified or 'Othered' and neocolonial Western agendas and images inform volunteers' perceptions of people in the global South (Baillie-

Smith and Laurie, 2011: 556; McGehee and Andereck, 2008: 18–19: Guttentag, 2009: 545–547; Sin, 2009: 496; Simpson, 2005; Brown and Hall, 2008; Caton and Santos, 2009; Palacios, 2010).

The Volunteer Tourism Industry

Volunteer tourism projects operate in many countries and are organized by a range of sending organizations including private companies, conservation and educational organizations and non-governmental organizations (NGOs) (Broad, 2003; Soderman and Snead, 2008; Raymond and Hall, 2008). A survey of over 300 volunteer tourism organizations worldwide concluded that the market caters to 1.6 million volunteer tourists a year, with a monetary value of between £832m and £1.3bn ($1.7bn–$2.6bn). Growth in the sector has been most marked since 1990 (ATLAS/TRAM, 2008: 5). There is a focus on gap year aged volunteer tourists, normally in the 18–25 age range, which make up the primary market (Simpson, 2005: 447; ATLAS/TRAM, 2008: 5; Wearing, 2010: 213; Jones, 2011, 535).

This focus represents how a significant number of young people seek to act upon their world, outside traditional political channels, in the realm of the moral consumption of holidays. In the UK and elsewhere gap year projects are encouraged through schools, universities and government. Jones (2005: 87) argues that participation on a gap year project can benefit the individual, who gains cross-cultural experience and develops as a global citizen with insights and experience beyond the parochial. Here volunteering is seen as a way of developing cultural sensitivity and a sense of 'global citizenship', with concepts of volunteering and citizenship increasingly part of the curriculum of schools and universities (Advisory Group on Citizenship, 1998; Bednarz, 2003; Standish, 2008; Baillie-Smith and Laurie, 2011). Gap years are now accredited, structured and praised by politicians for this contribution to citizenship (Jones, 2004, 2011; Lyons et al., 2012). Pearce and Coghlan (2008) suggest that in the UK gap years are seen as almost an obligatory post-compulsory education experience and this recent cultural shift is the source of many younger volunteer tourists. Simpson (2005) has argued that the gap year experience is also seen by many employers as desirable and can thus be considered as a training ground for future professionals who accumulate 'cultural capital' through their volunteer work.

According to a UK government commissioned report on gap year provision (defined in the report as 'a period of time between 3 and 24 months taken out of education or a work career', hence a wider category than volunteer tourism), internationally there are over 800 organizations offering overseas volunteer placements in 200 countries in the global North and South. In total these organizations offer around 350,000 placements opportunities annually (Jones, 2004). Tourism Concern, a UK based charity who tend to look specifically at development and community based tourism, estimate that there are now around sixty organizations in the UK offering volunteer tourism placements (Tourism

Concern, 2007: 1). These range from commercial companies to organizations operating in the NGO and voluntary sector. A 2007 Mintel study calculated that people undertaking volunteer projects abroad account for 10% of the UK's outbound tourism expenditure: £960 million annually (Travel Weekly, 2007). In 2010 a further UK study estimated that up to 500,000 gap year students volunteered abroad. Their main activities included teaching English, animal conservation and building homes in poor rural communities (Neeves and Birgnall, 2010).

The large number of organizations involved in the gap year sector makes it hard to accurately assess the absolute number of volunteering destinations, organizations and range of activities. Volunteer tourism activities range from community work, such as building a school or clinic (Raleigh International, 2009); to teaching English (Jakubiak, 2012); to conservation based projects that involve scientific research or ecological restoration such as reforestation and habitat protection (Wearing, 2004: 217). In many ways, the volunteer tourism phenomenon has become a 'rite of passage' (Wearing et al., 2008: 69) taken by increasing numbers of internationally mobile young people, in part, to do good, but also endorsed by commercial companies seeking professional employees with international experience and an appreciation of global issues.

Benefits to the Community or the Volunteer?

Despite many of the claims made for the positive impact of volunteers in host communities (Wearing, 2001, Wearing et al., 2005; Zahra and McIntosh, 2007; Ruhanen et al., 2008; Wearing and Ponting, 2009) others argue that the actual contribution to development is minimal and that the impacts on host communities are often assumed rather than researched (VSO, 2007; Clifton and Benson, 2006; Grey and Campbell, 2007; Barbieri et al., 2012). The lack of impact that the volunteer tourists have in host communities is often attributed to insufficient knowledge, inappropriate skills or weak qualifications to produce 'effective help' or even question the level of volunteers' altruistic intent (Salazar, 2004; Brown and Hall, 2008; McGehee and Andereck, 2009; Palacios, 2010: 863).

Volunteer tourists pay a significant fee for their programme. According to a report on UK gap year participants, the average UK gap-year traveller spends between £3,000–£4,000 on their trip (Neeves and Birgnall, 2010). If this money were directly donated to a local community it could pay a greater amount of local labour than the individual volunteer could provide (Butcher and Smith, 2010: 33). Guttentag (2009) argues that it should not be assumed that the volunteers' aim of conserving a community's surrounding environment is shared by the community itself. Citing a number of case studies, he argues that volunteers are frequently more focused on their own promotion of environmental values than appreciating the host community's desire for economic development. In this way it is suggested that volunteer projects may actually impede the development desired by the host population. Guttentag rejects Wearing's (2001: 172–174) assertion that volunteer tourism promotes a 'genuine exchange' between the volunteer and host communities from which mutual learning results. Indeed Richter and Norman (2010) have suggested that volunteer tourists' contributions are often brief and the work done is usually low-skilled in nature. As a result, volunteer tourism labour may undermine the local labour market. Such criticisms have also been voiced by the veteran UK based volunteer organization Voluntary Service Overseas, who favour long-term placements, utilizing skilled graduates, over short-term voluntary projects (VSO, 2007). Yet, as Simpson (2005) suggests the lack of requirement for any particular expertise is in itself an element of the appeal of many volunteer or gap projects. Volunteer tourists are able to experiment with their identity and take on varying roles within the host community with little or no attention paid to their qualifications other than that of being an enthusiastic volunteer (Hutnyk, 1996: 44: Devereux, 2008: 363).

A number of studies suggest that volunteer tourism should be seen within the context of a dominant neoliberal approach to development, where the main beneficiaries of volunteers' participation in international projects are corporate companies seeking young professional employees with experience of working with people from other cultures (Simpson, 2005; Baillie-Smith and Laurie, 2011; Jones, 2011). Here the demand of global businesses for professionals with experience of working in international environments is seen as a part of a neoliberal agenda. Neoliberalism is considered an ideology that favours free market solutions and individual enterprise over state or collective led economic and social policies, with governments and companies of pursuing an aggressive 'market fundamentalism' (Stiglitz, 2010). For Harvey the essence of neoliberal theory is support for a minimal state and stressing the virtues of privatization, masked by the rhetoric of liberty and individual freedom (Harvey, 2011). Critics charge neoliberals with ushering in a 'shock doctrine' approach to development (Klein, 2007) with corporate companies taking advantage of government privatization of provision of goods and services (Hertz, 2002).

It is argued that a neoliberal approach sees international development as less a structural or political issue and more one susceptible to the market solutions of trade and commerce (Stiglitz, 2003, Hertz, 2005). One solution posed to global inequalities is moral consumption, such as fair trade in goods and services, enabling consumers to force a more ethical agenda onto companies through exercising choice in favour of products that are seen as more moral or in some way 'fairer' (Nicholls and Opal, 2005; Paterson, 2006). Volunteer tourism has been criticized for providing commodified products to meet the demands of these moral consumers (Lyons et al., 2012; Tomazos and Cooper, 2012; Mostafanezhad, 2013).

It is certainly the case that many western companies and organizations welcome the experience gained though international volunteering seeing it as a 'rite of passage.' Yet it is open to question the extent to which this represents a neoliberal form of development practice (Vodopiveca and Jaffe, 2011: 112). If anything, contemporary international volunteering tends to be influenced more by post-development and neopopulist thinking, which links conservation and community well-being goals through small-scale projects, rather than economic development through structural change, international trade and commerce or even simple infrastructural development (Butcher and Smith, 2010). As such, it could be argued that volunteer tourism is less pursuit of a neoliberal development agenda but more a form of moral consumption that has taken the place of macro political outlooks that favour economic growth and social transformation of the global South. Today, such agendas are more likely to be eschewed as unsustainable or unrealistic (Escobar, 1995).

Decommodified Volunteer Tourism

In critiquing the aims and objectives of the commercial, commodified market for volunteer tourism products the work of Wearing (2001) has been particularly important in developing the concept of a decommodified form of volunteer tourism. This concept refers to not-for-profit organizations that offer products that are less informed by the need for profit making and more in tune with the needs of the host communities. Gray and Campbell suggest that the volunteer tourists desire for an authentic encounter with host communities is commercialized by profit seeking businesses and thus the desire to act altruistically is turned into a commodity to be commodified and sold (2007: 466).

In contrast, in its decommodified form, it is suggested that volunteer tourism offers a sustainable alternative to mass tourism; advocates note it for its potential to offer an opportunity for moral consumption of tourism products outside the 'dominant market-driven framework of commodified tourism and where profit objectives are secondary to a more altruistic desire to travel to assist communities' (Wearing, 2001: 12). Crucial to Wearing's conception of an ideal volunteer tourism is the involvement of the host community and a 'genuine exchange' of cultural practices, values and norms. Decommodified tourism products also enable host communities to define and manage development and conservation ideally including an 'ethics of care for nature' (Wearing, 2010).

Developing this concept further, Wearing and Ponting (2009) consider NGOs the best vehicle for delivering non commercial, not-for-profit ecotourism and volunteer tourism projects working with local communities in the developing world. In this way, it is argued that NGO volunteer tourism projects run counter to the 'commodified, normalizing and marketized nature of globalized Western tourism' (ibid., 257). In this sense then it is argued that volunteer tourism has the potential to act as 'ideal' ecotourism addressing many of the shortfalls and criticisms levelled at mainstream and commercial ecotourism projects, particularly accusations of 'greenwashing' (Wearing, 2001; Honey, 2002: 370; Buckley, 2003: xiv; Weaver and Lawton, 2007: 1174; Higgins-Desboilles, 2011: 565).

Advocates of a decommodified volunteer tourism acknowledge that the benefits accrued to the local community from volunteers' contributions are frequently limited. Yet they also suggest that the contribution to development cannot be measured simply in terms of the projects themselves. Through participation in a project the volunteer tourist makes 'a journey of self-discovery and self-understanding though the experience of life style alternatives' (Wearing et al., 2008: 70). For Pearce and Coghlan (2008: 132) volunteer tourism enriches the sending society by developing a 'pool of personnel with experiences and an embodied awareness of global issues'. Wearing (2001: 3) highlights the long-term impacts the experience of volunteering can have in developing people who will, in the course of their careers and lives, act morally in favour of those less well off. Thus the experience of volunteering becomes '... an ongoing process which extends far beyond the actual tourist visit'.

While this long term impact of the volunteer encounter may be realized, it is also acknowledged that many volunteer tourists seek to affect change as a part of a self-conscious shaping of their own identity or their own sense of 'self' (Matthews, 2008; Wickens, 2011). This narrative addresses the individual rather than the society visited. Wearing (2001: 2) suggests that 'the most important development that may occur in the volunteer experience is that of a personal nature, that of a greater awareness of the self'. From a study of volunteers in Kenya, Lepp (2008: 98) concludes that many volunteers 'discovered an intrinsic need for meaning and purpose in their lives'. Similarly, Brown and Lehto (2005) have argued that volunteering can result in the 'self' rejecting materialism in favour of a more moral outlook particularly to others in the global South. McGehee (2012: 101) suggests that participation in the volunteer project is the key element in the consciousness-raising of the individual participant and for Zahra and McIntosh (2007) a greater sense of social justice and responsibility can result from participation in volunteer tourism projects. In this sense participation on a volunteer project provides a moral encounter where issues of global inequalities and development (or lack of) are experienced by the volunteer tourist firsthand.

Conclusions

The emerging discourse of volunteer tourism is attractive because it offers young people the opportunity to experience and encounter moral questions through their interaction with poor communities in the global South (Zahra and McIntosh, 2007; Vodopivec and Jaffe, 2011). For advocates of a decommodified volunteer tourism consumption of these experiences offer opportunities outside the profit-seeking tourism industry to become aware of social inequalities, environmental and political issues or awareness of the causes of poverty, injustice and unsustainable development (McGehee, 2012; Devereux, 2008) with volunteer tourism seen as a further deepening of the moral concerns associated with ecotourism (Acott et al., 1998). Whilst the tangible benefits to host communities from volunteer projects is open to question (Richter and Norman, 2010; Barbieri et al., 2012) for both its commercial and decommodified advocates volunteers' self-improvement is a key benefit in terms of awareness of global inequalities and encouraging global citizenship (Raleigh International, 2009; Wearing and Ponting, 2009; Jones, 2011; Lyons et al., 2012). It is argued that communities hosting volunteer tourists become 'reflexive educators and interpreters' (Wearing and Ponting, 2009: 263); host communities thus provide sites of moral encounters for the visiting volunteer.

It may well be the case that NGOs aim to assist and empower communities in the developing world in contrast to more commercial volunteer tourism operations, however, this arrangement frequently involves community cooperation based on a pre-existing agenda rather than being premised on host communities' right to shape and define development agendas (Butcher, 2007: 74; Diprose, 2012: 190). The degree to which these communities have agreed to act as the site of moral encounter is unclear and the needs of the host community may be superseded by the interests of the volunteers or the funding NGO's priorities or agenda (Guttentag, 2009: 70). It seems advocates of decommodified, NGO based volunteer tourism projects as much as the more commercial, 'neoliberal' volunteer or gap year organizations rely on moral meaning being delivered to volunteers through these interactions, or encounters, with host communities in the global South.

Perhaps it would be better to see the discourse of volunteer tourism as a reversal of the 'politics of care' (Popak, 2006) and 'caring at a distance' (Silk, 2000, 2004) with host communities in the developing world acting not as passive receivers of volunteers' 'performances of care' (Sin, 2010: 987) or as 'needy beneficiaries' (Vodopivec and Jaffe, 2011: 13) but providers of moral encounters for paying tourists from the North. Why these moral meanings should be delivered by encounters with poor rural communities in the global South rather than at home; why a greater awareness of the self (Wearing, 2001); a greater sense of social justice and responsibility (Zahra and McIntosh, 2007) or simply positive change through personal experience (McGehee, 2012) cannot be formed in the volunteer's own country remain a critical moral question the discourse of volunteer tourism has yet to address.

References

Acott, T., La Trobe, H., and Howard, S. (1998). An Evaluation of Deep Ecotourism and Shallow Ecotourism. *Journal of Sustainable Tourism*, 6(3), 238–253.

Advisory Group on Citizenship (1998). *Education for Citizenship and the Teaching of Democracy in Schools: Final Report of the Advisory Group on Citizenship.* London: Qualifications and Curriculum Authority.

Association for Tourism and Leisure Education/Tourism Research and Marketing (ATLAS/TRAM) (2008). *Volunteer Tourism: A Global Analysis.* Arnhem: Association for Tourism and Leisure Education.

Baillie Smith, M., and Laurie, N. (2011). International Volunteering and Development: Global Citizenship and Neoliberal Professionalisation Today. *Transactions of the Institute of British Geographers*, 36, 545–559.

Barbieri, C., Santos, C., and Katsube, Y. (2012). Volunteer Tourism in Rwanda: Insights from Participant Observation. *Tourism Management*, 33(3), 509–516.

Barnett, C., Cloke, P., Clarke, N., and Malpass, A. (2005). Consuming Ethics: Articulating the Subjects and Spaces of Ethical Consumption. *Antipode*, 37(1), 23–45.

Bednarz, S. (2003). Citizenship in the Post-9/11 United States: A Role for Geography Education? *International Research in Geographical and Educational Education*, 12(1), 72–80.

Benson, A. (ed.) (2011). *Volunteer Tourism: Theoretical Frameworks and Practical Applications*. London: Routledge.

Broad, S. (2003). Living the Thai Life—A Case Study of Volunteer Tourism at the Gibbon Rehabilitation Project, Thailand. *Tourism Recreation Research*, 28(3), 73–82.

Broad, S., and Jenkins, J. (2008). Gibbons in their Midst? Conservation Volunteers' Motivations at the Gibbon Rehabilitation Project, Phuket, Thailand. In K. D. Lyons and S. Wearing (eds.), *Journeys of Discovery in Volunteer Tourism: International Case Study Perspectives*, pp. 72–85. Wallingford: CABI Publishing.

Brown, S. and Lehto, X. (2005). Travelling with a Purpose: Understanding the Motives and Benefits of Volunteer Vacationers. *Current Issues in Tourism*, 8(6), 479–496.

Brown, F., and Hall, D. (2008). Tourism and Development in the Global South: The Issues. *Third World Quarterly*, 29(5), 839–849.

Buckley, R. (2003). *Case Studies in Ecotourism*. Wallingford: CABI.

Buckley, R. (2008). *Ecotourism: Principles and Practice*. Wallingford: CABI.

Butcher, J. (2003). *The Moralization of Tourism: Sun, Sand ... and Saving the World?* London: Routledge.

Butcher, J. (2007). *Ecotourism, NGOs and Development*. London: Routledge.

Butcher, J., and Smith, P. (2010). 'Making a difference': Volunteer Tourism and Development. *Tourism Recreation Research*, 35(1), 27–36.

Callanan, M., and Thomas, S. (2005). Volunteer Tourism: Deconstructing Volunteer Activities within a Dynamic Environment. In M. Novelli (ed.) (2000). *Niche Tourism: Contemporary Issues and Trends*, pp. 183–200. New York: Elsevier.

Caton, K., and Santos, C. A. (2009). Images of the Other: Selling Study Abroad in a Post-colonial World. *Journal of Travel Research*, 48(2), 191–204.

Clifton, J., and Benson, A. (2006). Planning for Sustainable Ecotourism: The Case for Research Ecotourism in Developing Country Destinations. *Journal of Sustainable Tourism*, 14(3), 238–254.

Coghlan, A. (2006). Volunteer Tourism as an Emerging Trend or an Expansion of Ecotourism? A Look at Potential Clients' Perceptions of Volunteer Tourism Organisations. *International Journal of Nonprofit and Voluntary Sector Marketing*, 11(3), 225–237.

Coghlan, A. (2007). Towards an Integrated Typology of Volunteer Tourism Organisations. *Journal of Sustainable Tourism*, 15(3), 267–287.

Coghlan, A. (2008). Exploring the Role of Expedition Staff in Volunteer Tourism. *International Journal of Tourism Research*, 10, 183–191.

Conran, M. (2011). They Really Love Me! Intimacy in Volunteer Tourism. *Annals of Tourism Research*, 38(4), 1454–1473.

Cousins, J. A. (2007). The Role of UK-based Conservation Tourism Operators. *Tourism Management*, 28(4), 1020–1030.

Diprose, K. (2012). Critical Distance: Doing Development Education Through International Volunteering. *Area* 44(2), 186–192.

Devereux, P. (2008). International Volunteering for Development and Sustainability: Outdated Paternalism or a Radical Response to Globalisation? *Development in Practice*, 18(3), 357–370.

Duffy, R. (2002). *A Trip Too Far: Ecotourism, Politics and Exploitation*. London: Earthscan.

Escobar, A. (1995). *Encountering Development—The Making and Unmaking of the Third World*. Chichester: Princeton University Press.

Fennell, D. (2008). *Ecotourism*. London: Routledge.

Gray, N. J., and Campbell, L. M. (2007). A Decommodified Experience? Exploring Aesthetic, Economic and Ethical Values for Volunteer Ecotourism in Costa Rica. *Journal of Sustainable Tourism*, 15(5), 463–482.

Guttentag, D. A. (2009). The Possible Negative Impacts of Volunteer Tourism. *International Journal of Tourism Research*, 11(6), 537–551.

Guttentag, D. A. (2011). Volunteer Tourism: As Good as It Seems. *Tourism Recreation Research*, 36(1), 69–74.

Halpenny, E., and Caissie, L. (2003). Volunteering on Nature Conservation Projects: Volunteer Experiences, Attitudes and Values. *Tourism Recreation Research*, 28(3), 25–33.

Harvey, D. (2011). *The Enigma of Capital and the Crises of Capitalism*. London: Profile Books.

Hertz, N. (2002). *The Silent Takeover: Global Capitalism and the Death of Democracy*. London: Arrow Books.

Hertz, N. (2005). *IOU: The Debt Threat and Why We Must Defuse It*. London: Harper Perennial.

Higgins-Desboilles, F. (2011). Death by a Thousand Cuts: Governance and Environmental Trade-offs in Ecotourism Development, at Kangaroo Island, South Australia. *Journal of Sustainable Tourism*, 19(4/5), 553–570.

Higgins-Desboilles, F., and Russell-Mundine, G. (2008). Absences in the Volunteer Tourism Phenomenon: The Right to Travel, Solidarity Tours and Transformation Beyond the One-way. In K. D. Lyons and S. Wearing (eds.), *Journeys of Discovery in Volunteer Tourism: International Case Study Perspectives*, pp. 182–194. Wallingford: CABI Publishing.

Honey, M. (2002). Conclusions. In M. Honey (ed.) (2002). *Ecotourism and Certification*, pp. 357–71. Washington, DC: Island.

Hutnyk, J. (1996). *The Rumour of Calcutta: Tourism, Charity and the Poverty of Representation*. London: Zed Books.

Jackson, T. (ed.) (2006). *The Earthscan Reader on Sustainable Consumption.* London: Earthscan.

Jakubiak, C. (2012). 'English for the Global': Discourses in/of English Language Voluntourism. *International Journal of Qualitative Studies in Education*, 25(4), 435–451.

Jones, A. (2004). *Review of Gap Year Provision*. Department for Education and Skills (DfES), University of London.

Jones, A. (2005). Assessing International Youth Service Programmes in Low Income Countries. *Voluntary Action: The Journal of the Institute for Volunteering Research*, 7(2), 87–100.

Jones, A. (2011). Theorizing International Youth Volunteering: Training for Global (Corporate) Work? *Transactions of the Institute of British Geographers*, 36, 530–544.

Keese, J. R. (2011). The Geographies of Volunteer Tourism: Place Matters. *Tourism Geographies*, 13(2), 257–279.

Klein, N. (2007). *The Shock Doctrine: The Rise of Disaster Capitalism*. London: Allen Lane.

Krippendorf, J. (1987). *The Holiday Makers: Understanding the Impact of Leisure Travel*. Oxford: Heinemann.

Lepp, A. (2008). Discovering Self and Discovering Others through the Taita Discovery Centre Volunteer Tourism Programme, Kenya. In K. D. Lyons and S. Wearing (eds.), *Journeys of Discovery in Volunteer Tourism: International Case Study Perspectives*, pp. 86–100. Wallingford: CABI Publishing.

Lury, C. (1996). *Consumer Culture*. Cambridge: Polity.

Lyons, K. D., and Wearing, S. (eds.) (2008a). *Journeys of Discovery in Volunteer Tourism: International Case Study Perspectives*. Wallingford: CABI Publishing.

Lyons, K. D., and Wearing, S. (2008b). Volunteer Tourism as Alternative Tourism: Journeys beyond Otherness. In K. D. Lyons and S. Wearing (eds.), *Journeys of Discovery in Volunteer Tourism: International Case Study Perspectives*, pp. 3–11. Wallingford: CABI Publishing.

Lyons, K. D. and Wearing, S. (2008c). All for a Good Cause? The Blurred Boundaries of Volunteering and Tourism. In K. D. Lyons and S. Wearing (eds.), *Journeys of Discovery in Volunteer Tourism: International Case Study Perspectives*, pp. 147–154. Wallingford: CABI Publishing.

Lyons, K., Hanley, J., Wearing, S., and Neil, J. (2012). Gap Year Volunteer Tourism: Myths of Global Citizenship? *Annals of Tourism Research*, 39(1), 361–378.

Matthews, A. (2008). Negotiating Selves: Explaining the Impact of Local-global Interactions on Young Volunteer Travellers. In K. D. Lyons and S. Wearing (eds.), *Journeys of Discovery in Volunteer Tourism: International Case Study Perspectives*, pp. 101–117. Wallingford: CABI Publishing.

McGehee, N. G. (2002). Alternative Tourism and Social Movements. *Annals of Tourism Research*, 29(1), 124–143.

McGehee, N. G. (2012). Oppression, Emancipation and Volunteer Tourism: Research Propositions. *Annals of Tourism Research*, 39(1), 84–107.

McGehee, N. G., and Almeida Santos, C. (2005). Social Change, Discourse and Volunteer Tourism. *Annals of Tourism Research*, 32(3), 760–779.

McGehee, N. G., and Andereck, K. (2009). Volunteer Tourism and the 'Voluntoured': The Case of Tijuana, Mexico. *Journal of Sustainable Tourism*, 17(1), 39–51.

McGehee, N. G., and Andereck, K. (2008). 'Petting the Critters': Exploring the Complex Relationship between Volunteers and the Voluntoured in McDowell County, West Virginia, USA and Tijuana, Mexico. In K. D. Lyons and S. Wearing (eds.), *Journeys of Discovery in Volunteer Tourism: International Case Study Perspectives*, pp. 12–24. Wallingford: CABI Publishing.

Mostafanezhad, M. (2013). The Politics of Aesthetics in Volunteer Tourism. *Annals of Tourism Research*, 43, 150–169.

Mowforth, M., and Munt, I. (1998). *Tourism and Sustainability: New Tourism in the Third World*. London: Routledge.

Mustonen, P. (2005). Volunteer Tourism: Postmodern Pilgrimage? *Journal of Tourism and Cultural Change*, 3(3), 160–177.

Neeves, J., and Birgnall, M. (2010). Paying the Price for a Gap Year of Adventure, *The Guardian*, 26th June, http://www.guardian.co.uk/money/2010/jun/26/paying-price-gap-year-adventure accessed on 18.03.2013.

Nicholls, A., and Opal, C. (2005). *Fair Trade: Market-driven Ethical Consumption*. London: Sage.

Novelli, M. (2005). *Niche Tourism: Contemporary Issues, Trends and Cases*. Oxford: Butterworth-Heinemann.

Palacios, C. M. (2010). Volunteer Tourism, Development and Education in a Postcolonial World: Conceiving Global Connections Beyond Aid. *Journal of Sustainable Tourism*, 18(7), 861–878.

Paterson, M. (2006). *Consumption and Everyday Life*. London: Routledge.

Patullo, P. (1996). *Last Resort: The Cost of Tourism in the Caribbean*. London: Cassell.

Patullo, P., and Minelli, O. (2009). *The Ethical Travel Guide: Your Passport to Exciting Alternative Holidays*. London: Earthscan.

Pearce, P. L., and Coghlan, A. (2008). The Dynamics behind Volunteer Tourism. In K. D. Lyons and S. Wearing (eds.), *Journeys of Discovery in Volunteer Tourism: International Case Study Perspectives*, pp. 30–143. Wallingford: CABI Publishing.

Popke, J. (2006). Geography and Ethics: Everyday Mediations through Care and Consumption. *Progress in Human Geography*, 30, 504–512.

Raleigh International. 30 July 2009. *Raleigh and Department for Business, Innovation and Skills Launch Bursary Award for Recent Graduates*. News Release. http://www.raleighinternational.org/files/Raleigh%20Graduate%20Bursary%20Award%20official%20release%20FINAL.pdf, Accessed on 18.03.2013.

Raymond, E., and Hall, C. M. (2008). The Development of Cross-cultural (Mis)understanding through Volunteer Tourism. *Journal of Sustainable Tourism*, 16(5), 530–543.

Richter, L. M., and Norman, A. (2010). AIDS Orphan Tourism: A Threat to Young Children in Residential Care. *Vulnerable Children and Youth Studies: An International Interdisciplinary Journal for Research*, Policy and Care, 5(3), 217–229.

Rojek, C. (2001). Leisure and Life Politics, *Leisure Sciences*, 23, 115–125.

Ruhanen, L., Cooper, C., and Fayos-Sola, E. (2008). Volunteering Tourism Knowledge: A Case from the United Nations World Tourism Organization. In K. D. Lyons and S. Wearing (eds.), *Journeys of Discovery in Volunteer Tourism: International Case Study Perspectives*, pp. 25–35. Wallingford: CABI Publishing.

Salazar, N. (2004). Development Tourists vs Development Tourism: A Case Study. In A. Raj (ed.), *Tourist Behaviour: A Psychological Perspective*. New Delhi: Kanishka Publisher.

Scheyvens, R. (2002). *Tourism for Development: Empowering Communities*. Harlow, UK: Prentice Hall.

Silk, J. (1998). Caring at a Distance. *Ethics, Place and Environment*, 1(2), 165–182.

Silk, J. (2000). Caring at a Distance: (Im)partiality, Moral Motivation and the Ethics of Representation. *Ethics, Place and Environment*, 3(3), 303–322.

Silk, J. (2004). Caring at a Distance: Gift Theory, Aid Chains and Social Movements. *Social and Cultural Geography*, 5(2), 229–251.

Simpson, K. (2005). Dropping Out or Signing Up? The Professionalisation of Youth Travel. *Antipode*, 37(3), 447–469.

Sin, H. L. (2009). Volunteer Tourism—'Involve Me and I Will Learn'? *Annals of Tourism Research*, 36(3), 480–501.

Sin, H. L. (2010). Who Are We Responsible To? Locals' Tales of Volunteer Tourism. *Geoforum*, 41, 983–992.

Singh, T. V. (2004). *New Horizons in Tourism: Strange Experiences and Stranger Practices*. Wallingford, UK: CABI Publishing.

Smith, D. M. (1998). How Far Should We Care? On the Special Scope of Beneficence. *Progress in Human Geography*, 22(1), 15–38.

Smith, D. M. (2000). *Moral Geographies: Ethics in a World of Difference*. Edinburgh: Edinburgh University Press.

Soderman, N., and Snead, S. (2008). Opening the Gap: The Motivation of Gap Year Travellers to Volunteer in Latin America. In K. D. Lyons and S. Wearing (eds.), *Journeys of Discovery in Volunteer Tourism: International Case Study Perspectives*, pp. 118–119. Wallingford: CABI Publishing.

Standish, A. (2008). *Global Perspectives in the Geography Curriculum: Reviewing the Moral Case for Geography*. London: Routledge.

Stiglitz, J. (2003). *Globalization and its Discontents*. London: Penguin.

Stiglitz, J. (2010). *Freefall: Free Markets and the Sinking Global Economy*. London: Penguin.

Tourism Concern (2007). *Briefing Paper*. London: Tourism Concern.

Travel Weekly (30th August, 2007). Volunteer Tourism: Is it Really Helping? http://www.travelweekly.co.uk/Articles/2007/08/30/25031/volunteer-tourism-is-it-really-helping-30-aug-2007.html accessed on 18.03.2013.

Tomazos, K., and Cooper, W. (2012). Volunteer Tourism: At the Crossroads of Commercialization and Service. *Current Issues in Tourism*, 15(5), 405–425.

Vodopiveca, B., and Jaffeb, R. (2011). Save the World in a Week: Volunteer Tourism, Development and Difference. *European Journal of Development Research*, 23, 111–128.

Voluntary Service Overseas (2007). Press release: *Ditch (Un)worthy Causes, VSO Advises Gap Year Students*. 14 August 2007.

Vrasti, W. (2009). 'Love and Anger in a Small Place: Ethnographic Improvisation on the Politics of Volunteer Tourism'. Paper presented at the annual meeting of the ISA's Annual Convention 'Exploring the Past, Anticipating the future', New York, USA, Feb 15, 2009 http://www.allacademic.com/meta/p313978_index.html accessed on 18.03.2013.

Wearing, S. (2001). *Volunteer Tourism: Experiences that Make a Difference*. Wallingford: CABI Publishing.

Wearing, S. (2004). Examining Best Practice in Volunteer Tourism. In R. A. Stebbins and M. Graham (eds.), *Volunteering as Leisure/Leisure as Volunteering*, Oxford: Wallingford.

Wearing, S. (2010). A Response to Jim Butcher and Peter Smith's Paper 'Making a Difference': Volunteer Tourism and Development. *Tourism Recreation Research*, 35(2), 213–215.

Wearing, S., and Neil, J. (2009). *Ecotourism Impacts, Potentials and Possibilities*. Oxford: Butterworth-Heinemann.

Wearing, S., and Ponting, J. (2009). Breaking Down the System: How Volunteer Tourism Contributes to New Ways of Viewing Commodified Tourism. In T. Jamal and M. Robinson, *The Sage Handbook of Tourism Studies*, pp. 254–267. London: Sage.

Wearing, S., Deville, A., and Lyons, K. (2008). The Volunteer's Journey through Leisure and the Self. In K. D. Lyons and S. Wearing (eds.), *Journeys of Discovery in Volunteer Tourism: International Case Study Perspectives*, pp. 63–71. Wallingford: CABI Publishing.

Wearing, S., McDonald, M., and Ponting, J. (2005). Building a Decommodified Research Paradigm in Tourism: The Contribution of NGOs. *Journal of Sustainable Tourism*, 13(5), 424–435.

Weaver, D. (2008). *Ecotourism: An Introduction*. 2nd edition. Brisbane: Wiley.

Weaver, D., and Lawton, L. (2007). Twenty Years On: The State of Contemporary Ecotourism Research. *Tourism Management*, 28(5), 1168–1179.

Wickens, E. (2011). Journeys of the Self: Volunteer Tourists in Nepal. In A. Benson, *Volunteer Tourism: Theoretical Frameworks and Practical Applications*. London: Routledge.

Zahra, A., and McIntosh, A. J. (2007). Volunteer Tourism: Evidence of Cathartic Tourist Experiences. *Tourism Recreation Research*, 32(1), 115–119.

Chapter 4

The Re-Enchantment of Development: Creating Value for Volunteers in Nepal

Heather Hindman

Introduction

In the first few years of the 1950s, Nepal experienced the first summiting of Mt. Everest, the overthrow of an over one-hundred year long dynastic domination and the arrival of Western aid and diplomatic entourages. Thus, from the very beginning, Western tourism and Western aid have been deeply linked in the history of the nation-state and, with the exception of the rising role of remittance funds, Nepal's economic success has largely hinged upon the country's successful navigation of its relations with these two foreign industries. The arrival of the new millennium brought a greater conjoining of foreign tourism and aid as a result of global changes as well as events specific to Nepal. The pressure to engage in moral acts as part of tourism to Nepal has its obvious and initial motive in the economic disparity that is inherent in the disjuncture between tourist-sending nations and Nepal, and that disparity is part of the attraction of the country as a destination as well. Yet, in this chapter I suggest that tourists who, in many different ways, seek to give back to Nepal do so under conditions they often misunderstand and their actions have unintended effects on Nepal, the development industry and the very idea of "ethical tourism" across the globe.

Garbage strewn streets, beggars and failing infrastructure are sites that confront the tourist from the moment of arrival, and these visible and ever-present illustrations of poverty motivate many visitors to Nepal to find some way to give back to the country, while other visitors initiate their visit to Nepal with the intent of focusing their time on volunteer activities. Here I focus not on the need for poverty eradication in Nepal or other debates over the merit of international development in the country (cf. Shrestha, 1997; Panday, 2011), but on the infrastructure in both home countries and Nepal that makes volunteer charity activity in Nepal possible as well as the limits that relying on this new class of amateur aid workers places on the kind of development that it is possible to do. In juxtaposing the contemporary rise of voluntourism with an earlier practice of youth service, the early years of the Peace Corps, I suggest that the struggles and lessons of early Peace Corps volunteers reflects concerns that are surfacing about the impact of touristic leisure aid workers upon Nepal and highlight the power that visitors have to dictate what problems are addressed and which are neglected.

**Figure 4.1   Cow and flaming garbage in Kathmandu.
                Photo: Author, May 2012**

In the area of Kathmandu that has served budget tourists since in 1970s, Thamel, many businesses support the non-package tourist and several organizations focus specifically on providing home-stays as well as short-term volunteer opportunities for foreigners. These business exist alongside, and in some ways blend in with, the shops offering rafting trips, visits to Lhasa and trekking guides. In the 1990s, few foreign visitors came to Nepal expressly for the purposes of volunteering. There was less infrastructure for such formal voluntourism trips and Nepal presented special challenges. In interviews with one agency seeking to facilitate short-term volunteer experiences for tourists on longer visits to Nepal in the late 1990s, the volunteer coordinator complained that there was a shortage of opportunities. The same economic disparity that pulled at the heartstrings of visiting Westerners made their (relatively) unskilled labour valueless. Especially given that many tourists wished to participate in activities that would allow them to stay in Kathmandu—volunteering during the day and enjoying the nightlife with traveler-friends at the end of the day—there were more volunteers than charities interested in their labour. The short duration of their visits also deterred many agencies from utilizing even their donated time, given the language barriers and lack of technical skills of most visitors. The volunteer placement agency—which charged a small fee to those seeking its services—found some schools willing to work with tourists who would come in for a few days to teach foreign languages, but little beyond this. Finally, Ilana, the young German tourist who had formed this agency as an off-shoot of a trekking guide charity, found a way to entice local NGOs to work with tourists—to have the visitors pay for their voluntourism experience. It was only when agencies were incentivized with foreign currency that they were willing to cope with foreign tourists' labour. Although Ilana still found some organizations, particularly those outside of Kathmandu, that were willing to accept short-term volunteers without recompense, and occasionally foreigners with technical skills—especially medical training—would contact her office and she found them easy to place, it was only with this new format of for-pay volunteering that she was able to find relatively equal numbers of positions and volunteers.

The expectations of "pay-to-not-play" instituted by Ilana's small enterprise in Kathmandu is now familiar practice for many young people in the West seeking to volunteer abroad. Organizations offer to package overseas volunteering programs for church groups, schools and individuals, taking care of housing, transport, legal issues and placement, for fees that vary from almost incidental to the costs of a year's private school education or a luxury vacation, depending upon the location, services provided and kind of work. These voluntour vacations also often include cultural and historical experiences, thus recreating the package tour, but with "caring for orphans" replacing "learn to weave traditional baskets." While some of the fees charged to tourists are devoted to guide salaries and airport transportation that are a part of many package tours, some are directly attendant to the expenses incurred by organizations in utilizing "free labour." Hiring volunteers is not a expense-free pathway for employers. The management and training of inexperienced workers begets practices that became controversial in the US in the 2010s, as interns sued their "employers," noting that they were exploiting their unpaid market labour (Philipps, 2008) under the guise of providing training or experience (Glatt and Footman *v.* Fox Searchlight Pictures, 2011). For more and more young voluntourists in Nepal, these experiences are seen in such light—as internships, resume lines and productive "time-on" when law school applications fail. The European term "gap year" seems increasingly suitable as many voluntourists are pursuing overseas travel and work due to a lack of domestic opportunities. Given the economic flows that are entailed in much voluntourism these days, and certainly in Nepal, the idea of paying to work suggests the need for a rethinking of who is benefiting from this labour, to what their work contributes, and what is changing about the development organizations, hospitals and schools who take in these unpaid workers.

Who is the Human in Humanitarian Interventions?

In an article Peter Buffett rather uncharitably titled *The Charitable-Industrial Complex*, the philanthropist himself questions who are the real beneficiaries of the monies invested in "giving back" or "conscience laundering" (Buffett, 2013).

While some scholarship has been devoted to "green washing" and other critiques of corporate social responsibility, I suggest that similar critical examinations are necessary of individual acts of social good, in this case through volunteering in Global South locations like Nepal. While wishing to carefully avoid an overall condemnation of such intended social goods, which have undeniable benefits, I want to bring attention to how voluntourism in Nepal is framed in ways that create value for the volunteers and to suggest that the requirements produced by voluntourists' preference some forms of intervention in local problems over others changes what support is offered to Global South citizens. When voluntourists transform themselves from tourists to aid workers to customers (of an experience), careful attention should be directed to whose needs are served by the volunteer encounter (see Barbieri et al., 2012: 515). Furthermore, the interests, desires and skill sets of these short-term workers limit the kind of work that is possible, with preference often given to hands-on care work (see Mostafanezhad, 2013a). Thus in the rise of the use of tourist labour as part of the development industry in Nepal, two expectations emerge, both of which emanate from the volunteer, first the framing of the experience (the production of titles and certificates of completion) and secondly the kind of work that will be done (often work with children and nature).

Community service, charity, humanitarian actions and ethical consumption have had to replace the role of the state in an era where even non-"failed states" offer little in the form of services for citizens (Snellinger and Shneiderman, 2014). This commonplace reading of civil society filling in for the state in an era of neoliberalism finds a distinctive expression the contemporary United States, and to some degree other Western nations. Inderpal Grewal provides a trenchant critique and exploration of this form of the expectation of "humanitarian citizenship" in her examination of how U.S. exceptionalism and a requirement to be caring members of the public has brought together religion, the state, civil society and nationalism in a command that in order to be a "real" citizen one must participate in particular forms of volunteer activities. She notes that in the very term humanitarianism, the focus is put on the giver, such that these practices are "as much about self-making and the biopolitical as it is about a world in which such self-making is seen as essential to the welfare [of Others]" and that the result is that this new form of citizenship-through-charity "removes those who cannot become humanitarians, often low-income, from such citizenship" (Grewal 2014). Grewal finds this ideology played out in the U.S. government, as well as the general public, such as in fascination with Greg Mortenson's *Three Cups of Tea*, the penchant for "peer-to-peer" forms of giving and the abject status attributed to domestic Others in need of help, as was the case during Hurricane Katrina. While there is undoubtedly good done in the name of celebrity humanitarian outreach and religious philanthropic tours, I suggest, following Grewal and others, that the benefits attained by the "aiders" must be attended to and particularly how activities such as voluntourism and ethical consumption are constructed to meet the needs of the "givers" or "consumers" as much as those of the recipient Others (see Igoe, 2010).

Concern that tourists/volunteers/consumers benefit more from their experience than those that they are offering to "help" has become a familiar critique in the voluntourism literature. Less attention has been focused on wage workers who benefit or lose as a result of this new population of people willing to do some jobs for free (or even pay for the privilege), but only under particular conditions. Aid work is, as much as it is often obscured as such, ultimately work, and many people make a living doing activities not dissimilar from those labours undertaken by voluntourists (Hindman, 2013). It is excess of time and/or money that allows some to work for the pleasure of "giving back" and this creates a particular tension for those who are engaged in care work or other forms of labour that are by others seen as leisure. The ability of many who participated in computing technology in its early years to make enough money to retire into philanthropy before middle age has made visible the exchanges of well-compensated (if ethically suspect) labours for ones that are cast as having intrinsic pleasures that make monetary compensation unnecessary.

Yet the utilization of casual labourers in roles formerly held by well-trained professionals requires more mediating labour, in the form of facilitators and managers. It is this new class who benefits the most from a rise in voluntourism. Visitors, for whom their work in Nepal is often one element of other adventures, often demand forms of facilitation, support and accommodation that were not required by professional aid workers. Thus, there is more travel planning, hosting and management required, work done by people such as Ilana, which has become much more formal and professionalized in the intervening years. Furthermore, this new form of labour reduces the continuity within organizations and as several scholars have noted, has led to a rise in NGO management degrees and a greater number of non-profit human resources workers who must facilitate the many comings and goings of workers (see Lewis, 2011).

"Peace Corps types only stay around long enough to realize they're not helping anyone" (Dicaprio 2006—*Blood Diamond*)

To illustrate the difficulties that inure in asking volunteers to do development labour, I want to look to an historical example, the Peace Corps in the 1960s and 1970s. This institution was challenged by the limited technical skills of those who sought out volunteering for the Peace Corps and the way in which volunteers, in their own perceptions as well as those of their evaluators, often benefited more than the communities in which they were placed. In his in-depth analysis of the first groups of Peace Corps workers to visit Nepal, of which he was a part, Jim Fisher interprets the initial charge as having three components: "1) providing trained manpower to developing countries, 2) increasing understanding of America in other countries, and 3) increasing understanding of other countries in America" (Fisher, 2013: 12). While his reflection on the paths and adventures

of early Peace Corps workers suggests that much change occurred, he somewhat reluctantly concludes that "[w]e thought we were going to save the world, but most of us came to the gradual realization that we were only, or at least mainly, saving ourselves. We thought we had answers to other people's problems, but we came away with more answers to our own problems" (Fisher, 2013: 181). Fisher's intimate reflection is supported by the data gathered as part of the statistical drive that was a central part of the early Peace Corps under Sargent Shriver, where a survey of 7,000 returned volunteers conducted in the 1960s reveals that while 92 percent thought their time abroad had been very valuable to them, only 25 percent thought it very valuable for the foreign country they visited (Blatchford, 1970). This perhaps had to do with the frustration experienced by these early volunteers who were unclear about their mission in their host country, the strong expectation of some sort of measurable success by Peace Corps officials and the often limited training in technical skills, which were most in demand overseas. In the 1960s the majority of those who participated in the Peace Corps were from New England liberal arts colleges and often were "B.A. generalists," with some teaching experience at the most. While there were many noble intentions held by both the program initiators and early volunteers, what such generalist could accomplish in on-the-ground development programs was limited and volunteers were often cast into positions in which they were destined to fail, as they lacked the technical skills they were supposed to be imparting to locals (Fischer, 1998). The desires for "doing good" that were a key motivation of these pioneers were undeniable, yet they were unable to conjoin their own abilities, the needs and motives of the local population (that were strongly prioritized by the early Peace Corps) and the expectation of concrete results that could be reported to detractors, as well as supporters, in Washington.

Volunteers were not silent in expressing their frustration upon return and only a few years into its history, many called for radical reform of the Peace Corps. Here I focus on only two elements of the debate that took place in the late 1960s and early 1970s. First, some suggested that volunteers themselves should be seen as the product of the Peace Corps experience, not so much as aid workers supporting foreign lands, but as a new kind of American citizen. One author suggested that the problem is the inadequacy of contemporary higher education to prepare young people for citizenship, and that volunteering should be seen as a required part of American and world citizenship (Wofford, 1966). This idea of the expectation of volunteer service as a part of what it is to be an American citizen, championed by Sergent Shriver, in many ways sounds like a more optimistic version of Inderpal Grewal's "humanitarian citizen." The second change recommended for the Peace Corps was a call for greater use of the very technical professionals that were conceived as part of the initial charge—a move away from the "B.A. generalist" to recruiting those with specialized skills, those who could actually improve medical training, repair vehicles, weld and engineer bridges and roads. It was these needs that many of the early Peace Corps workers saw as most in demand, and yet which their own background as English majors gave them few skills to address. Ambivalence about the Peace Corps continues to the present, but here I only want to suggest that in this landmark example of using volunteer labour to engage in international development activities, at least in its early years, it was often the volunteers who received the most benefit from their involvement and that those attracted (at least initially) to the Peace Corps tended to have general, rather than technical skills, thus limiting the kind of work they were able to undertake.

There is one additional pattern to extract from these early struggles in the Peace Corps's utilization of young volunteers on development projects. Development, in its many guises, is subject to the whims of fashion, or changing research, depending upon how one sees the shift. While technical expertise, such as intensive farming and use of pesticides, irrigation and fertilizer, was considered the "best practices" of agricultural aid in this mid-century period, the prevalent ideology shifted over time towards ideas of sustainable development and the support of traditional farming practices. Contemporarily, many development professionals complain of the need to continually re-write their grants and publicity statements to conform to the fashion for "women in development (WID)" projects or "good governance" (Hindman, 2013). In the early Peace Corps, in keeping with the Point Four objectives of providing technical skills to the developing world, the focus was on providing expertise to places that were seen to lack advanced training in such fields. These shifts in fashion are justified by research, but largely driven by the priorities and agenda of the funders. For example, a recent "good governance" program in Nepal, sponsored by Dell Corporation, while directed at a diverse set of ends including government accountability, increased youth participation and civil society, seems to emerge with projects and staff centered upon technological solutions to such challenges through e-governance. Volunteers, by their willingness to give time, are in some ways funders, and thus set priorities. In the early years of Peace Corps, it was not merely the skills of volunteers that were incompatible with the goals of the U.S. government, but the goals of many volunteers different from those of their "employers." Thus, to return to contemporary Nepal, I want to ask the question of how the skills and well as the goals of voluntourists (who by their contribution of labour are "funders") have the potential to clash with the goals and needs of the country, creating a new fashion in aid.

Labour, Leisure and the Goals of Voluntourism

As many scholars of alternative tourism have noted, most of the literature on the volunteer activities of tourists has followed the tourists and attention has focused on the personal development outcomes of their visits, rather than their (positive or negative) impact on the community (cf. Salazar, 2004; Sherraden et al., 2008). Thus, scholars have followed the moving people and grounded their research in the visitors, rather than their local context, and even in those studies devoted to "community impact," the community has been those helped,

Figure 4.2   The garden of the 1905 restaurant. Photo: Author, April 2012

rather than the development field. Here I want to observe how transient labour, like voluntourists, is changing the aid community in Nepal. Thus, the question turns from the (legitimate) question of if volunteers are doing their hosts any good (which the current consensus appears to be in the negative) or even if the personal growth of the tourist justifies their intrusion into a "developing" nation (which appears up for debate), but how these individuals are shaping the work it is possible to do in Nepal as well as who is doing it.

The garden of the 1905 Restaurant was usually bustling on Saturday afternoon. The Saturday morning farmers market attracted many expatriates and elite locals with offerings of organic vegetables, locally made cheese and fruit preserves. These markets have been held in Kathmandu for more than a decade, usually catering to foreigners, and have long provided a location for entrepreneurs, both Nepali and foreign, to market goods desired by visitors. Formerly, it was diplomatic and development spouses who were the customers, but by 2012 the main consumers and many of the sellers might be termed voluntourists. This was especially true by the afternoon when the market dispersed and young volunteers stayed on to share a bottle of wine on the grassy field. The same collection of a dozen or more, young, mainly European, visitors would regularly occupy the area near the pond, exchanging stories of their week, discussing global events and recent books read. While each had taken a slightly different pathway to arrive in Kathmandu, all were happy to share the label volunteer but none wanted to adopt the moniker tourist (cf. Mostafanezhad 2013b).

James was one of the most regular—and most vocal—attendees at this informal gathering. He was likely one of the oldest members of the group, but still in his early 30s. His visit to Kathmandu was both one of the longest, as he was planning on staying for eight months, and the only one fully planned from abroad as a volunteer trip exclusively to Nepal. This period fit well with his schedule as a change of specialization in medical school had required this gap before his residency was to begin and he was eager to fill it with something that would be good for his resume, his soul and his relaxation. "With my experience, they said it would be easy to place me," he said about his visit to the European office of an organization that specialized in finding voluntourists opportunities. He was one of the few of those present who was compensated for his time, receiving housing and a small stipend. Others struggled to make ends meet, even in Nepal, as they had to pay for their own lodging, food and expenses, "but at least its cheaper than being a tourist" one woman observed. As 1905 was just a few blocks from the tourist district of Kathmandu—a place that was frequently visited by many of those present, but also a source of derision—their distinction from tourists was common topic of conversation. This discussion was often initiated by the arrival of a traveling friend of one of the volunteers. Several commented on how their schoolmates saw their presence in Nepal as a good excuse for visiting the country. While some took the visit of a friend from home as an excuse to take time off from their work to tour the country, others were either unable or unwilling to abandon their positions for a week or two. Several people remarked on the irony of this situation, as their own initial plan had been to be a "carefree traveler," but the beauty and poverty of Nepal or just luck of opportunity, cast them into this new role as labourer.

The lawn group expanded when the market shut down in the afternoon. New arrivals included one woman who had been working a booth for the charity that was her volunteer opportunity, which sold jams and pickles as part of a social entrepreneurship endeavor to provide women who had experienced domestic abuse with new job skills. Few of the women served by the organization spoke English, and she spoke no Nepali, thus her skills were most useful as a sales person either at the market or at other charity-related shops in Kathmandu. There were also arrivals from a booth that collected donations just outside the gate of 1905 for a program to spay and neuter street dogs in Kathmandu. The booth was usually manned by three of the six volunteers that the organization had at any given time, most of whom approached the organization once they were in Nepal, often having learned of the opportunity from friends who were already working there. These volunteers shared the skills and liabilities of many of the casual volunteers in Nepal: they lacked the technical abilities or language skills to do the core work of the organization, but excelled in soft skills and the ability to sell the cause to other foreigners. As has been noted with other voluntourist situations, work with children and animals, or teaching English, were the main jobs open to this group (see Wickens, 2010: 44).

Figure 4.3 **The abandoned offices of USAID in the Rabi Bhawan area of Kathmandu. Photo: Author, August 2010**

The End of Aid as We Know It

Although orphanages, schools and hospitals certainly benefit from the unpaid labour of volunteering visitors, here I want to focus on examining what aid work and development projects might be lost as organizations seek to take advantage of voluntourists. As I suggest above, it is not uncommon for donor priorities to dictate what projects get done, but considering voluntourists as donors casts this changeability in a new light. To see the transformation, I turn to the workplace of many of those who used to visit the farmers market but are much less numerous than in the past. In 2007, USAID was in the process of packing up its long-time offices in Kathmandu to relocate to a building the organization would share with the US Embassy and other official Mission activities. Part of the motivation for the move was concern over the age of the old palace in which they were housed, which did not meet US government standards for either earthquake resistance nor security concerns. Yet, it was also an issue of space. The direct and permanent staff of USAID based in Kathmandu was dwindling, and the large, in-compound houses and proximity to the major international school was less attractive to incoming workers. The new building would have fewer offices and none of the residential facilities of the old building. Greg, who had worked for years at USAID, and his wife Sarah, who worked at the international school, were some of the last to move out of their in-compound house. Greg had seen many colleagues leave over the past years, but saw the change in location as reflective of a greater change taking place. Greg's training was in civil engineering and hydrology, and he had been central to the expansion of Nepal's hydroelectric power facilities. Nepal has great potential as a source of hydropower, with large glacial mountains, and yet has always lacked the local technical experts to utilize the technology. Yet, Greg worried that projects like his would be impossible in the future, "they're hiring kids," he lamented, discussing the new arrivals in his office, most of whom were focused on writing grants and drafting RFPs (requests for proposals). The geeky atmosphere of technical professionals was being replaced by managers and accountants. His own children had decided against getting technical degrees, even though they wanted to follow in their father's path, and obtained business credentials instead. While the new offices being built for USAID would be filled with specialists in contract management, his wife's job was also being eliminated, in favor of volunteers. Sarah was once a regular at the old farmers market in Kathmandu, but couples like Greg and Sarah had vanished by 2012, to be replaced by James and his friends. This shift was not merely social, but also entailed a shift in the kinds of aid work that it was possible to do. That social entrepreneurship, projects like skill development for victims of domestic violence, has been one of the fashionable directions of international aid for the last decade might be attributable to research, but may also have something to do with who is now engaged in international aid work. The voluntourists at 1905 enjoyed being able to work with women, children and animals, as well as the marketing element that was both reminiscent of the jobs to which they might return, and offered an opportunity to socialize with other foreigners. It is thus James and his friends, through their abilities and desires, who are deciding what is best for Nepal's future.

References

Barbieri, C., Santos, C., and Katsube, Y. (2012). Volunteer Tourism: On-the-ground Observations from Rwanda. *Tourism Management*, 33, 509–516.

Blatchford, J. (1970). The Peace Corps: Making It in the Seventies. *Foreign Affairs*, 49(1), 122–135.

Buffet, P. (2013). The Charitable-Industrial Complex. *New York Times*, July 27, A15.

Butcher, J., and Smith, P. (2010). 'Making a Difference': Volunteer Tourism and Development. *Tourism Recreation Research*, 35(1), 27–36.

Fischer, F. (1998). *Making Them Like Us: Peace Corps Volunteers in the 1960s*. Washington, DC: Smithsonian Institution Press.

Fisher, J. (2013). *At Home in the World: Globalization and the Peace Corps in Nepal*. Bangkok, Thailand: Orchid Press.

Grewal, I. (2014). American Humanitarian Citizenship: The "Soft" Power of Empire. In S. Ponzanesi (ed.), *Gender, Globalization and Violence: Postcolonial Conflict Zones*. New York: Routledge. Cited from manuscript copy.

Hindman, H. (2013). *Mediating the Global: Expatria's Forms and Consequences in Kathmandu*. Palo Alto: Stanford University Press.

Igoe, J. (2010). The Spectacle of Nature in the Global Economy of Appearances: Anthropological Engagements with the Spectacular Mediations of Transnational Conservation. *Critique of Anthropology*, 30(4), 375–397.

Lewis, D. (2011). Tidy Concepts, Messy Lives: Defining Tensions in the Domestic and Overseas Careers of UK Non-Governmental Professionals. In D. Mosse (ed.), *Adventures in Aidland*, pp. 177–197. New York: Berghahn Books.

Liechty, M. (2012). The "Age of Hippies": Neaplis Make Sense of Budget Tourists in the 1960s and 1970s. *Studies in Nepali History and Society*, 17(2), 211–262.

Mostafanezhad, M. (2013a). "Getting in Touch with your Inner Angelina": Celebrity Humanitarianism and the Cultural Politics of Gendered Generosity in Volunteer Tourism. *Third World Quarterly*, 34(3), 485–499.

Mostafanezhad, M. (2013b). Locating the Tourist in Volunteer Tourism. *Current Issues in Tourism*, DOI: 10.1080/13683500.2013.793301.

Palacios, C. (2010). Volunteer Tourism, Development and Education in a Postcolonial World: Conceiving Global Connections Beyond Aid. *Journal of Sustainable Tourism*, 18(7), 861–878.

Panday, D. (2011). *Looking at Development and Donors: Essays from Nepal*. Kathamndu, Nepal: Martin Chautari.

Philipps, L. (2008). Silent Partners: The Role of Unpaid Market Labor in Families. *Feminist Economics*, 14(2), 37–57.

Rapoport, L. (1965). On Undefined Project, An Undefined Person. *Peace Corps Volunteer*, March 1965: 18.

Salazar, N. (2004). Developmental Tourists vs. Development Tourism: A Case Study. In A. Raj (ed.), *Tourist Behavior: Psychological Perspective*, pp. 85–107. New Delhi: Kanishka.

Sherraden, M., Lough, B., and McBride, A. (2008). Effects of International Volunteering and Service: Individual and Institutional Predictors. *Voluntas*, 19, 395–421.

Sin, H. L. (2010). Who are we responsible to? Locals' tales of volunteer tourism. *Geoforum*, 41: 983–992.

Snellinger, A. and Shneiderman, S. (2014). Framing the Issues: The Politics of "Post-conflict". *Fieldsights—Hot Spots, Cultural Anthropology Online*. Accessed March 24, 2014, http://www.culanth.org/fieldsights/500-framing-the-issues-the-politics-of-post-conflict.

Wickens, E. (2010). Journeys of the Self: Volunteer Tourists in Nepal. In Angela Benson (ed.), *Volunteer Tourism: Theoretical Frameworks and Practical Applications*, pp. 42–52. Hoboken: Taylor and Francis.

Wofford, H. (1966). The Future of the Peace Corp. *The ANNALS of the American Academy of Political and Social Science*, 36(5), 129–146.

Chapter 5
Tourism Development, Architectures of Escape and the Passive Beloved in Contemporary Yucatán (México)

Matilde Córdoba Azcárate

Introduction

This chapter analyses the active role that tourism planning plays in the configuration of a vulnerable moral economy of mutual dissociation in Yucatán, México. Following Andrew Sayer (2003, 2004: 2), I define moral economies as economic activities that are influenced and structured by moral dispositions and norms, which are, in turn, "compromised, overridden or reinforced by economic pressures." In Yucatán, tourism has created a moral economy predicated upon discourses of sustainable development but sustained on spatial segregation and enclosed architectures of escape. This moral economy produces weak and instrumental tourist-local encounters that result in a disengagement from both traditional and contemporary Maya cultural practices. More importantly, it stimulates "the passive beloved phenomenon" defined by Richard Sennett (2001: 3) as "the truce of leaving one another alone, the peace of mutual indifference." I argue that this mutual dissociation aggravates the region's vulnerability to economic, political and environmental crises thus challenging its long-term sustainability.

The chapter builds on ongoing multi-sited ethnographic research on tourism and development practices in Yucatán. The first section provides a brief historical contextualization of how tourism has been used as a national economic strategy for development in the region. This section presents the concepts of the "passive beloved" and "imaginaries of tourist escape" that lead the discussion. The second and third sections analyze the region's oldest and newest types of tourism ventures—Cancún's all-inclusive resorts and *The Haciendas* guilt-free luxury hotels—as paradigmatic examples advancing the landscape of mutual dissociation and indifference. The chapter concludes highlighting the importance of addressing moral issues in tourism and development studies in the context of current financial and environmental crises.

Tourism *as* Development: Mutual Dissociation and Architectures of Scape

Development through tourism has become the most powerful ordering practice organizing local, regional and global systems of mobility for goods, capital, labor and people in Yucatán. The industry's power is such, that after the *henequén* industry, tourism can be considered the new region's mono-crop.[1] In 1974, the ex-novo creation of Cancún on the Caribbean coast by the Federal Government was a watershed event in the deployment of tourism as a development tool in the region. Since then, development has been synonymous with modernization and the mass tourism industry of sea, sand and sun has been used as its hegemonic vehicle. Recently, economic growth resulting from tourism has been accompanied by discourses of sustainability, heritage preservation, and local participation. Coinciding with a global wave praising more responsible forms of tourism, official tourism discourses have moved away from the sun, sea, sand and sex tourism model to appeal to "travelling, trekking and trucking new moral tourists" (Butcher, 2003: 13). Alternative tourism models as ecotourism, cultural, archeological tourism and luxury tourism have emerged and they have quickly populated the region's tourism landscape. However, and in spite of these discourses, alternative and hegemonic tourism models have proved to be dependent upon practices of spatial segregation, enforced enclosures and transient tourist-locals relations (Córdoba Azcárate, 2011). In so doing, tourism *as* development has generated an uneven moral economy governed by what Richard Sennett (2001) has called the "passive beloved phenomenon."

The "passive beloved phenomenon" is defined by three major characteristics. First, it is the result of the volatility of international firms and investments and their constant threat to leave for more profitable places. Second, it entails the avoidance of corporate civil responsibility towards space and people. And third, it is defined by a generalized lack of commitment to social justice at an institutional and individual level. The combination of these three elements generates social and economic landscapes organized by a mutual dissociation or indifference to the here and now, and towards others (Sennett, 1990). That is, a space in which individuals and institutions are unchallenged and unencumbered by the presence of others (Lathan, 1999).

Although Sennett is referring to urban spaces and notions of Western citizenship, the passive beloved phenomenon is pervasive in those rural and urban areas of southern Mexico where tourism is present. Mutual dissociation is here rooted in the idea of the tourist escape and gets fully materialized in tourism planning. All-inclusive resorts and guilt-free luxury resorts can be seen as "architectures of escape" where this moral economy of denial of place and others becomes fully

---

1   *Henequén* (sisal) is an agave plant. The production of sisal-fiber ropes in industrial quantities for exportation to USA was Yucatán's major economic activity from mid nineteenth century until the mid-twentieth century. Due to its centrality in the regional and national economy, *henequén* was known as the Mexican "green gold."

realized (Shaw, 2007). As the next sections illustrate, these architectures are tied to different "imaginaries of escape"—from the ordinary and into the past–that consolidate selective entitlements to place and cultural resources (Salazar, 2011). These entitlements have developed as a result of processes of privatization and enclosure of land and resources as well as upon the establishment of a system of transient social relations. Taken together, these ventures provide a comprehensive and diachronic evidence of different modalities of tourism in the region as well as of their social, economic and moral consequences.

All-inclusive Resorts in a "Come and Go" City

Cancún was planned, designed and built by the Federal Government as a market device to absorb transnational capital, and a strategic tool in the state's modernization plans for rural and indigenous communities (Castellanos, 2011: xviii). With a population that has grown from 100 inhabitants in 1974 to the current population of well over 600,000, the city has become the first tourist destination of Latin America, receiving nearly four million tourists and over 65,000 cruise visitors annually. Tourism in Cancún produces one-third of the Mexican tourist GDP and it is the major source of labor and income for 80 percent of its inhabitants, a third of which are Maya migrants (Sectur, 2010).

Cancún's main idiosyncrasy is that it was planned from the start as a dual tourist enclave in which tourists and workers were expected to remain invisible to each other. To achieve this, the Mexican National Fund for Tourism Development, created two distinct zones: a Hotel Zone, or *Cancún Island*, a city for tourists built upon the barrier that separates the Caribbean Sea from the Nichupté Lagoon, and Cancún City or the *Model City*, built inland on the other side of the lagoon, for workers and infrastructure provision (Torres and Momsen, 2006).

As a result of this original spatial and functional segregation, Cancún has evolved as a city with two distinctive landscapes. The Hotel Zone's highly protected and policed landscape, home of all-inclusive hotels, high-rise condominiums and other tourist infrastructures, and mainly populated by hyper-mobile "gringos." And Cancún City's overpopulated and unregulated landscape, characterized by different types of formal and informal architectures, home of Mexican middle-class tourist workers and of highly vulnerable informal indigenous settlements with annual population growth rates of over twenty percent. Or to put it in other words, a fortified enclave and socially homogeneous environment, and a heterogeneous, racialized and ghettoized city.

In Cancún, tourists' desires to escape from the ordinary to a paradisiacal Caribbean beach have been morphologically and architectonically achieved through complex sets of physical barriers and immaterial boundaries. Massive privatizations and enclosures of public spaces such as the beach have been accomplished in the name of maintaining the image of the destination as an idealized Caribbean beachscape in the tourism global market. One of the most prominent material barriers producing this dreamed Caribbean beachscape involves the use of tourism architectures, particularly all-inclusive resorts.

All-inclusive resorts are built on the narrow oceanfront corridor of the Hotel Zone. They have been placed immediately next to each other, thus allowing little space for accessing, or and even seeing, the beach. Each hotel is firmly enclosed through the use of walls, fences and gates creating a massive barrier that make public access to the beach only possible at nine sites along nearly twenty-five kilometers of beachfront. In addition to these tangible physical barriers, the enclosure of the Hotel Zone is effectively achieved through a number of immaterial, but equally effective, boundaries marking socio-economic status and race (Low, 2006). The conspicuous difference between "gringos," affluent and typically white-skinned North American and European tourists, and the brown-skinned, indigenous locals often act as an insurmountable boundary for the latter. Immaterial boundaries are constantly at play when trying to access the beach, walking on it or when deciding where to go shopping. As one young local from Guadalajara who periodically visits Cancún in his holidays put it "when I am on my own I am always stopped at the gate of hotels and restaurants because of my brown skin and my car plate … they think I am a worker and I am not supposed to be here … I always have to wait at the gate for them to check." As a result of these enclosures, the beach, which under Mexican law is a Federal public space, has been *de facto* privatized for the consumption of tourists and locals infrequently enter the Hotel Zone for reasons other than work.

All-inclusive resorts have become standardized and self-contained habitats for private consumption characterized by the regimentation of people, capital, and objects within tightly controlled and monitored spatial circuits. As self-contained resorts offering full board accommodation, drinks and entertainment activities for a fixed price paid in advance to tour operators, all-inclusive hotels' philosophy of seclusion explicitly aims to satisfy tourists' desires for escape and contribute to their detachment from local culture. The fear of the outside is a recurrent strategy used by hotel workers and managers to keep tourists within their secluded spaces, or as they put it, "to keep tourists captive." It is estimated that over eighty-five percent of all-inclusive clients never leave the hotel's installations and when they do they remain in the shopping malls of the Hotel Zone (interview, October 2011). Fear of the outside and a desire of escape from the ordinary are met with pre-packaged artificial encounters with the "Maya world" in thematic parks. In so doing, they facilitate tourism experiences that are indifferent to place and otherness. As one Spanish tourist put it, "this (the resort) is an island. We are secure here. We don't need to travel so far to see poverty or to have a bad experience. I don't want to know about that in my holidays!"

Within these gated architectures, tourists and workers' encounters are minimal, highly monitored and instrumental. As a hotel worker said, "we are not allowed to disturb guests with our conversation." Most workers at the Hotel Zone are part of the 22% of the city's population that after forty years of tourism development is still living in irregular settlements, with precarious basic infrastructures, and located in extremely environmentally and socially vulnerable areas. The majority of hotel workers are Maya migrants from inland communities who only live in the city during tourist seasons. During these seasons, they work on endless shifts in jobs characterized by "low wages, repetitive motion, limited job promotions, lack of economic security and the reliance of racialized bodies" typical of the *maquila* system in the north of the country and reproduced in Cancún's hotel industry (Castellanos, 2011: 30). And yet, despite impoverished living and hard working conditions, Cancún's population is not unionized or organized in resistance. Instead, they seem to dwell in a sort of a generalized acquiescence. The reason for this can be found in the region's extreme dependence on the avatars of the Hotel Zone. Typically referred to by locals as "the goose of the golden eggs"; an "engine to be fed"; the Hotel Zone is seen as an area "to be protected" and respected as a restricted space for outsiders and tourist consumption. Workers establish an instrumental relation to the area, regarding their labor at the service economy as a source of a complementary seasonal income to the traditional agricultural system in their home communities where their social networks are still firmly established.

This detachment has transformed Cancún into "a come and go city" (*ciudad de paso*), characterized by transient relations and a pervasive sense of "rootlessness" (*desarraigo*) which crystallize in instrumental relations to the city and its spaces. That is, in a mutual indifference *vis-à-vis* the city, and *vis-à-vis* one another. These processes of enclosure enable, maintain and extend this detachment to the city to tourists and corporations. Tourists travel to Cancún to encounter the imaginary of the tourist escape from the everyday. Government and corporations reproduce this imaginary through all-inclusive resorts and the enclosure of the beach. The result is a vulnerable and fragmented city where indifference to place and others rule.

Guilt Free Indigenous Luxury Resorts: Elision of Uneven Pasts

If Cancún was the pioneering tourism venture in Yucatán, *The Haciendas* is its "newest luxury offer to the world" (Yucatán Today, 2009). *The Haciendas* is the name given to a private project led in the mid 2000s by the former chairman of Banamex, in partnership with the world's largest luxury hotel operator, Starwoods Luxury Collection, to transform ex-haciendas *henequeneras* into luxury hotels. To date, five haciendas have been fully restored as luxury hotels in inland Yucatán.[2] These haciendas are advertised as Premium and Grand Tourism. They have been promoted as luxury cultural tourism alternatives and marketed

---

2 Hacienda Temozón Sur, Hacienda Santa Rosa and Hacienda San José in the state of Yucatán, and Hacienda Uayamón and Hacienda Puerta Campeche in the neighboring state of Campeche. See Córdoba Azcárate (2013) for a detailed ethnographic account of the transformation of Hacienda Temozón Sur into a luxury hotel.

as guilt free luxury resorts. That is, luxury hotels where tourists can spend their money knowing, as one client put it "that something good comes out of it for local populations."

Haciendas were agricultural estates based in the production, manufacturing and exportation of *henequén*. In Yucatán, they were operated by *hacendados* or landowners, and had a dependent labor force, *peones*, whose working conditions have been described as regimes of semi-slavery. As in other Latin American haciendas, means of production "were employed not only for capital accumulation but also to support the status aspirations of the owner" (Wolf and Mintz, 1957: 380), which in Yucatán, were closely connected with a European elite mentality.

The transformation of haciendas into hotels for the luxury market has required a selective construction of enclosed, exclusive, aestheticized spaces following the culture and values of the oligarchy of *hacendados* during *henequén* times. These enclosures help to materialize a moral economy of mutual dissociation within their walls as well as outside of them. This moral economy is sustained by an imaginary escape into the past that is articulated through various material elements and social practices, like a careful craftsmanship of nature, a museification and aesthetization of *hacendado's* everyday life and objects, and the disciplining and professionalization of tourist-locals encounters. These material arrangements and social practices embed tourists in a fantasy escape to the past that becomes instrumental in promoting indifference towards place and others.

Restoration processes have privileged the recovery of those buildings within *The Haciendas* that were linked with the *hacendados* everyday life, like the *Casa Principal*. The selective equation of the Casa Principal with the hacienda as a totality produces an image of *The Haciendas* as romanticized scenarios (MacCannell, 1999) in which tourists' experiences and imaginaries are univocally equated to those of *hacendados'* elite and European mentalities. Moreover, the equation of the hacienda with the *hacendado's* lifestyle has been accomplished at the expense of eliminating all those living and work spaces and practices that link haciendas to the their past as productive and non-egalitarian places. No reference is made to the marginal living conditions in which their labor force was and still is living in being the only allusions to this past highly aestheticized portrayal of a privileged mobile elite, as for example, the ones shown in the machine houses of several haciendas, now transformed into conference rooms.

The selective reconstruction and aestheticization of the past is also evident in the way *The Haciendas* design and represent "tropical nature." Following French formal gardening, *The Haciendas'* have constructed an image of nature following mathematical formulas, where geometry, monumentality, perspective and the controlled movement of bodies are the rules. Elevated structures allow a panoptic control over spaces and activities; careful layouts, daily fumigation and collection of leaves manage to craft an idyllic representation of the tropical jungle. This crafted environment contrasts with contemporary Yucatec landscapes lying just a few meters away from most haciendas. These are characterized by hundreds of hectares of abandoned *henequén* fields and generalized illegal waste dumps, including land-filling, which evince serious waste management problems and reveal larger environmental and health problems such as desertification and dengue.

The staged and professionalized encounter with indigenous others is another element helping to perform the passive beloved phenomenon that characterizes the detachment of tourists from contemporary Maya cultural practices. One of the spaces where these encounters take place is in *The Haciendas'* spas, where they offer traditional body massages (*sobadas*). These massages involve the privatization and commodification of communal resources and traditional practices to promote forms of self-indulgent tourist consumption. Massages take place in acclimatized spas or sinkholes (*cenotes*) that were used as communal resources, both because of their attachment to Maya traditional religious practices, and because of their use as public spaces of leisure for communities. Within *The Haciendas*, however, *cenotes* have been cut off from their uses as religious and leisure spaces and have been privatized for the exclusive use of tourists. In them, the practices of midwifes (*parteras*) and healers (*sobadoras*) have been re-signified losing their traditional meaning and symbolism as practices performed by old expert rural women to help women during pregnancy and labor. Inside *The Haciendas*, young indigenous women who have been trained to perform Western styled massages, perform *sobadas* as pleasure-seeking experiences that advocate the isolation, shelter and exclusive treatment of tourists' selves in a very similar fashion to Western spas and old-style seaside resorts.

Despite discourses of guilt-free and responsible consumption, escaping to the past in one of these privatized gated and embellished luxury resorts sets in motion a selective use of natural resources and cultural practices. It generates staged scenarios for tourist-local encounters where tourists are removed from contemporary Yucatán and are never challenged or encumbered by the presence of others. In spite of sustainable discourses, all five municipalities where *The Haciendas* are located still are classified, after twelve years of community development, as "highly marginal areas" where over 80 percent of homes lack access to basic services thus questioning the idea that luxury can be a sustainable and socially just road to development (Coneval, 2010).

Conclusions

In her most recent work, Caton (2012: 1920) elaborates on the importance of addressing moral issues in tourist studies. She states, "if I can relax in a cool swimming pool as a visitor in your community while you, as a resident of that community, lacks clean water to drink, then there is clearly a problem." This problem escalates when relaxing in exclusive swimming pools, within privatized spaces, is normalized *both* by tourists and locals who seem to accept that water to drink or to swim, and cultural traditions and spaces, should be sacrificed in the name of tourism and economic development.

No matter how old or new tourism developments are in Yucatán, they have proven to reproduce a moral economy of mutual dissociation. This moral economy is entangled in different imaginaries of tourist escape—from the ordinary, into the past—that have created asymmetrical entitlements to land and resources such as the beach, sinkholes or traditional healing practices. The cases of Cancún and *The Haciendas* have illustrated how these imaginaries produce indifference through the idealization of environments and resources like the Caribbean beach, or through the elision and aesthetization of the past, that result in a lack of engagement with place and others. Such regimes of indifference are upheld and reproduced in practice through spatially segregated tourism planning, enclosed architectures and the disciplining of the indigenous bodies of those who cater for tourists.

Privatization, enclosure and disciplining of otherness are deeply motivated by global economic forces in this region. Pressures to remain a global Caribbean beach destination and pressures to remain a historically unique Mexican enclave pave the way to uneven tourism ventures and they press populations, who find in tourism their only economic alternative, to comply with them. Current financial, environmental, health and violence crisis add a patina of greater uncertainty for these economically dependent populations on tourism, making the destination's vulnerability more clamoring.

Attending to moral issues like the ones addressed here is of most importance when tourism is articulated as a development tool at the governmental level and when the sustainability of natural and cultural resources and practices is at stake (Smith and Duffy, 2003; Lea, 1993; Tribe 2009). Addressing moral questions should go beyond cautioning or advocating tourism as a bad or good development strategy to address the larger issue of *how* responsibility towards other peoples and places is created or, in this case, erased, in and through tourism practices. How is *indifference* achieved in practice through tourism? What are the material and social practices informing and reproducing it? If we still believe that tourism can be a way to move out of impoverished and precarious existences, discourses, practices and material arrangements, *indifference* should be at the center of our studies. Only in so doing, socially just agendas can be deployed and sustainability achieved.

References

Butcher, J. (2003). *The Moralization of Tourism: Sun, Sand ... and Saving the World?* London: Routledge.

Castellanos, M. (2011). *A Return to Servitude. Maya Migration and the Tourist Trade in Cancún.* Minneapolis: University of Minnesota Press.

Consejo Nacional de Evaluación de la Política de Desarrollo Social, CONEVAL (2010).

Córdoba Azcárate, M. (2011). 'Thanks God, this is not Cancún!' Alternative Tourism Imaginaries in Yucatán (México). *Journal of Tourism and Cultural Change*, 9(3), 183–200.

Córdoba Azcárate, M. (2013). The Uneven Pragmatics of "Affordable" Luxury Tourism in Inland Yucatán, México. In T. Birtchnell and J. Caletrio (eds.), *Elite Mobilities*, pp. 149–175. London: Routledge.

Caton, K. (2012). Taking the Moral Turn in Tourism Studies. *Annals of Tourism Research*, 39(4), 1906–1928.

Indicadores de Carencia Social por Municipio. Abalá. México: CONEVAL.

Lathan, A. (1999). Powers of Engagement: On Being Engaged, Being Indifferent, and Urban Life. *Area*, 31(2), 161–168.

Lea, J. (1993). Tourism Development Ethics in the Third World. *Annals of Tourism Research*, 20, 701–715.

Low, S. (2006). Towards a Theory of Urban Fragmentation: A Cross-Cultural Analysis of Fear, Privatization, and the State. *Cybergeo: European Journal of Geography*. At: http://cybergeo.revues.org/3207 [Last Accessed 8th November 2012].

MacCannell, D. (1999). *The Tourist: A New Theory of The Leisure Class*. Berkeley: University of California Press.

Salazar, N. (2011). *Envisioning Eden: Mobilizing Imaginaries in Tourism and Beyond*. Oxford: Berghahn.

Sayer, A. (2003). (De-)Commodification, Consumer Culture and Moral Economy. *Environment and Planning D: Society and Space*, 21, 341–357.

Sayer, A. (2004). "Moral Economy," published by the Department of Sociology, Lancaster University, Lancaster LA1 4YL, UK. At http://www.comp.lancs.ac.uk/sociology/papers/sayer-moral-economy.pdf [Last Accessed 8th November 2012].

Secretaria de Turismo México, SECTUR (2010). *Compendio estadístico del turismo en México*. Available from: CD. Secretaria de Turismo. México.

Sennettt, R. (1990). *The Conscience of the Eye: The Design and Social Life of Cities*. London: Faber and Faber.

Sennettt, R. (2001). "New Capitalism, New Isolation. A Flexible City of Strangers," *Le Monde Diplomatique*. At: http://Mondediplo.Com/2001/02/16cities [Last Accessed 8th November 2012].

Shaw, W. (2007). *Cities of Whiteness*. London: Wiley-Blackwell.

Smith, M., and Duffy, R. (2003). *The Ethics of Tourism Development*. London: Routledge.

Torres, R., and Momsen, J. (2006). "Gringolandia": Cancún and the American Tourist. In N. Bloom (ed.), *Adventures into México: American Tourism Beyond the Border*, pp. 58–76. Lanham, MD: Rowman & Littlefield.

Tribe, J. (ed.) (2009). *Philosophical Issues in Tourism*. Bristol: Channel View.

Wolf, E., and Mintz, S. (1957). Haciendas and Plantations in Middle America and the Antilles, *Social and Economic Studies*, 6, 380–412.

Yucatán Today (2009). "Hacienda Hotels??" At: http://yucatantoday.com/en/topics/hacienda-hotels [Last Accessed 8 November 2012].

SECTION 2

Embodied Tourism Encounters

Chapter 6

Reproductive Fugitives, Fertility 'Exiles' or Just Parents? Assessing Possible Approaches to the Governance of Cross-Border Fertility Tourism

Shelley K. Grant

Introduction

Besides the conspicuous growth in family travel for emotional reward (Kluin and Lehto, 2012) and educational self-discovery (Santos and Yan, 2010), the geographies of tourism are equally shaped by the routinized but largely concealed patterns of global travel by prospective parents seeking to fulfill their intimate desires for family building. The avenues for obtaining reproductive assistance continue to multiply in ways that imply a corresponding increase in process accessibility. Yet, even the most uncomplicated cases of assisted family building often require parents to obtain various advanced medical procedures, to reply upon rapid communication systems and to traverse long distances to and from service provider destinations. Surprisingly little consensus exists within cultures on the standards needed to regulate parental travel to receive these vital, socially constitutive processes.

Presently, the governance of family building practices varies widely across methods and often fails to explicitly extend to family building that is dependent upon cross border reproductive contracting. Some inconsistencies in process standards emerge from shifts in the perceived value of reproductive 'tourist encounters' (Crouch et al., 2001), as conceived on the parental level and at broader scales of analysis. Other discrepancies arise from culturally derived quasi-legal or purely moral thoughts about internationalized family building overall. The differences between legal and moral evaluations are especially evident when reproduction appears to transgress traditional biological connections among kin or presume the definition of parental 'fitness' as married and heterosexual. In this chapter, I think through three hypothetical offenses frequently associated with parental election to engage in reproductive tourism. In evaluating their potential transgressions against the current practice realities, I articulate the need for continued attention to the nature of the violation presumed in the exercise of intimate parental interests.

Defining the Practice Across Scales and Methods

Arguably, reproductive tourism is one of the most controversial forms of medical tourism. It involves travel by 'candidate service recipients from one institution, jurisdiction, or country where treatment is not available to another institution, jurisdiction, or country where they can obtain the kind of medically assisted reproduction they desire' (Pennings, 2002, p. 337). Although the phenomenon includes intra- as well as international processes, both are well-established practices. This is evidenced in the evolution from the relatively awkward term 'procreative tourism', initially used in 1991 by bioethicists Knoppers and Le-Bris, to more specific descriptors such as 'fertility tourism' (Spar, 2005) or 'travel ART', used variously by policy analysts at the United Nations (Smith-Cavros, 2010) and the World Health Organization (Fathalla, 2001) and elsewhere. Despite slight variations in meaning, the overall presumption is that procreative tourism encompasses travel to obtain techniques of *in vitro* fertilization (IVF) techniques and tests such as *pre-implantation genetic diagnosis* (or PGD). In reality, this assumed meaning narrowly excludes the significant travel required to complete analogous family building processes.

In response, my understanding of reproductive tourism includes processes of inter-country child adoption and child surrogacy. A cross-method survey indicates that transnational methods are undeniably similar in average cost ranges, required levels of service provider contracting and use of multiple technologies. Assessed at the family level, multinational studies show that parents with medical conditions of infertility frequently consider a variety of reproductive options during the course of their decision making process (Selman, 2006, p. 202). Based on this, I argue that globalized methods are similarly constituted across scales, in ways that speak to the construction of subjectivities for global categories of parents forced to choose among a specific range of options.

Reading Across the Intersecting Realities of Policy and Procreation

Many misunderstandings about the proliferation of reproductive tourism arise from the absence of accurate information about current process patterns. I will initially review three under-examined facts about the phenomenon to support a subsequent reframing of the current depiction of prospective parents. The first point is that cross-border reproduction is no longer a marginalized practice. Since the mid-2000s, reports issued by the European Society for Human Reproduction and Embryology (ESHRE) indicate that reproductive tourism is now an 'entrenched phenomenon' with families in the US, across the EU and other economically developed areas (Shenfield et al., 2010; Billari et al., 2007). They claim that cross-border reproductive contracting for ART processes now involves travel by prospective parents from over 30 nations to around 130 inter-regional sites within the EU. These figures overlap with protocols set by the *Hague Convention on*

Protection of Children and Co-operation in Respect of Intercountry Adoption that permit international child adoptions among 89 member and non-member ratifying nations to the Hague Conference on Private International Law (HCCH). Even without the addition of child surrogacy data, these numbers provisionally attest to the breadth of cross-border family building contracting across methods.

The second critical point is that most economically developed nations now provide families with substantial levels of social welfare assistance, tax exclusions and other benefits to aid family building efforts. State assisted family building not only supports the wishes of parents but also benefits the sovereign interests of countries with chronically low replacement birth rates and high incidences of medical infertility among female populations of child bearing age. To provide an example of the potential influence of assistance, the US *Adoption Promotion and Stability Act of 1996* (H.R. 3286) and the *Economic Growth and Tax Relief Act of 2001* allowed US residents to claim up to $10,600 per year in tax exemptions for the adoption of a foreign child. Until 2009, the US received the highest annual number of child immigrations for purposes of family placement. In effect, the tax measures collectively halved the estimated cost to complete international child adoption, making the cross-border method nearly equivalent to the US March of Dimes (2008) estimated costs for an uncomplicated birth through natural delivery.

Based on a statistical review of multinational family building trends, the *Organization for Economic Co-Operation and Development* (OECD) published a 2005 report that verified the correlation between national standards for social, fiscal and labour market policies and the changes in fertility rates (D'Addio and d'Ercole, 2005). The report further suggested that the social assistance policies have increased the reliance of some European nations on cross border reproductive contracting for population maintenance. Evidencing this dependency, more recent studies on family growth in Denmark estimate that the successful use of assisted reproductive technologies may contribute to just over 5 percent of the total child population (Shaikh, 2010). Similarly, in 2012 the UK Office of National Statistics (ONS) reported that the number of births to 'advanced age' parents have contributed to a reversal in long-range population projections to above-replacement birth levels. Importantly, this excludes data for population increases resulting from inter-country child adoptions or child surrogacy arrangements.

The third, and final, point is that the categories of parents most frequently known to engage in cross-border reproduction are often unable to receive assistance through domestic channels (Porter et al., 2007). Domestic restrictions on assistance are frequently based on factors such as parental age, sexual orientation, marital status and even medical history. The economic downturn of the late 2000s has further altered patterns in national social welfare spending in ways that now force adjustments in the allocation of assistance to various parent groups. For instance, authorities in the UK, Netherlands, France, the US, Italy and Germany have passed measures that limit or eliminate funding entirely for infertility treatments to women over the age of 42 (Netherlands) and some nations fail to recognize the child adoptions or ARTs contracted by same-sex parents

(France) (Wardle, 2006). Even further, ESHRE studies suggest that parents may be applying skills of consumer spending to compare the services offered by a growing cadre of global providers (Pennings, 2002). The inconsistencies in access to family building assistance respond not only to concerns for child welfare and security, but also to the moral economies developing around this form of travel. It exposes an undervalued relationship between the multinational growth in numbers of parents 'electing' to engage in reproductive tourism and the national 'mandates' that force specific parental groups to engage in reproductive tourism. To explore this distinction, I turn now to examine the intersecting rules of law and the extra-legal responses that shape cultural considerations of reproductive tourism.

Exploring the Culpability in Cross-Border Reproduction

Policy makers and political theorists are clearly divided about the level of stringency required to regulate the reproductive travel of parents. Political theorists Franco Furger and Francis Fukuyama (2007) call for an extension of reproductive regulations that mimic the ethical parameters established for technology use under the terms of multinational human rights accords. More radically, political scientist Leonard Fleck (2009) proposes the concept of health care 'rationing' to ensure a 'just' and democratic allocation of scarce state social welfare resources. Speaking directly to the idea of parent culpability, Sven Bergman (2011) suggests that reproductive tourism exemplifies a 'circumventive' political agency by parents. Countering this, James Fossett (2007) notes the potential difficulty in establishing standards for a singular morality across cultures, while Brian Salter and Charlotte Salter (2007) caution against the unintended perpetuation of cultural differences and hierarchies in the governance of ART use. Rather than dismissing the exercise of parental interests within reproductive tourism, I instead wish to emphasize the distinction between governance by law and the moral circumscription of intimate activities through the interpretation of legal standards.

To further explore this difference, I consider three quasi-legal hypothetical or charges against reproductive tourism drawn from a review of perceptions about the moral economies of these practices. The three charges of *criminality*, *irresponsibility* and *immorality* aptly characterize the core elements of responses. In following each, I especially consider the political participation of parents in their global exercise of nationally guaranteed individual interests. Following a review of each charge, I then explore alternatives to the current conceptions of reproductive tourism ethics that involve the construction of a globalized civil society.

Charge #1: Reproductive Tourism is a 'Criminal' Act

In a 2001, UK journalist George Monbiot commented, in the UK *Guardian* newspaper op-ed piece, on the disquieting advances in globalized reproductive medicine that enable women to bear children well into their 60s, particularly after receiving fertility treatments at foreign centers. Speaking to the 'strange fear of older mothers', Monbiot stated,

> I can't help feeling that an underlying revulsion still informs the debate about the ethics of reproduction ... To suggest that late births are unethical, we have first to say whom they have wronged. Otherwise our complaints boil down to this: no blood please, we're British.

Humor aside, his statement raises two points about travel reproduction that contribute to its perceived offense. The first is that reproduction assisted by foreign agents is not a sexual activity that actually violates the current rule of law. The second is that the social discomfort created by travel reproduction and by certain classes of parents may be norm defying, but not the same as a binding legal prohibition.

In reality, the UK and US legal standards generally disfavour state intervention in family building in ways that might prevent reproductive tourism from constituting a crime. Under US law, sexual offenses normally involve the assault or battery of a victim in non-consensual, involuntary intimate physical acts (or *actus reus*) where the violator is aware of the victim's lack of consent (termed *mens rea*). Sexual offences involve the victimization of certain populations in cases of adult or statutory (minor) rape or crimes of pedophilia. Unlike sex offenses involving the victimization of children or women, the criminalization of reproductive tourism involves the subjectification of parents under intersecting standards of legal and moral authority (Ong, 1996; Butler, 1990).

The law also increasingly fails to recognize differences across family types. For instance, the International Criminal Court under the Rome Statute Explanatory Memorandum (of 1998) (A/CONF.183/9 of 17 July 1998) declared that forced sterilization constitutes a violation of protected human rights. Similarly, high courts in the US and elsewhere have extended protections for privacy to include same sex-partners and unmarried individuals seeking access to methods of contraception under *Griswold v. Connecticut* 381 U.S. 479 (1965) and *Eisenstadt v. Baird*, 405 U.S. 438 (1972). Although not an exhaustive or strict consideration of the legal standards regarding sex crimes and state non-intervention, I do mean to suggest that the legal precedence does not affirm the conclusion that reproductive tourism constitutes a crime.

Charge #2: Reproductive Tourism is Irresponsible

This scenario presumes that parents traveling to receive reproductive support have committed a civil tort by obviating national prohibitions or restrictions on domestically permissible care. The parental offence is a defiance of the legally defined scope of private contracting abilities. Many of the current policies on reproductive practice contracting aim to reduce fraud in the arrangements formed between parents and foreign service providers. For instance, this preventative policy intent guides the provisions on family building contracting set forth by the HCCH as in the standards for child adoption processes (*Hague Convention of 29 May 1993 on Protection of Children and Co-operation in Respect of Intercountry Adoption*) and for surrogacy arrangements (*Private Internat'l Law Issues Surrounding the Status of Children, Incl. Issues Arising From Internat'l Surrogacy Arrangements*, Prel. Doc. No 11 2011). Similarly, the UK restrictions on cross-border family building, first articulated within the Report of the Warnock Committee (1984, 1985), aim to protect prospective parents from the abusive use of reproductive technologies. The views of the committee speak to the necessity for informed consent within reproductive contracting, as extended in the later *FIGO Committee for the Ethical Aspects of Human Reproduction and Women's Health Guidelines* (Milliez and Milliez, 2009), which recommended that patient consent be required for all reproductive healthcare treatments. Under these policies, parental election to contract with foreign providers violates national laws directed at the social welfare protection of individual citizens. Seen thus, the activities of prospective parents are 'illegal' and transform tourists into a multinational collective of civil disobedients, as suggested by Rattner et al. (2003).

On the other hand, reproductive tourism can be interpreted as a violation of national social policies aimed at limiting health care costs in the future, particularly those associated with failed or high-risk infertility procedures. In this case, the perceived harm in travel reproduction is the negligence of parents both to assume expanded levels of social responsibility within their private reproductive practices as well as the exposure of society to increases in future health care maintenance costs.

Although this view prevails in European states that routinely assume higher levels of responsibility for providing public social welfare and health care assistance, it is also growing more common in the US where private health care insurance and reproductive contracting are the norm. Summed up in a 2010 UK *Daily Mail* article, the failure to regulate the private reproductive contracting of parental populations with international service providers 'will open floodgates unless age limit is enshrined in law' (MacFarlane, 2010). The implication here is that laws are required to prevent the social irresponsibility of prospective parents.

Understood temporally, the violation of parental social irresponsibility takes on new meaning. With the proliferation in cross-border reproductive process contracting, the UK Human Fertilization and Embryology Authority (HFEA) has championed the consideration of changes to the 2008 Act (c 22) that would additionally dictate the maximum patient age at which UK patients may receive state assisted reproductive treatments domestically. In the current Section 13 (5) of the 2008 Act, the law states: 'A woman shall not be provided with treatment services unless account has been taken of the welfare of any child who may be born as a result of the treatment (including the need of that child for supportive parenting), and of any other child who may be affected by the birth'. This language implies that parental disobedience threatens to harm an unborn child, essentially punishing parents for an unrealized human rights violation and evoking the enforcement of predictive punishments against still innocent individuals as depicted in the science fiction film the 'Minority Report' (2002).

Certainly, this imperative carries a different meaning for 'advanced age' parents than for same-sex other parental groups because arguments of lifespan and health conditions are critical to medical and personal decision making. Yet, the legal recognition of future criminality this suggests is unsettling. It is dangerous to singularly presume that travel tourism will give rise to social welfare costs without also considering the potential for these practices to result in social welfare benefits through tax base increases.

Charge #3: Reproductive Tourism is Immoral

In some ways, this charge most accurately reflects the inconsistencies in the interpretation of reproductive process standards. The notion of immorality recognizes the emotional and extra-legal concerns infusing many cultural valuations of assisted reproduction as child commodification (Zelizer, 1985) in adoption or unregulated biocapital flows (Franklin and Ragone, 1998). Essentially, to claim immorality suggests that reproductive tourism is a 'bad' form of global consumption. Conversely, it also implies that 'good' international participation altruistically involves acts such as supporting children's rights established under the *United Nations Declaration on the Rights of the Child* (1989) and within the localized work of the United Nations Children's Fund (UNICEF).

In situating the debate on procreative travel on moral grounds, the accusation of parental desires begs for a more spatially nuanced and pluralist interpretation of law, rather than the universalization of absolute standards (Pennings, 2002). Borrowing concepts from political geographers Clive Barnett and Murray Low (2004), I suggest the possibility for devising ethical standards to generally support responsible international consumption by non-state actors. Recognizing that family building is comprised of multiple processes of consumption and production, I advocate a broader recognition of groups possessing family building faculty.

Conclusions: Unchartered Areas of Governance

In the end, the difficulty in presuming reproductive tourism to be an offense hinges on the fact that this is a relatively unchartered area of social governance. This realization extends the ideas of social scientist John Tribe (2006) on the necessity for interdisciplinarity in assessing tourist practices and the need for a recognition of 'multiple truths' about tourist practices. It challenges the notion that reproductive tourism is a singularly minded performance and suggests the need to protect individual interests to enable diverse processes of social constitution.

While reproductive tourism, challenges current norms of individual market participation, the access to reproductive options also aids in the construction of a global civil society. Speaking to this constitutive aspect of tourism, human rights theorist Alison Brysk (2005) notes the difficulty in identifying individual private wrongs occurring in the expansion of civil societies. She states that 'when abuse crosses borders, it does not always wear a uniform' (Brysk, 2005, p. 1). She further suggests effective methods of 'norm innovation', particularly in the transnational governance of private actors, may require systems 'build upon existing standards and frameworks' (p. 3) and that 'human rights for global civil society carry a critical new content, questioning and sometimes reconstructing deeply embedded boundaries between public and private social arenas' (Brysk, 2005, p. 3). In reflection, Brysk's comments critically expose the imperative to practically evaluate the politicization of cross border reproductive processes in reference to seemingly unrelated factors of family difference and cultural fears.

In the end, my evaluation of the moral economies of reproductive tourism necessarily challenges many universalized conceptions of equity and justice. It is an unlikely blend of libertarianism and a notion of 'feminist fundamentalism' raised by legal scholar Mary Ann Case (2011). In exploring the notion of 'feminist fundamentalism,' Case suggests that the regulatory parameters around reproductive practices must explicitly maintain protections for the legal interests of individuals in non-traditional family configurations. Taking this thought further, I believe the failure to protect the prospective parents, harms civil societies on multiple scales. Even worse, the disregard of interests endangers the decision making capacity of individuals engaged in multi-scaled reproductive processes. The tension between the cultural mores and legally imposed parameters is most apparent in the intimate tourist activities of particular prospective parents. This exposes a fragility in the democratic protections for individuals participating in spatially extended reproductive activities. In practice, the debates on reproductive practice governance will likely expand to new and more scintillating areas before ultimately determining common ideals for the scope of reproductive choice and social responsibility governance.

References

Barnett, C., and Low, M. (2004). *Spaces of Democracy: Geographical Perspectives on Citizenship, Participation and Representation*. London: Sage.

Bergmann, S. (2011). Fertility Tourism: Circumventive Routes that Enable Access to Reproductive Technologies and Substances. *Signs*, 36(2), 280–289.

Brysk, A. (2005). *Human Rights and Private Wrongs: Constructing Global Civil Society*. New York: Routledge.

Butler, J. (1990). *Gender Trouble*. London: Routledge.

Case, M. A. (2011). Feminist Fundamentalism as an Individual and Constitutional Commitment. *American University Journal of Gender Social Policy and the Law*, 19(2), 549–576.

Crouch, D., Aronsson, L., and Wahlstrom, L. (2001). Tourist Encounters. *Tourist Studies*, 1(3), 253–270.

D'Addio, A. C., and d'Ercole, M. M. (2005). Trends and Determinants of Fertility Rates in OECD Countries: The Role of Policies. *Social, Employment and Migration Working Paper No. 27* OECD. DELS/ELSA/WD/SEM(2005)6.

Fathalla, M. (2001). Current Challenges in Assisted Reproduction. In *Current Practices and Controversies in Assisted Reproduction*. Report of a Meeting on 'Medical, Ethical and Social Aspects of Assisted Reproduction', held at WHO Headquarters in Geneva, Switzerland, 17–21 September 2011, ed. Effy Vayena et al., 3–14. Geneva: WHO.

Franklin, S., and Ragoné, H. (1998). *Reproducing Reproduction: Kinship, Power, and Technological Innovation*. Philadelphia: University of Pennsylvania Press.

Furger, F., and Fukuyama, F. (2007). A Proposal for Modernizing the Regulation of Human Biotechnologies. *Hastings Center Report*, 37(4), 16–20.

Kluin, J. Y., and Lehto, X. Y. (2012). Measuring Family Reunion Travel Motivations. *Annals of Tourism Research*, 39(2), 820–841.

Knoppers, B. M., and Le Bris, S. (1993). Ethical and Legal Concerns: Reproductive Technologies 1990–1993. *Current Opinion in Obstetrics & Gynecology*, 5(5), 630–635.

MacFarlane, J. (2010). Woman, 59, Becomes the Oldest Person to Ever be Offered IVF Treatment by a British Clinic. *Daily Mail* newspaper [online]. Available at: http://www.dailymail.co.uk [accessed: 16 Feb. 2012].

Milliez, J., and Milliez, J. (2009). Fertility Centers and Who They should Treat: FIGO Committee for the Ethical Aspects of Human Reproduction and Women's Health. *International Journal of Gynecology & Obstetrics* 107(2).

Monbiot, G. Our Strange Fear of Older Mothers: No Longer Attractive to Men, They're Treated as an Offence Against Nature. *Guardian UK* newspaper [online]. Available at: http://www.guardian.co.uk [accessed: 19 Feb. 2012].

Ong, A. (1987). Cultural Citizenship as Subject-making: Immigrants Negotiate Racial and Cultural Boundaries in the US. *Current Anthropology*, 37, 737–762.

ONS (2012). *Statistical Bulletin: Births in England and Wales by Parents' Country of Birth*. 30 August. Available at: http://www.ons.gov.uk [accessed: 20 Oct. 2012].

Porter, M., Peddie, V., and Bhattacharya, S. (2007). Debate: Do Upper Age Limits need to be Imposed on Women Receiving Assisted Reproduction Treatment? *Human Fertility*, 10, 87–92.

Rattner, A., Yagil, D., and Pedahzur, A. (2001). Not Bound by the Law: Legal Disobedience in Israeli Society. *Behavioral Sciences & the Law*, 19(2), 265–283.

Salter, B. and Salter, C. (2007). Bioethics and the Global Moral Economy: The Cultural Politics of Human Embryonic Stem Cell Science. *Science, Technology, & Human Values*, 32(5), 554–581.

Santos, C., and Yan, G. (2010). Genealogical Tourism: A Phenomenological Examination. *Journal of Travel Research*, 49(1), 56–67.

Selman, P. (2006). Trends in Intercountry Adoption: Analysis of Data From 20 Receiving Countries, 1998–2004. *Journal of Population Research*, 23(2), 183–204.

Shaikh, N. (2010). Danish Government Cuts Funding for IVF. 6/5/2010. *BioNews* [online] 561. Available at: http://www.bionews.org.uk/page_62080.asp. [accessed: 4 Oct. 2011].

Shusett, R. (2002). *Minority Report*. Universal City, CA: DreamWorks Pictures.

Smith-Cavros, C. (2010). Fertility and Inequality Across Borders: Assisted Reproductive Technology and Globalization. *Social Compass*, 4, 466–475.

Spar, D. (2005). Reproductive Tourism and the Regulatory Map. *New England Journal of Medicine*, 352(6).

Tribe, J. (2006). The Truth about Tourism. *Annals of Tourism Research*, 33(2), 360–381.

Wardle, L. (2006). Global Perspective on Procreation and Parentage by Assisted Reproduction. *Cap. U. L. Rev.*, 35(2), 413–478.

Warnock Committee (1984). *Br Med J (Clin Res Ed)*. 1984 July 28. 289(6439), 238–239.

Warnock, M. (1985). The Warnock Report. *Br Med J (Clin Res Ed)*. 1985 Jul 20; 291(6489), 187–190.

Zelizer, V. A. R. (1985). Pricing the Priceless Child: The Changing Social Value of Children. New York: Basic Books.

Chapter 7

Gazing at Kayan Female Bodies as Embodied Others in Myanmar

Anne-Marie d'Hauteserre

Introduction

As one concentrates on the demands of one's multiple identities does one have any time for considerations such as how to negotiate moral cross-cultural relations? How purposive is tourism and this desire for 'off the beaten track' experiences? By 1955 Claude Lévi-Strauss had already mulled over the motivations of the 'self-less traveller'. He struggled whenever his work led him to research 'other' societies with what travelling to 'different lands' and to encounter 'others' is supposed to mean. My tentative response was prompted when a group of us were led to gaze upon 'traditions' that are etched in the bodies of women who are photographed for their difference, though no one seemed to question what I believed was the oppressive and gendered nature of the practice. No one questioned either their forced displacement from their original homes to Regina Hill Village.

I use this 'moment of experience' (Nelson, 2003) with Kayan women who wear brass neckbands to examine what morality our embodied tourism encounters embrace (even when reduced to *gazing* upon and *recording* practices). The neckbands, which weigh three to eight kilos, crush the shoulder blades and collar bones of their wearers, hence, I believe, effectively constrain these women. Yet, they are required to perform for tourists in villages established by the Myanmar Junta. Do globalization forces throw cultures together in such a way that "the outer experience is cut off from the inner experience" so that different ethnic groups jostle each other but remain unresponsive to each other's existence (Castells, 1983, p. 7)? Relational capacities are signified unequally whatever space they occur in. Encountering 'others' when travelling, in the street at home, or on the screen may lead to the belief that a face to face conversation is occurring when, however, the exchange is only a simulacrum that reinforces stereotypes (d'Hauteserre, 2004; O'Reilly, 2005). These 'others' are rendered familiar but remain hardly known.

This chapter explores how capital and cultural circuits exploit local difference and particularity by commodifying them for consumption as 'unique' elements tourists can add to their cultural capital. Lyotard (2005, p. 18) confirms that "cultural capitalism has found the market for singularities." Literary and other conventions prepare us for differences, which we now recognize as stereotypically conventional. The hegemony of 'profitability' (global capitalism) obfuscates heterogeneity and

Figure 7.1   Long-necked Kayan woman

incommensurability but does not resolve differences. International growth of ethnic markets represents a western-directed 'cosmopolitanization' of selected cultural traits commoditized and standardized for the global market (d'Hauteserre, 2009).

Space is recreated for consumption by global image flows directed to privileged 'cosmopolitans' (tourists) so that moral responsibilities about such commodification and consumption are left to individual actors. Moral questions have often been considered merely incidental, except in a few cases. Gibson-Graham (2006) demonstrate how to create different kinds of subjectivities, more open to dialogue with others, based on ethical practices of the self. They promote a "diverse community economy" (p. 95) which they define as a moral space of becoming and "being-in-common" and argue that this space questions "how to share meaning and finding ways to be together in the world" (p. 82). Remote (read 'until now marginal') landscapes have become the ultimate destination, especially if they are 'wild and pristine' or they are inhabited by an 'authentically primitive or different' group of humans. Can tourism, as it moves towards such 'post modernist' forms, provide more enlightened encounters with the rest of the world (McCannell, 2011)?

This chapter first describes the original encounter with the Kayan women of a government tourist village in eastern Myanmar and their aesthetisized turn on the world stage. The methodology and the theoretical framework that follow support the discussion on the role and, or place of the transactional processes that define how the tropics and their inhabitants are imagined. The methodology engages with the emotional turn in the critical social sciences (Widdowfield, 2000). Lyotard's and Levinas's work frame the discussion on the morality of tourist practices. The chapter then examines whether tourists can behave morally in the course of encounters in remote destinations when facing oppressive political practices that also maintain gendered cultural practices.

Visiting Regina Hill Village

It was with great excitement during a field trip in Southeast Asia that we received the news of a stop where our group of touring academics would be able to photograph women who wear brass neckbands (Figure 7.1). Regina Hill Village, located near Tachileik, Myanmar, had been set up by the Myanmar government to accommodate tourist visits. The village remains based on the colonial model of 'exhibition' of primitiveness and tradition for Western publics through commoditization of 'difference' (Minca, 2006; Morton, 2000). When our group arrived, the female residents of the village and their children started to gather in front of their houses. About four Akha women who adorn their traditional clothing with pieces of silver of varying sizes were first captured on camera, then five Kayan women. The Kayan women also wore brass rings fitted just under the knee. We followed the two groups to a small stage (a raised platform facing rows of benches) further up the hill, where they performed dances to recorded music. The older Kayan women sat on the side waiting to pose with the visitors. The younger ones barely moved while a CD player diffused some ethnic music; the Akha, were more mobile during their dances.

The village was the scene for me of a most reprehensible practice, a major form of gendered political oppression. It seemed difficult not to recognize the embodied resistance of the Kayan women. The women's gestures, especially of the older ones who wore the tallest neckbands, expressed their discontent and to some extent the constraints the adornments they have to wear impose. Such a visit had not been considered before setting off on the trip so I had not been able to put in an ethics application at my university to interview the women or the field trip participants. In any case no interpretation or explanations were offered. No translators or guides were available to respond to queries or to question the women. There were no other opportunities or time to interact with the residents of the village.

We remained in the village for just twenty minutes. The next day, we visited a museum dedicated to opium where an information panel spelt the history, the reasons (recognized here as one among several versions) and the consequences of the practice of wearing neckbands. This information though was available only a day after our visit to Regina Hill Village. The explanation confirmed some of the resistance I had read on the bodies of the Kayan women. I do recognize that an ethnographic study of the Kayan practice of wearing the heavy neck rings may reveal the degree to which it is considered oppressive by the women themselves but also whether they wish to be 'liberated' from performing in a government village created for the very purpose of exhibiting such a practice. Earning a living from tourism may also have released these women from difficult agricultural toil. However such a study could not take place.

One of the women in the village did not wear a neckband but it seemed that she could have worn one previously because her shoulders were exceptionally straight and her neck appeared as long as those of the two older women in the village who still wore the rings. Her movements bore the imprint of wearing those neck devices. I mention this here to record what I interpreted as a possible form of resistance to the practice, an 'utterance' of agency (Lyotard, 1988). These bands can be removed because they do not separate the vertebrae and the weakened, atrophied muscles can be retrained. The crushing of the bones cannot be undone. Some of these women who live in Thailand have admitted to physical discomfort, even in sleep and that they only wear the bands to increase family income (*Standards*, 2001; Nicholson, 2007). The Kayan were actively encouraged to cross the border (*Standards,* 2001) into Thailand but had to respond to the Thai government's demand that they keep up the practice as tourism attractions.

MacCannell challenges the assumption that tourism enlightens its practitioners. He seeks to "inspire more intense, creative and ethical engagement with the act of sightseeing" (2011, p. xi). MacCannell discusses ethics of gazing, as a practical application of morals to a specific form of tourist performance. My emphasis is on the morality of tourism encounters, including gazing. I wish to question the motivations of those who 'gaze' upon (or maintain a subject to object relation with others) rather than seek embodied encounters (a subject to subject interaction). If encounters are not given but produced by the experience of the protagonists, is understanding oppression (of any kind) related to differing geometries of power? Seabrook (2005) exemplified such an understanding when discussing the consequences of the 2004 Indian Ocean Tsunami: only western tourists deaths were recounted as individual tragedies in the western press. Should this form of encounter, limited to the gaze without contesting the unjust practices witnessed, be condoned or condemned? For gazing seems to tip the balance towards acquiescence and even approval of oppressive practices.

Framework

This chapter examines how embodied emotional dynamics are triggered when tourists encounter certain practices. Emotions as ways of knowing have become relevant in geographical research (Anderson and Harrison, 2006; Davidson, Bondi and Smith, 2005; Ettlinger 2009), including feminist research, since "they inform every aspect of our lives" (Davidson et al. 2005, p. 10). I use emotion here not as just a personal feeling but rather as a line of force, a capacity to act. It supported my determination to research further about tourism and the morality of encountering cultural and, or political practices that to me as a Western woman signify some kind of oppression.

I agree with Kwan (2007, p. 22) that attention to emotions in research can "lead to a more just world." Emotion directed my subjective reflection on female oppression and gendered marginalization. If tourists did not seem to enjoy gazing at certain practices without reflecting on the particular place they are staged in or on the consequences of the practices on the well-being of those performing for the visitors, it might lead to less oppression in many arenas, starting with a reduction in violence against women. Tourist destinations evoke a range of emotions, from excitement to trepidation (Urry, 2005) so that moving between cultural settings can exacerbate emotional dynamics, engendering different kinds of relational flows. Tourism has great emotive capacity even if (or because/when) it is encountered as a cultural product so it is necessary to recognize the emotional power of some forms of experience and to question how moral they are.

Tourism is used by many governments to encourage isolated communities to create wealth and improve their standard of living. Regina Hill Village is sponsored by the Myanmar government because the attractivity of its residents resides in their 'inability' to progress. Attention to politics of rank and gender within communities can give us a key to the use of control and violence as exercises of authority. Treiner (2006, p. 84) confirms that "women are but objects in the hands of men ... the 'respect' of female bodies is highly mutable: males are only concerned with their ability (right) to control them." The removal of Kayan women to Regina Hill Village by the Myanmar government severed their ties with the origins of their 'difference', concealing political reasons to separate them from the rest of their ethnic group. Gazing upon their neckbands obfuscates this abuse as well as the devastating human rights abuse record of the Myanmar government. Its appropriation and forced objectification of the women's alterity, at the same time, enabled it to earn revenues from foreign tourists' gazing. Was it moral to contribute to such earnings when the women only received paltry tips for posing for photographs?

Tourism is an integral part of the global 'libidinal economic system', an economy that exploits and releases desires and feelings (Lyotard, 1974). By privileging appearance, might today's libidinized economic order relieve its consumers of any guilt? Including the guilt I felt for visiting a country under an authoritarian Junta, which may have coloured my interpretation of the practice of neckband wearing? Indigenous participation occurs often as no more than 'staging their presence', an "untainted by modernity" add-on to capitalist projects (Din, 1997; Zeppel, 2006). They are represented as "existing in a relation of pure immediacy to the world and to themselves" (Mbembe, 2001). Change for them is impossible. Yet, mobility is very important to most tourists, who "appear to revel in jet-propelled speed and intensity" (O' Reilly, 2005, p. 153). Does such mobility avoid unnecessary involvement? Kennedy (2005, p. 231) confirms that "local people are surprisingly invisible in the text" of the postcards sent home. Morality seems to have vanished in the speed and movement of modern life.

Female suffering throughout the world is still not sufficiently recognized, including in the West (Ockrent, 2006). Progress towards gender equality in most parts of the world is still way below what the United Nations Commission on the Status of Women set up in 1946 promised (Momsen, 2004; Ockrent, 2006). Why can we not recognize how the majority of women are "exploited, beaten, raped, bought, repudiated, worked mercilessly? Condemned to remain silent, to be forgotten? Despicable and worthless" (Ockrent, 2006, p. 8)? Following Henderson (2008, p. 29) "should one feel hopeful in the case of another's misfortune" or outrageously angry? Henderson does admonish that "we can—and *should*—be angered by affronts to common human dignity" (2008, p. 30). Is there no right to live without inflicted pain, physical or moral (as in forced displacement because of a cultural practice attractive to tourists)? I agree with Davis (2004, p. 308) that "an absence of outrage might indicate ... denial of the suffering of others ... which is endemic to the western world."

How ethical is it to gaze on certain practices that seem to cause suffering to those gazed upon, and to record some of these practices for further viewing? Lyotard (1988) forces our attention upon the injustice of using criteria of performance that are insensitive to radically differing notions of aesthetics or morals. This incommensurability of 'ways of living' throws all interaction where different cultural spheres meet into power struggles: what is the just course of action and is any action even possible? How is a legitimate response determined?

Lyotard assures us that there is no universal rule as to what a just action might be, nor can we blame the rise of differing responses. Connolly (1987, p. 138) warns that "any authoritative set of norms and standards is at best an ambiguous achievement: it excludes and denigrates that which does not fit into its confines" but it is well-nigh impossible to resist the "powerful human urge to suppress disharmonies," or to prone liberation. Even if moral behaviour is considered a form of dialectic of solidarity which privileges care and communication one must recognize the diversity of moral belief and the relativity of moral truth (Deigh, 2010; Chappell, 2009).

Gazing and, or recording a different, even seemingly oppressive, practice might then make it not seem oppressive to all. If "the repressed of today is the body" (Anzieu, 1989, p. 64), if oppressive gender practices have effectively been displaced from view in the West so we hardly recognize their existence and their effects (e.g. rape and physical violence; major 'aesthetic surgery' or drastic dieting to conform to 'social' body norms), they will be even less visible to the ephemeral gaze of most visitors. Krishnamurti (1996, p. 109) adds that since "we are always interpreting what we [see]," rather than giving it our total attention, "obviously that does not bring about understanding." It does make it difficult to recognize an order imposed by cultural means, i.e. to perceive repression or oppression in others.

Though one is never sure of truly pursuing what is just, one must seek justice (Lyotard et al., 1989), even if Wheeler (2005, p. 264) wonders whether we "are ready to wholeheartedly ... really care." Levinas confirms that "the human is the return to ... its capacity to fear injustice more than death, to prefer to suffer than to commit injustice" (cited in Hand, 1989, p. 85). Morality requires a response to suffering, especially if it is unjust, to eliminate it or at least reduce it. Aquinas (1947) acquiesces that anger can be a desire for just vengeance for things done unjustly against others that cause injury. Levinas and Lyotard encourage an attitude that embraces difference rather than confront it antagonistically. The morality of care, which is followed here, enjoins one not to hurt others and that morality provides the possibility of solving conflicts. Authors agree that causing harm, even indirectly (as by encouraging the continuation of a hurtful practice such as forced displacement), is considered selfish and immoral as it shows a lack of concern (Chappell, 2009).

Levinas goes a step further when he exclaimed, following the massacres at Sabra and Chatilla in 1982: "my *self*, I repeat, is never absolved from responsibility towards the Other" (cited in Hand, 1989, p. 291). For Levinas we are not just accountable to the Other, we are in his/her debt since we owe our being to others, "an original responsibility of man (sic!) for the other person" (p. 290). Levinas believes in the infinite responsibility of the individual to the Other. He adds, the relationship with the Other, however, is not necessarily idyllic or harmonious, or in sympathy; we are not called to put ourselves in the Other's place. The indebtedness is asymmetrical, based on the primacy of the Other's right to exist.

Geometries of Power in Embodied Encounters

The suffering that this 'difference' caused did not seem to register as an abject practice with other members of the group. However, tourists surely cannot leave such an encounter untouched. Maybe, recording could be assimilated to a reminder so later reflections might lead to action. Could it be morally justified to just gaze and not seek an embodied relation, a true interaction? Viewing (gazing) is a matter of authorizing power: vision relies on an invisible frame that organizes how we see (Macphee, 2002), so it often disregards local (indigenous) reality. I agree with Lyotard (2005) that visitors who refuse to absorb local culture and its values impose disrespect, a form of violence. One of the main attributes of the gaze is its blindness (Macphee, 2002), as in the unseen (and rarely disclosed) violence used to open up more new destinations in the developing world (Mowforth and Munt, 2009; *Guardian Weekly* 2008).

Gazing objectifies the racialized essence of different cultures, since they are presented as titillating spectacle. They continue to be figments of western imagination, stereotypically conceived as exotic paradise (d'Hauteserre, 2006; Mowforth and Munt, 2009). They are thus hardly locations in which to raise matters of oppression and suffering. Susan Sontag had already remarked that "the medium which conveys distress ends up by neutralizing it" (1979, p. 109), "it aestheticise[s] the injuries of class, race and sex" (p. 178). The oppressiveness of the practice can then be ignored as its objectification quells the search for the imaginary aroused by the culture industry. So visitors take photographs, which only prolong the gaze, to communicate their practices, composing images of their act of visiting (Crang, 1999), in the village and of the dancers and last, posing as "objects of their own gazing" with the women.

This village which displaced the women from their original homes recontextualizes female otherness for easy consumption. This recontextualization, the very removal of the women from their home territory, transforms their cultural practices into an abstract, disembodied spectacle. The staging obfuscates any form of oppression or pleasure that it might represent for the females subjected to it. It encourages distanciated judgement by those who witness the practice. The scene, removed from the original event (the imposition of the neckband in the home village) can thus never truly account for the event either (Lyotard, 1988). Nor does it account for the suffering caused by displacement to this new location.

Theatricality, just like photography (Sontag, 1979), militates against intensity of empathy for suffering on the part of the audience. It encourages an absence of emotion or even of questioning the appropriateness of witnessing the practice. Just as museum exhibits cannot truly reveal the lived past, the women offer but an aestheticized version of their culture. Presentation for visual consumption transformed the practice into an abstract, disembodied spectacle in which the body of the hosts is ignored. A twenty minute encounter can hardly go beyond objectifying possession: interaction was reduced to an exchange relation between signs, rather than a genuine, embodied encounter.

These encounters are in fact bundled as a western practice that contributes to the creation of self-identities. They are constructed on western parameters, that render them requisite to satisfy western tastes, and that do not include any desire for interaction with the local people. 'Lifestyle entrepreneurism' (travelling to build personal identities) rather than morals (respect for place specific values) governs relations between tourists and hosts. Conran (2006) asks for better communication between the two groups which I translate as a call for a subject to subject relationship. Visitors (like myself) need to manifest respect towards the indigenous people encountered to overcome these kinds of violence.

Conclusions

The problem of dealing with oppression remains. As Larner (2008, p. 149) argues, "we are not outside these ethical and political processes, indeed we may in some cases be major contributors to them." Opening up spaces for negotiation of (gender or political) rights does need to steer clear of pitfalls as the desire to engage with such issues can lead to appropriating their representation. I cannot, however, disconnect what I lived 'out there' from my practices at home, to be relegated into an excludable and forgettable 'category'—for instance, a photo folder on a hard drive—any more than I can abide by the continuation of what I believe are oppressive practices wherever they occur.

There never is just one way to morally respond to cultural differences. The wearing of the neckbands has become a source of revenue for the military government of Myanmar who has displaced those members of ethnic minorities most likely to be attractive to foreign tourists. It has led to a double oppression: the severance of their ties with their ethnic minority and the possibility to resist the government as well as being forced to continue wearing neckbands as a tourist attraction. Kayan women who fled to Thailand to escape that appropriation and forced objectification found themselves in the same predicament (Khaikaew, 2005; Rose, 2007). In 2008, the Thai government refused to allow those Kayan women who had obtained refugee status in New Zealand to leave as that government would lose an important but cheap tourist attraction (New Zealand Herald, February 4 2008, p. A11). Continued gazing at these women, does not erase the inequity of power relations that govern their lives. Relational modes other than gazing at displaced groups because of a particularly 'interesting' cultural trait should provide revenues other than minuscule tips.

Such moral investigation might lead to the recognition that others are not mere objects to be apprehended through gazing (even if prolonged through photography) but subjects, agents of their own becoming, producers of the performances they offer. Tourists, as they objectify possession though gazing, impose disrespect, a form of violence, as they refuse to absorb local culture and its values (Lyotard, 2005). Our representations, or those encouraged by the market place, should not reduce others to stereotypes, be they of barbarity, primitiveness or exotic mystery. These clichés conveniently obfuscate inequitable exploitation by developed economies, but also by individuals who come from those privileged areas (Gregory, 2003; Brennan, 2004).

Incorporating reflexivity and emotion can enhance a moral approach to 'difference' without claiming moral right or definitive conclusions. Different relational modes would permit tourists to truly appreciate cultural diversity by, for example, returning subjective agency to 'others' as their embodied presence is fleshed out. It requires taking responsibility to break through the power geometries that reduce 'other cultures' and their practitioners to stereotypes. Relationality between bodies, for example, a politics of generosity, of welcoming, of indebtedness, implies a rejection of all forms of 'difference—as—antagonism'.

Acknowledgements

A professional development and a travel grant from the University of Waikato for which I am very grateful financed my participation in the fieldtrip in Myanmar.

References

Anderson, B., and Harrison, P. (2006). Questioning Affect and Emotion. *Area*, 38(3), 333–335.

Anzieu, D. (1989). *The Skin Ego*. London: Karnac.

Aquinas, Thomas (1947). *Summa Theologica*. [online] Available at: <http://www.ccel.org/a/aquinas/summa/FS/FS047.html> [Accessed 3 October 2011].

Brennan, D. (2004). *What's Love Got to Do with It?* Durham, NC: Duke University Press.

Castells, M. (1983). Crisis, Planning and the Quality of Life: Managing the New Historical Relationships between Space and Society. *Environment and Planning D: Society and Space*, 1(1), 1–14.

Chappell, T. (2009). *Ethics and Experience*. Durham: Acumen.

Connolly, W. (1987). *Politics and Ambiguity*. Madison, WI: University of Wisconsin Press.

Conran, M. (2006). Beyond Authenticity: Exploring Intimacy in the Touristic Encounter in Thailand. *Tourism Geographies*, 8(3), 274–285.

Crang, M. (1999). Knowing Tourism and Practices of Vision. In D. Crouch (ed.), *Leisure/Tourism Geographies*, pp. 238–256. London: Routledge.

Davidson, J., Bondi, L., and Smith, M. (eds.) (2005). *Emotional Geographies*. Aldershot: Ashgate.

Davis, K. (2004). Responses to W. Njambi. *Feminist Theory*, 5(3), 305–311.

Deigh, J. (2010). *An Introduction to Ethics*. Cambridge: Cambridge University Press.

D'Hauteserre, A.-M. (2004). Postcolonialism, Colonialism and Tourism. In A. Lew, C. M. Hall and A. Williams (eds.), *A Companion to Tourism*, pp. 235–245. Oxford: Blackwell.

D'Hauteserre, A.-M. (2006). Landscapes of the Tropics. In T. Terkenli and A.-M. d'Hauteserre (eds.), *Landscapes of the New Cultural Economy*, pp. 149–169. Dordrecht: Springer.

D'Hauteserre, A.-M. (2009). L'altérité et le tourisme: construction du soi et d'une identité sociale, *Espace, Populations, Sociétés*, 2009(2), 279–291.

Din, K. (1997). Indigenization of Tourism Development: Some Constraints and Possibilities. In M. Oppermann (ed.), *Pacific Rim Tourism*, pp. 76–83. Wallingford, UK: CAB International.

Ettlinger, N. (2009). Whose Capitalism? Mean Discourse and/or Actions of the Heart. *Emotion, Space and Society*, 2(1), 92–97.

Gibson-Graham, J. K. (2006). *Postcapitalist Politics*. Minneapolis: University of Minnesota Press.

Gregory, S. (2003). Men in Paradise: Sex Tourism and the Political Economy of Masculinity. In D. Moore, J. Kosek and A. Pandian (eds.), *Race, Nature and the Politics of Difference*, pp. 323–355. Durham, NC: Duke University Press.

Guardian Weekly (The) (2008). Sale of the Century. *Weekly Review*, 2 May, pp. 23–25.

Hand, S. (1989). *The Levinas Reader*. Oxford: Blackwell.

Henderson, V. (2008). Is There Hope for Anger? The Politics of Spatializing and (Re)producing an Emotion. *Emotion, Space and Society*, 1(1), 28–37.

Kennedy, C. (2005). Just Perfect: The Pragmatics of Evaluation in Holiday Postcards. In A. Jaworski and A. Pritchard (eds.), *Discourse, Communication and Tourism*, pp. 223–246. Toronto: Channel View Publications.

Khaikaew, T. (2005). Neck Rings carry Promise of a Better Life. [online] Available at: <http://www.s-t.com/daily/07-00/07-31-00/a13wn082.htm> [Accessed 29 August 2005].

Krishnamurti, J. (1996). *Total Freedom: The Essential Krishnamurti*. San Francisco: Harper.

Kwan, M. P. (2007). Affecting Geospatial Technologies: Toward a Feminist Politics of Emotion, *The Professional Geographer*, 59(1), 22–34.

Larner, W. (2008). The Musings of a 'Reluctant Subject'. *Emotion, Space and Society*, 1(2), 148–149.

Lévi-Strauss, C. (1955). *Tristes tropiques*. Paris: Plon.

Lyotard, J.-F. (1974). *Economie libidinale*. Paris: Les Editions de Minuit.

Lyotard, J.-F. (1988). *The différend: Phrases in dispute*. Minneapolis: University of Minnesota Press. Translator: G. van den Abbeele.

Lyotard, J.-F. (2005). *Moralités postmodernes*. Paris: Galilée.

Lyotard, J.-F., Derrida, J., Descombes, V., Kortian, G., Lacoue-Labarthe, Ph. and Nancy, J. L. (1989). *La Faculté de juger*. Paris: Les Editions de Minuit.

MacCannell, D. (2011). *The Ethics of Sightseeing*. Berkeley: University of California Press.

MacPhee, G. (2002). *The Architecture of the Visible*. London: Continuum.

Mbembe, A. (2001). *On the Postcolony*. Berkeley: University of California Press.

Minca, C. (2006). Re-inventing the "Square": Post Colonial Geographies and Tourist Narratives in Jamaa el Fna, Marrakech. In C. Minca and T. Oakes (eds.), *Travels in Paradox*, pp. 155–184. Lanham, MD: Rowan & Littlefield Publishers.

Momsen, J. H. (2004). *Gender and Development*. London: Routledge.

Morton, P. (2000). *Hybrid Modernities*. Cambridge, MA: MIT Press.

Mowforth, M., and Munt, I. (2009). *Tourism and Sustainability*. London: Routledge.

Nelson, J. A. (2003). How Did "the Moral" get Split from "the Economic"? In D. Barker and E. Kuiper (eds.), *Toward a Feminist Philosophy of Economics*, pp. 134–141. London: Routledge.

Nicholson, M. (2007). Thailand's Long-necked Women, [online] Available at: <http://thailand-travel.suite101.com/article.cfm/thailands_longnecked_women> [Accessed 30 August 2007].

Ockrent, C. (ed.) (2006). *Le livre noir de la condition des femmes*. Paris: XO Editions.

O'Reilly, C. (2005). Tourist or Traveller? Narrating Backpacker Identity. In A. Jaworski and A. Pritchard (eds.), *Discourse, Communication and Tourism*, pp. 150–172. Toronto: Channel View Publications.

Rose, M. (2007). Human Zoo: Neck-ringing Refugees, [online] Available at: <http://www.newint.org/issue264/update.htm> [Accessed 30 August 2007].

Seabrook, J. (2005). In Death Imperialism Lives On, *The Guardian Weekly*, Jan 7–13, p. 13.

Sontag, S. (1979). *On Photography*. New York: Farrar, Straus and Giroux, c.1977.

Standards (2001). Defining "Comfort": Padaung Women in Thailand, [online] Available at: <http://www.colorado.edu/journals/standards/V7N2/EDITORIAL/editorial.html> [Accessed 15 September 2007].

Treiner, S. (2006). Au nom de l'"honneur": crimes dans le monde musulman. In C. Okrent (ed.), *Le livre noir de la condition des femmes*, pp. 80–89. Paris: XO Editions.

Urry, J. (2005). The Place of Emotions within Place. In J. Davidson, L. Bondi and M. Smith (eds.), *Emotional Geographies*, pp. 77–86. London: Routledge.

Wheeler, B. (2005). Ecotourism/Egotourism Development. In C. M. Hall and S. Boyd (eds.), *Nature Based Tourism in Peripheral Areas*, pp. 262–281. Clevedon: Channel View Press.

Widdowfield, R. (2000). The Place of Emotions in Academic Research, *Area*, 32(2), 199–208.

Zeppel, H. (2006). *Indigenous Ecotourism: Sustainable Development and Management*. Wallingford, UK: CABI.S

Chapter 8

Moral Ambivalence in English Language Voluntourism

Cori Jakubiak

Introduction

Volunteer tourism has been defined as "volunteer[ing] in an organized way to undertake holidays that … involve aiding or alleviating the material poverty of some groups in society" (Wearing, 2001: 1). Although recently appropriated in domestic contexts (Villano, 2009), volunteer tourism in academic literature indexes unskilled, temporally shallow travel that moves primarily in a Global North-South flow (Callanan and Thomas, 2005). While some volunteer tourism projects may involve assisting in orphanages or building physical structures, English language teaching is a common project option (Butcher and Smith, 2010). Within English language teaching via volunteer tourism, or what I call *English language voluntourism*, one's primary task is to teach English as a foreign language in settings that vary by placement site.

Research on volunteer tourism defined broadly suggests that the phenomenon operates within a *moral economy*: "a tangled circulation of money, people, labor, and emotions that creates complex webs of possibility and connection, but which also contains points of friction and disillusionment" (Sinervo, 2011: 6). That is, although many volunteer tourists are motivated primarily by affect and a desire for intimacy with distant others (Conran, 2006), their efforts take place within an individualistic, arguably neoliberal, formation that sustains rather than promotes redistributive justice (Conran, 2011; Jakubiak, 2012). In the context of English language voluntourism specifically, participants volunteer their time to teach English in the names of economic development, humanitarian aid, and international education, *inter alia*. Thus, issues of native-speaker privilege, teacher professionalization, and ideologies of language as a commodity add new dimensions to extant moral terrain.

To be sure, numerous factors complicate efforts to understand English language voluntourism—its purposes and goals as well as its effects on host communities and visiting volunteers. These factors include: conflicting claims made about the efficacy of English language voluntourism; unverified assertions by public policy organizations such as the US Brookings Institute that unlimited expansion of international voluntary service is both desirable and necessary (2006); and, most broadly, the historical complexities of Global North intervention in the South, particularly in the name of development (Escobar, 1995). Framed within these wider complications, this chapter presents findings from a larger research study that investigated the following questions: how do in-service and former English language voluntourism programme participants define *development*? What do they understand *development* to mean, and, further, what forms do they see development taking in the programmes in which they participate(d)? In exploring these two broad questions, I seek to understand the ways in which English language voluntourists conceive of themselves as participants in development work.

While many participants in English language voluntourism programmes do, indeed, view these programmes as development (see Jakubiak, 2012), this chapter reveals that such views do not go uncontested. Many in-service and former programme participants suggest that English language voluntourism does not achieve its stated mission—that is, teaching English—and therefore does not constitute development. Although the voices of such "dissenting" volunteer tourism programme participants are not frequently heard, I share them here to illustrate how even within neoliberal development paradigms such as volunteer tourism (Conran, 2011), individual actors working *within* these formations can open up spaces of moral resistance. Following Caton's (2012: 1907) call for tourism research to take the moral turn and address "the human imaginative and discursive capacity for considering how things should be, as opposed to describing how things are," I draw upon participants' voices to suggest what a more morally responsible English language voluntourism might look like. Before explicating my study's findings, however, I first situate English language voluntourism within a body of related research.

English Language Voluntourism: Embodied "Help"

English language voluntourism is a practice in which native speakers of prestige-variety English (Kachru, 1997) such as American Standard or British Standard English teach English as a foreign language on a short-term basis in the Global South as an alternative form of travel. Although some faith-based organizations sponsor short-term English language teaching as mission work (Snow, 2001), this study focuses on non-sectarian English language voluntourism as sponsored by private corporations and non-governmental organizations (NGOs). Whether characterized as "making a meaningful contribution to international education" (WorldTeach, n.d.) or increasing "educational and employment prospects for people who would not normally have the opportunity to learn English" (Cross-Cultural Solutions, n.d.), English language voluntourism, as depicted by sponsoring NGOs and corporations, provides positive benefits for local communities and constitutes development aid. English language voluntourism programmes are often linked to the websites of organizations such as the U.S. federal initiative, Volunteers for Prosperity, a division of the United States

Agency for International Development, and Idealist.org. These groups support the United Nations' Millennium Development Goals, a list of social initiatives that are based on a pro-growth, economically-oriented approach to development (Global Volunteers, 2008).

Consistent with other forms of volunteer tourism, the requirements for participation on most English language voluntourism programmes are minimal. Neither formal educator credentials nor prior teaching experience are generally required; one need not even possess a college degree. Instead, organizations stress participants' native English language speaking skills as well as their good intentions. As Projects Abroad (n.d.) claims, "Your own ideas and initiative will be welcomed by our partner schools .... [A] lack of formal qualifications can be more than made up for with plenty of enthusiasm and commitment"; similarly, WorldTeach (n.d.) states that "Prior teaching experience is helpful but not required. Flexibility and enthusiasm are pluses!" Teaching in the English language voluntourism context, then, does not rely on expertise in second language acquisition or pedagogical content knowledge. Rather, the primary vehicles through which English is ostensibly delivered via volunteer tourism are participants' innate language knowledge skills and their biding enthusiasm.

The enthusiasm called for in English language voluntourism, moreover, is distinctly *embodied*. Contra tourism that focuses on the gaze (Urry, 2002), volunteer tourism is marketed as an embodied practice. Hugging children, painting physical structures, and holding hands with people in host sites are common images associated with volunteer tourism in general (Sinervo, 2011). In English language voluntourism specifically, promotional materials link teaching to corporeal actions such as smiling, dancing, and dramatization. In illustration, i-to-i volunteering states that "Helping the children with special needs on [our] project[s] will undoubtedly bring you the biggest smiles possible when you sing, dance and help to enrich their lives with your enthusiasm" (n.d.).

Akin to performative, embodied tourism practices such as dancing in the sun to rave music (Saldanha, 2005) or bungee jumping (Cater and Cloke, 2007), English language voluntourism interpellates participants as able-bodied, intrepid, and rife with stamina. To judge from the language of promotional materials, English language voluntourism is less about guided language instruction than the insertion of energetic Global North bodies into what is cast as the exhausted South. Per Cross-Cultural Solutions (n.d.), "Your fluency in English motivates working adults and recent graduates to practice their English and improve career options. Your stay may be short, but ... [y]ou can bring new energy and enthusiasm to community members." English language voluntourism participants are thus charged not primarily with second language teaching, but with embodying enthusiasm as a way to motivate the ostensibly downtrodden. Still, English's allure as a global language provides an overarching frame for this embodied enthusiasm—a discussion to which I now turn.

The English Language As/For Development

Critiques of volunteer tourism as development suggest that the phenomenon represents *life politics*: a way for individuals to exercise social agency in a world in which grand narratives and collective political platforms seem irrelevant (Butcher and Smith, 2010). Particularly since the turn of the twenty-first century, making "green" consumer choices or purchasing so-called moral vacations have displaced other, less market-based, forms of social action (Butcher, 2003). Thus, volunteer tourism both constitutes and is constituted by neoliberalism: it relies on private, individual behaviors (often consumptive ones) rather than public channels or structural reform as a way to redress social problems (Conran, 2011).

Corporate and NGO promotion of the English language as a development tool links volunteer tourism to neoliberalism in other ways, too. For one, oft-cited phrases such as "global English," "English as the world's lingua franca," and English as the "universal" language obscure larger questions about the origins of English as a world language and elide the fact English operates in the interests of some, mainly corporate, interests better than others (Phillipson, 2000). Second, images of and discussions about English often associate the language with technology, modernization, and jobs in the knowledge economy. Throughout the Global South, English is seen by many people as a valuable form of symbolic capital, and students often study the language in the hopes of going overseas (Niño-Murcia, 2003). However, while discourse around the English language is rife with images of the Global North, it is thin on the truth of immigration: "Those who 'invest' in English language cultural capital have in practice little or no access to its marketplace," Niño-Murcia (2003: 138) notes in reference to learners in Peru. Despite rhetoric that links the English language to global opportunity, business, and technology, earning entrée to where "development" already exists is rarely part of the English language learning package.

While discourses connecting English to immigration and ideas of development may offer false hope to individuals in places like Peru, elsewhere entire nations have put their money on the "English as development" horse to little payoff. In Tanzania, for example, all secondary schools are conducted in an English language medium. Consequently, students often fail to grasp complex content in classes like science because of linguistic barriers. Additionally, many classrooms are highly undemocratic, as students with strong English language skills dominate class discussions (Brock-Utne, 2002). Similarly parental demand has produced extensive English language schooling in Hong Kong in the last few decades. As a result, English language education has displaced other, potentially more useful, subjects, like Cantonese, in K-12 academic curricula (Pennycook, 1994).

In sum, the rhetoric of English as development—especially as it bears upon English language voluntourism, which views English spread as neutral and beneficent—affirms rather than challenges neoliberal prerogatives. For one, the construction of English as a commodity that can be given by way of enthusiastic, uncredentialled volunteers neglects the complex sociocultural nature of language teaching and learning and shifts the effects of volatile job markets onto individuals in the name of "lifelong learning" (Block and Cameron, 2002). Second, English language voluntourism's uncritical positioning of English as the global language ignores the structural and political forces that propel language shift (Phillipson, 2000). Finally, as a form of life politics, English language voluntourism sees development work as doable by well-meaning individuals acting outside of political structures. Like exaggerated claims of globalization that predict an inevitable, new world order in which all people will be equally competitive and prosperous (Ohmae, 1999), English language voluntourism's "English as development" discourse is simplistically alluring. As Niño-Murcia (2003: 139) writes, the rhetoric of "English for development"

> is ... an example of overgeneralized globalist analysis. It projects the "world English" phenomenon as if it were a unitary universal, audible from all geographic and sociocultural difference. It simplistically places globalization discourse into a teleological sequence: "someday we will all be globalized" and "we will all speak English"—a dubious prophecy, but an irresistible one, because it contains a much-needed metaphor for hope.

This "metaphor for hope" undergirds English language voluntourism. Not only do people throughout the Global South hope to learn English to further their job prospects, but well-meaning volunteers hope that they can teach others the English language as a way of fostering development. This latter notion, though, often comes to be contested. Before turning to participants' voices, however, I first explicate my research methods.

Study Methods

The study presented in this chapter is part of a larger, multi-sited ethnography (Marcus, 1995) that spanned the course of two and a half years. In 2007, I conducted participant observation for two months in Costa Rica as a volunteer English language teacher under the auspices of an NGO-sponsored programme. In 2008, I worked in the NGO's US home offices for five weeks as a programme assistant, and in 2009, I returned to the NGO's home offices for ten days to conduct a series of retrospective interviews with programme alumni.

Data for the study presented in this chapter consist exclusively of 34 interview transcripts. While volunteering in Costa Rica, I conducted 16 open-ended, semi-structured interviews with 14 other members of my 21-person volunteer cohort (two participants were interviewed twice). Participants were selected using a process of convenience sampling (Patton, 2002). Interview questions were drawn from a pre-established protocol that sought to explore participants' motivations for having volunteered; their perceptions of the purposes of English teaching/learning in the host country and/or the local community; and their understandings of English language voluntourism as development. All interviews in Costa Rica lasted between 30 and 45 minutes, were audio-recorded, and were later transcribed for analysis. The other 20 interviews were those conducted with former programme participants in January 2009. Questions for these interviews were taken from a protocol similar to that used in Costa Rica. A process of purposeful sampling (Patton, 2002) was used to recruit interview participants who had volunteered in the last two years and resided near the NGO home office. As in Costa Rica, all interviews were audio-recorded and later transcribed for analysis.

In both interview settings (Costa Rica and the US), participants' identity categories were consistent with research in volunteer tourism at large, which suggests that participants in programmes such as volunteer tourism are likely to be female and under 30 (Heath, 2007). Out of 31 total participants (3 of my interview participants were interviewed in both 2007 and 2009), 19 identified as female; all but 1 were under thirty.

Interview transcripts were analyzed using a constructivist, grounded theory approach (Charmaz, 2006). Following a recursive process that involved initial, or open, coding, writing analytical memos, and focused coding (Emerson, Fretz, and Shaw, 1995), I ultimately generated three superordinate categories that expressed the different ways in which participants talked about development. Superordinate categories were generated inductively (based on ideas in interviewees' talk) and deductively (based on ideas implicit in the interview questions or present in academic literature). I discuss the first superordinate category, *English language voluntourism as development*, elsewhere (see Jakubiak, 2012). The other two superordinate categories were *English language voluntourism is not development: English language voluntourism as ineffectual* and *English language voluntourism is not development: development as something else*. Data from the first superordinate category, *English language voluntourism is not development: English language voluntourism as ineffectual* forms the focus of this chapter, which I discuss below.

English Language Voluntourism as Ineffectual

Of the 50 percent of study participants who reported that English language voluntourism is not development, 88 percent offered that English language voluntourism is too weak on the ground in terms of English language teaching to generate substantive social or economic change in host communities. Many in-service and former programme participants had been the exclusive English language resource in their host sites, and they observed that their communities had little or no way to continue English language learning at the end of a volunteer's tenure. Thus, claims that these programmes reliably deliver English language skills to people in the Global South are tenuous. As Stacey, a former programme participant in Ecuador, explained,

> [T]he reality is that like, like, the village doesn't really have any means to continue English language learning …. [M]aybe people who are teaching in Quito and are doing, like, more advanced classes are—are, have different experiences. But at least, being in the village, I didn't feel like I was furthering anyone's economic capabilities …. Like, here's kids who are going from Quechua class to English class, and Quechua they hear from their parents all the time, and English they hear for eight weeks over the summer. (January 28, 2009)

Stacey sees short-term, volunteer-taught English classes as impractical in a small, under-resourced community. The local schools in her placement site were already stretched thin promoting Spanish-Quechua bilingualism—a hard-won victory, incidentally, for indigenous groups in South America (Hornberger, 1998). Thus, Stacy questions the efficacy of adding a third, isolated, eight-week English language course into the mix.

Stacy's comment, however, that "maybe people who are teaching in Quito are having different experiences" suggests that short-term, volunteer-taught English courses might be more impactful in an ongoing, structured teaching/ learning setting in which people already know or use English with regularity. Indeed, Taylor, the one participant in my study who *did* teach in Ecuador's capital city, taught advanced level English to local professionals who needed language proficiency certificates for salary raises or job promotions. As Stacey imagines, the Quito volunteer placement site was in an established private school. This setting helped to offset Taylor's limited pedagogical experience by providing structured lessons, textbooks, and curricula. Despite these benefits to Taylor and her students, though, Taylor insisted that her volunteer situation was "non-traditional" and in some ways, very disappointing. She explained:

> I taught at [a private school], which also was, I think, sort of a non-traditional experience, because it was very, very organized. It's run by an American couple—the husband is actually Ecuadorian—but, they go back and forth between the US, and the wife is American …. It's like, it's very organized—you have to, like, sign up to—like 48 hours in advance to make copies. They had scheduled movie days … they had tests you had to, like, give certain days, and they, like, made the tests for you, and you taught from *Interchange* [a book]. So it was very—it was very different from a lot of, some of the other [volunteer] experiences …. I was sort of, like, a little sad when I went, because a lot of my students like weren't as, like, warm and like, you know, like, taking me home like some of the other sites. (June 27, 2008)

Taylor's interpretation of the urban volunteer experience as "non-traditional" because, among other reasons, she had a lot of teaching support (something seemingly desirable for an inexperienced teacher) confirms research suggesting that what volunteer tourism sells to participants, more than anything, is geographic and cultural *difference* (Simpson, 2004). The opportunity to live and work in an exotic, even poor, place where one will struggle to "deliver" development and be warmly welcomed by local people forms the backbone of volunteer tourism's allure. "What a warm, welcoming, and energetic community we entered," a volunteer states in a Global Volunteers (2008: 13) brochure. "I've not felt as appreciated as a teacher in 11 years of teaching in the States as I did during two weeks in Crete!" Taylor's description of her organized, instructionally-focused, urban experience as "non-traditional" reveals the extent to which English language voluntourism is not primarily about educational impact. Rather, volunteers arrive expecting to "be taken home." If and when this doesn't occur, one's experience is classified as "non-traditional" and even disappointing.

Other former programmeme participants also viewed English language voluntourism as ineffectual. Like Stacey, who saw her teaching role as limited, Karen thought that the structure of her English courses was disjointed and unsustainable. When asked about the larger purpose of English language voluntourism in rural Poland, her placement site, Karen responded:

> [H]onestly, I don't feel like … it does very much …. [I]n terms of actually making a significant difference in teaching English, I mean, the fact that it's summer and people go on vacation and you have random kids coming in and out and it's not that long anyway—you're teaching for, like, six weeks—I don't think that it … makes a difference in terms of English. I, maybe I'm not supposed to think that, but. (January 28, 2009)

Karen's reflections are grounded in the observation that student attendance in volunteer-taught, short-term English language courses can be and is often spotty. In order for any education-related programme to be effectual, students must at least be in attendance.

More pointedly, though, is Karen's reticence to share her negative opinion about English language voluntourism's educational impact. For one, it suggests that frank discussions of English language voluntourism's classroom outcomes are rare if not discouraged among participants. Second, Karen's framing of a critical perspective on English language voluntourism as ineffectual prohibits the dialogue from moving forward. Any discussion of how English language teaching under English language voluntourism *might* be more impactful, effective, or useful is shut down before it can begin.

Participants' comments also touched on the overall brevity of volunteer tourism. Participants in this study engaged in two-month long programmes, inclusive of a week-long orientation and a mid-service conference. Consequently, most participants taught for approximately six weeks, a time frame they perceived as prohibitive to language teaching and learning. Amanda, a former programme participant in Costa Rica, gave voice to this concern as follows:

> I'm just thinking about the, the statement, "education for international development." It sounds kind of like a magic equation, where, you know, you

give them more education, and then, they're equipped and they're developed and they do their own thing. Along the ground it's a little bit of a slower process. If you're only there for two months, you're spending the first couple of weeks getting to know people and getting to know your students, to be the most effective, you know, person in the classroom that you can be. And you spend the last month getting ready to say goodbye. So, it leaves very little time to, to actually impart anything. (January 27, 2009)

If the development driven by English language voluntourism relies on local people actually acquiring English language skills, time itself may make this proposition untenable. The US Foreign Service Institute, for example, suggests that 8 weeks, or 240 hours, of intensive language training are required for an adult to achieve minimum speaking proficiency in an Group 1 language (an additional language that shares roots with one's primary language) (Hadley, 2001). Given that English language courses in the voluntourism context can be as little as one hour a day or a week for one to six weeks, it is hard to imagine that English language acquisition occurs in a rigorous, consistent way by way of a volunteer's efforts.

Along with the observations that English language teaching within voluntourism can be unsustainable, disorganized, and brief, participants also saw English language voluntourism as ineffectual because of general teaching difficulties. These difficulties included structural challenges as well as classroom ones, particularly as 29 of this study's 31 participants were not credentialed educators and possessed little to no prior teaching experience. Participants spoke about complexities ranging from a lack of knowledge about curricula to discomfort with displacing local teachers. Joanne, a former programme participant in Costa Rica, spoke to these tensions like so:

> It was only much later that I—well, maybe a few months later—that I started thinking about in, in the bigger scheme of things, the fact that the English teachers that they have don't speak English. And so they've just had me come in, sweep—you know, it's fun for them. It's like—sort of like summer vacation, because I, I don't give them tests that they're responsible—like, I give them tests, but it doesn't have any bearing on their actual, like, school grade. So it's like—it's fun. The, you know, the young ... American girl comes and does lots of games with them. But then they go back and have English class with a teacher who doesn't speak English and have to take national exams for which I haven't prepared them, because no one's told me what they're supposed to be learning or what the exam is. (January 30, 2009)

Here, Joanne reveals tacit knowledge of major concepts in teaching and learning—concepts that are missing in the instructional settings of many English language voluntourism programmes. For one, she sees a lack of accountability as prohibitive to language acquisition. Research in second language education suggests that purposeful, ongoing, formative and summative assessment (for example, homework, conferences, and tests) can be as important to school-based language acquisition as the process of instruction itself (Folse, 2004). Therefore, Joanne's discomfort with simply "playing games" is warranted. Ongoing and continual evaluations can not only provide incentives for students to engage with classroom material but also provide teachers with essential information about whether their students are learning.

Joanne's reflection on what happens when a short-term, native English language speaker displaces a local teacher, moreover, refers to important, if rarely discussed, issues. As Joanne intimates, who, exactly, *is* responsible if and when students do poorly on a national English examination after a volunteer's departure? What are the personal and professional effects on local teachers when young, non-certified outsiders usurp their classes? Research on the roles of native English language speakers as English teachers suggests that the consequences are many (Block and Cameron, 2002). Mainly, the practice perpetuates the "native speaker myth" (Phillipson, 1992): the idealization of prestige-variety, (often White) native English language speakers as having innate knowledge of English and as best qualified to teach it.

Moreover, given that most participants in English language voluntourism programmes are not certified teachers, the English language classrooms in which they work become politically-charged sites. In the context of volunteer tourism, participants try on professional identities that they don't possess and experiment with those identities on real people (Simpson, 2004). Such experimentation not only risks exacerbating already inequitable conditions between the Global North and South (Hutnyk, 1996), but it also raises broader moral concerns. Akin to how the most under-resourced schools in the US have greatest number of unqualified, inexperienced teachers (Darling-Hammond, 2010), a fact that reflects what "is" but not what "ought to be" (Caton, 2012), English language voluntourism's placement of unqualified volunteers in vulnerable peoples' classrooms as primary teachers is a form of educational malfeasance. People most in need of the opportunities brought by way of education deserve the most qualified, highly experienced teachers— not the least. Inadvertently following Smith (2000), who avers that moral progress in human geography involves an insistent effort toward creating a more equal world, the participants in this study point out that English language voluntourism, as a development initiative, does not level educational experiences worldwide.

Finally, participants in this study viewed English language voluntourism as ineffectual for other reasons, too. While participants like Joanne were distressed by a lack of curricular knowledge and concerned about displacing local teachers, some participants were disenchanted with the overall instructional format of English language voluntourism. Shelly, a former programme participant in China, was concerned about English language voluntourism's "immersion," or English-only, approach to language teaching. She commented:

> I think the whole concept of sort of volunteer English teaching when you don't really speak the other language is so difficult. Because [in the US], they, you, you know, you talk about having immersion classes, but the fact is, you don't put a teacher who has no knowledge of the language that students speak in to try to teach them a language that they don't speak .... One of my classes, none of them had ever learned any English. I didn't know any Mandarin when I arrived, and it was just crazy. I was like, "Hi, hi, hi"—like, for the whole week. (January 29, 2009)

Total immersion, or what is termed the *natural approach* (Krashen, 1982) to language instruction, is sometimes employed in second language educational settings. However, recent research on language teaching and learning suggests that liberal use of the students' primary home language is important in introductory level language classrooms (Echevarría, Vogt, and Short, 2008). Shelly's observation that the "immersion" approach among beginning language learners led to reductive wheel-spinning suggests an intuitive understanding that English language voluntourism is often not methodologically sound.

For participants like Joanne and Shelly, then, time in the classroom under the auspices of an English language voluntourism programme was not time engaged in effective English language instruction. Joanne felt that her lack of curricular knowledge as well as teacher authority prohibited her from preparing her students for national examinations. For Shelly, the lack of a mutual, communicative medium between teacher and students reduced language instruction to the basic. For these and similarly-minded programme participants, English language voluntourism is not development because it fails to deliver quality language instruction. If development in the Global South ostensibly occurs as a result of English language teaching, English language voluntourism does not deliver.

Conclusions

To conclude, I discuss the ways in which data in this study reflect an important, though rarely discussed, outcome of English language voluntourism. My findings suggest that many English language voluntourists complete their programmes critical of the experience: specifically, of the pedagogical foundations on which English language voluntourism is based. As a result, they cannot say they engaged in meaningful development work. These findings prompt another set of questions.

For one, how might the development of critical perspectives on English language voluntourism's pedagogical premises be a positive outcome of participation? If, as my data suggest, English language voluntourism is not development (in the economic-growth sense) but rather the growth and development of visiting Global North volunteers, what should this development be? If the goal of English language voluntourism is indeed "life changing experiences" (Teaching and Projects Abroad, n.d.), sponsors and stakeholders alike should make clear whose life is changed and how. My study's findings suggest that volunteers' disciplinary majors, for example, may impact volunteers' perceptions; many of the most vocal criticisms of English language voluntourism came from anthropology, education, and humanities students. How and in what ways do volunteer-sponsoring organizations take college majors into account when selecting or preparing volunteers?

Second, what is to be made of the fact that if and when English language voluntourists become critical of these programmes' pedagogical foundations, they are often afraid to voice their critiques? The consistency with which participants in this study expressed hesitancy, insecurity, and even apology for critical views suggests they received the message that developing these views is wrong. Perhaps this is a consequence of the promotional literature; perhaps this is a consequence of broader, reductive trends in Global North education, which promote an uncritical acceptance of content knowledge rather than critical thinking (Spring, 2004). Whatever the case, it is disconcerting that critical views are reported cautiously.

Foucault (1976/1978: 27) writes that "silence itself—the things one declines to say, or is forbidden to name ... is less the absolute limit of a discourse ... than an element that functions alongside the things said." Despite English language voluntourism's persistence on framing itself as a time of "meaningful experiences" (Cross-Cultural Solutions n.d.), meaning itself seems to be circumscribed. Participants' critiques—of short-term English language teaching, of displacing local teachers, of English-only pedagogy—comprise a part of the volunteer tourism phenomenon. Failing to attend to this critique is a failure to engage with what English language voluntourism is and does. Advocates of a more moral world order would be wise to attend to *all* the voices that constitute, and are created by, this same experience. As the data in this study suggest, the various stakeholders in English language voluntourism programmes often hold contradictory views. Rather than being incommensurate, these differences may constitute a space in which the beginnings of alternative kinds of social change, and, indeed, more moral encounters in tourism might occur.

References

Block, D., and Cameron, D. (eds.) (2002). *Globalization and Language Teaching*. New York: Routledge.

Brock-Utne, B. (2002). *Language, Democracy, and Education in Africa*. Uppsala: Nordiska Afrikainstitutet.

Butcher, J. (2003). *The Moralization of Tourism: Sun, Sand ... and Saving the World?* London: Routledge.

Butcher, J., and Smith, P. (2010). Making a Difference: Volunteer Tourism and Development. *Tourism Recreation Research*, 35(1), 27–36.

Cater, C., and Cloke, P. (2007). Bodies in Action: The Performativity of Adventure Tourism. *Anthropology Today*, 23(6), 13–16.

Caton, K. (2012). Taking the Moral Turn in Tourism Studies. *Annals of Tourism Research*, 39(4), 1206–1928.

Charmaz, K. (2006). *Constructing Grounded Theory: A Practical Guide Through Qualitative Analysis*. Los Angeles: Sage.

Conran, M. (2011). They Really Love Me! Intimacy in Volunteer Tourism. *Annals of Tourism Research*, 38(4), 1454–1473.

Conran, M. (2006). Beyond Authenticity: Exploring Intimacy in the Touristic Encounter in Thailand. *Tourism Geographies*, 8(3), 274–285.

Cross-Cultural Solutions (n.d.). *Cross-Cultural Solutions* [Brochure]. New Rochelle, NY: Author.

Darling-Hammond, L. (2010). *The Flat World and Education: How America's Commitment to Equity will Determine Our Future*. New York: Teachers College Press.

Echevarría, J., Vogt, M., and Short, D. J. (2008). *Making Content Comprehensible for English Learners: The SIOP Model*. Boston: Pearson.

Emerson, R. M., Fretz, R. I., and Shaw, L. L. (1995). *Writing Ethnographic Fieldnotes*. Chicago: The University of Chicago Press.

Escobar, A. (1995). *Encountering Development: The Making and Unmaking of the Third World*. Princeton, NJ: Princeton University Press.

Folse, K. (2004). *Vocabulary Myths: Applying Second Language Research to Classroom Teaching*. Ann Arbor, MI: University of Michigan Press.

Foucault, M. (1978). *The History of Sexuality, volume 1: An Introduction* (R. Hurley, Trans.). New York: Vintage Books (original work published 1976).

Global Service Corps. (n.d.) Global Service Corps. Accessed May 6, 2009 from www.globalservicecorps.org.

Global Volunteers (2008). *Adventures in Service* [Brochure]. St Paul, MN: Author.

Hadley, A. O. (2001). *Teaching Language in Context*, 3rd edn. Boston: Heinle and Heinle Publishers.

Heath, S. (2007). Widening the Gap: Pre-university Gap Years and the "Economy of Experience." *British Journal of Sociology of Education*, 28, 89–103.

Hornberger, N. (1998). Language Policy, Language Education, Language Rights: Indigenous, Immigrant, and International Perspectives. *Language in Society*, 27, 439–458.

Hutnyk, J. (1996). *The Rumour of Calcutta: Tourism, Charity, and the Poverty of Representation*. London: Zed.

Jakubiak, C. (2012). "English for the Global": Discourses in/of English Language Voluntourism. *Journal of Qualitative Studies in Education*, 25(4), 435–351.

Kachru, B. (1997). World Englishes 2000: Resources for research and teaching. In L. E. Smith and M. L. Forman (eds.), *World Englishes*, pp. 209–251. Honolulu: University of Hawaii Press.

Krashen, S. (1982). *Principles and Practice in Second Language Acquisition*. New York: Pergamon Press.

Marcus, G. (1995). Ethnography in/of the World System: The Emergence of Multi-sited Ethnography. *Annual Review of Anthropology*, 24, 95–117.

Niño-Murcia, M. (2003). "English is like the dollar": Hard Currency Ideology and the Status of English in Peru. *World Englishes*, 22(2), 121–142.

Ohmae, K. (1999). *The Borderless World: Power and Strategy in the Interlinked Economy* (Revised ed.). New York: HarperBusiness.

Patton, M. Q. (2002). *Qualitative Research and Evaluation Methods*, 3rd edn. Thousand Oaks, CA: Sage.

Pennycook, A. (1994). *The Cultural Politics of English as an International Language*. London: Longman.

Phillipson, R. (1992). *Linguistic Imperialism*. Oxford, UK: Oxford University Press.

Phillipson, R. (2000). English in the New World Order: Variations on a Theme of Linguistic Imperialism and "World" English. In T. Ricento (ed.), *Ideology, Politics, and Language Policies: Focus on English*, pp. 87–106. Philadelphia, PA: John Benjamins Publishing Company.

Projects Abroad (n.d.). *Volunteer and Intern Abroad* [Brochure]. New York: Author.

Rieffel, L., and Zalud, S. (2006). International Volunteering: Smart Power. (Policy Brief No. 155). Washington, DC: Brookings Institution.

Saldanha, A. (2005). Trance and Visibility at Dawn: Racial Dynamics in Goa's Rave Scene. *Social and Cultural Geography*, 6(5), 707–721.

Simpson, K. (2004). 'Doing Development': The Gap Year, Volunteer Tourists and a Popular Practice of Development. *Journal of International Development*, 16, 681–692.

Sinervo, A. (2011). Connection and Disillusion: The Moral Economy of Volunteer Tourism in Cusco, Peru. *Childhoods Today*, 5(2), 1–23.

Smith, D. M. (2000). Moral Progress in Human Geography: Transcending the Place of Good Fortune. *Progress in Human Geography*, 24(1), 1–18.

Snow, D. (2001). *English Teaching as Christian Mission: An Applied Theology*. Scottdale, PA: Herald Press.

Spring, J. (2004). *How Educational Ideologies are Shaping Global Society: Intergovernmental Organizations, NGOs, and the Decline of the Nation-state*. Mahwah, NJ: Lawrence Erlbaum Associates.

Teaching and Projects Abroad (n.d.). *Teaching and Projects Abroad: Life-changing Opportunities* [Brochure]. West Sussex, UK: Author.

Urry, J. (2002). *The Tourist Gaze*, 2nd edn. London: Sage.

Villano, M. (2009). Silver-spoon Voluntourism: Luxury Hotels offer Day Trips to Help Vacationers Connect with Communities. *Time*, November 16.

Wearing, S. (2001). *Volunteer Tourism: Experiences that Make a Difference*. Wallingford: CABI Publishing.

WorldTeach (n.d.). WorldTeach. Accessed May 10, 2009 from www.worldteach. org.

Chapter 9

Moral Lessons from a Storied Past in New York City

Elissa J. Sampson

Introduction: Welcome to the Lower East Side

To retrofit an old tenement building for touring in 1994, the Lower East Side Tenement Museum in New York City re-created historic residential apartments within a living neighborhood. The Museum's historic tenement—97 Orchard Street—is located at an intersection of a rapidly gentrifying area of the old Jewish Lower East Side with a visibly growing immigrant Chinatown. For many visitors, the Tenement Museum is part of a Lower Manhattan immigration triad in which the Museum marks the first immigrant housing destination in partnership with the National Park Services' better known sites of immigration, the Statue of Liberty and Ellis Island. The Museum serves as a site of heritage tourism for immigrant descendants, including American Jews for whom the neighborhood is seen as a site of American origin, particularly for families that arrived before World War I.

The Lower East Side's story as the 'gateway to America' is typically portrayed as one of rapid immigrant absorption and urbanization taking place in what was once (circa 1911) the world's densest slum. The Museum's national landmark building at 97 Orchard Street is situated in an area where many neighborhood residents live in tenements, multi-story New York apartment buildings initially associated with the urban poor from the 1860s on. Visitors buy tickets to take interpreted apartment tours and hear stories of long-gone residents associated with a past age of once-controversial massive American immigration.[1] As a museum built around touring, it participates in the broader commodification of a living neighborhood within a downtown destination economy. The Museum's tourism is a small part of a local culture of consumption seen in the Lower East Side's boutiques, hotels, restaurants, bars and clubs in what was once a poor ethnic neighborhood conveniently wedged between Midtown and Wall Street.

In late 2001, the Tenement Museum attempted to expand beyond its 97 Orchard Street national historic landmark by having New York State acquire the building next door through eminent domain. The Museum hoped to double its visitor traffic by jointly selling tickets with Liberty National Park. 99 Orchard, its one-time

---

1 Over twenty million mainly European "New Immigrants" came to New York from 1850 to 1924.

twin and neighbor, was now a newly renovated and inhabited tenement whose street-level restaurant employed Fujianese workers.[2] In the ensuing controversy the Museum's re-creation of historic immigration was portrayed as happening at the expense of living immigrants. By 2002, this fight had generated significant national news coverage. The New York Daily News noted:

> Local entrepreneur Liang says Congee Village's ... business has skyrocketed since he expanded it into Holtzman's cellar. Condemnation would put about 20 immigrant workers out of a job at a time when the Asian American Foundation estimates about 1,000 Chinese New Yorkers were left unemployed by the World Trade Center attack (Kates, 2002: 2).

Museum opponents made good use of spatial and immigrant-themed dynamics by posting signs in Mandarin and English protesting 'Eminent Domain Abuse', and holding solidarity visits and demonstrations at the building in question. One sign read 'Don't ERASE living history with artificial history.'

The events of 2002 are a micro-history set in a storied topos of immigration— a tale rich with ironic juxtapositions of empathy, museumification, and gentrification. All of this took place on an Orchard Street otherwise eerily quiet, since most shoppers were scared away after September 11, 2001. Residents and merchants alike were just becoming aware that the city wanted Lower Manhattan to be restructured as a visitor arts and entertainment area. Ethnic heritage tourism in the Lower East Side was expanding along with its economic restructuring as a rapidly changing downtown neighborhood. Its allure as a poor historic place of immigrant memory and culture now intersected with its increasing appeal as a gentrifying area.

The Moral Economy of Tourism in the Showcasing of Past Life

The Museum's connection to its neighborhood's ethnic enclaves reflects this commodification even as the Museum sought to combine tourism with the delivery of bundled moral lessons. Re-created tenements are morally exemplary and their lessons for outside visitors are often attuned to generations who have never lived in them. The Museum saw its messages as reinforced by connections between the sympathetic immigrant past shown in its apartments and a visible immigrant

---

2   99 Orchard Street was long owned by the disputative fourth generation Lower East Side Holtzman family who brought in a Fujianese partner, Peter Liang. In July of 2001, they renovated the building to allow Liang's Congee Village restaurant to be carved out of the back side of the building to expand into a wider, and more visibly Chinese, Allen Street. The owners also created fifteen tiny studio apartments whose new tenants paid over $1,600 monthly rent, thus making the building profitable and impossibly expensive for most neighborhood residents.

present surrounding its 97 Orchard Street location. Its liberal activist founders saw their project as harnessing history to advance an ethical political agenda of 'tolerance' towards new immigrants through the portrayal of older immigrant life. As Wendy Brown (2008) has dryly noted, liberal discourses of tolerance that evoke moral values can also be seen as producing and pointing to its discursive and social limits. Thus 97 Orchard's depiction raises a key moral question: How were local living communities represented in (or occluded by) a building interpreted by a Museum (1994) of past immigrant life whose multi-cultural mission was one of 'tolerance and historic perspective'?[3]

In short, the story of how a museum of immigrant life has attempted to exercise eminent domain is a case study in the moral economy of tourism. Andrew Sayer (2004: 2) defines 'moral economy' as 'the study of how economic activities of all kinds are influenced and structured by moral dispositions and norms, and how in turn those norms may be compromised, overridden or reinforced by economic pressures.' Here what is understood to be economically moral can be that which what is seen as normatively appropriate behavior in a given context. As Sayer (2004: 12) notes, 'ethical valuation and economic valuation may sometimes be in tension.' Thus, use by host communities of the normatively moral in discourses of tourism may aid community actors in exercising agency by contesting economic pressure in framing institutional dynamics as contextually inappropriate.

The Tenement Museum is highly dependent on the heritage tourists who compose most of its adult visitors; in seeking to convey its message of tolerance to its audience it has tailored its tours of past immigrant life so as to encourage empathy for more recent immigrants. 97 Orchard Street's tours often stressed commonalities of hardship seen in tenement life to encourage descendants of past immigrants to feel a sense of ethical responsibility to newer immigrants. In its *Piecing It Together* tour from 2002, the guide is prompted to state: 'Even though the immigrant groups have changed, the experience of tenements and the garment industry are much the same' (2002, 2005: 3). The tension between these conflicting pressures came to a head in 2002 in its dealings with the neighborhood's newer migrant groups. In effect, the Museum avowed that accommodating more visitors was also advocating for new immigrants.

The 'Story'

By mid-2002 the Museum's attempt at eminent domain garnered enough opposition to prevent it from going forward. When the Museum's earlier offers to buy its neighboring building at below market rate were refused in the fall of

---

3   The Museum's mission was updated in 2011 under new management and no longer uses the term tolerance. The same 2002 *Daily News* article quoted above also described the Museum as 'devoted to celebrating 19th and early 20th century immigration' and 'the dreams that motivate today's immigrants …' (1).

2001, its administrators convinced a quasi-state agency to use eminent domain to condemn 99 Orchard Street. The arguments focused initially on the Museum's need to accommodate more visitors. Its director stressed the Museum's role as a National Park Service (NPS) affiliate serving visitors.

> 'We cannot accommodate any portion of the 5 million visitors who go to Ellis Island and the Statue of Liberty every year,' said Ruth Abram, president of the Lower East Side Tenement Museum. 'We're already turning people away.' With 99 Orchard St., the museum would be able to accommodate an additional 200,000 guests a year … (Jensen, 2002).

In a public statement read posted on the Museum's website and submitted to the local Community Board, Abram (2002) also explained that 'The Museum needs 99 Orchard Street because it is a sister building and shares a party wall.'

National media were quick to comment on the irony of an immigrant history museum's becoming the target of immigrant protest. The Museum appeared to be placing its own interests—getting more people through the door, increasing revenue—over those for whom it purportedly advocated. Accordingly the Museum was cast as violating moral norms associated with Lower East Side immigrant life and proper neighborly behavior as well as with violating its raison d'être of advocacy for new immigrants. This criticism spilled over into a debate on the Museum's authenticity that challenged its attested values given its behavior in the very place that it termed the United States' most important immigrant neighborhood.

On January 4, 2002, the right-wing New York Post published a piece titled 'Museum in Bizarre Bid to Wreck Building' (Lehmann, 2002) implying that it was discrediting authentic historic national landmarks. The Museum's proposal to tear down and re-create four of 99 Orchard's tenement apartments was termed a touristic 'Disney World Creation' by a building owner. The right-wing Wall Street Journal (Comment: Museums, 2002: A12) questioned the reality of the Museum as a reconstructed, ergo dead, presentation of history: 'The two buildings on Orchard Street share a common past, but one is devoted to nostalgically … invoke the immigrant experience, while the other has real people living real lives in a real building.' The moral value of the Museum's commemorating and memorializing the past was thus relegated to an inauthentic state-supported nostalgia. An article that then appeared on February 6, 2002 in the Jewish Daily Forward went on to further quote the disputative Holtzman family: '"They're make-believe history," said Mr. Holtzman, motioning to the museum …. "We are history"' (Keys, 2002).

As the visibility of the Museum's re-creation of the past expanded so did concerns as to whether its expansion should have priority over contemporary uses. The New York Times (Haberman, 2002: B1) noted, under the headline 'Your Tired, Your Poor, Your Building?' that 'The renters may not be the tired, poor and huddled masses of yesteryear. But there they are all the same.' The *Los Angeles*

Times captured a local reaction voiced by Community Board 3's (CB3) manager: "'They want to create a virtual tenement museum in a neighborhood that already has tenements'" (Getlin, 2002: A.14). At a raucous Community Board hearing, a tenant at 99 Orchard asked, "'What are they going to tell the tourists of 99 Orchard Street? This is the history of the people who lived here before we evicted them?'" (Sayrafiezadeh, 2003).

New York's Daily News chortled: 'As one resident put it, "It's the immigrant museum vs. the immigrants, the newcomers vs. the old-timers'" (Kates, 2002). The tangible benefits of the Museum's advocacy for new immigrants seemed unclear even as more generally its moral right to prioritize the showcasing of past lives at the expense of the present was questioned. The appropriateness of its behavior undermined both its authenticity and moral claims in representing past and contemporary immigrant experience and interests. Five years later, a Museum News article (2007: 78–79) still cited the Tenement Museum actions to explain why perceived authenticity and 'realness' for museums necessarily depends on adhering to attested moral values.

The Museum's actions in evoking the public interest standard of eminent domain also raised issues about the moral appropriateness of the state's role as well as of how the Museum served the interest of the State. The Villager, a liberal downtown newspaper, commented, 'The Lower East Side Tenement Museum is good for New York. That is at least according to the Empire State Economic Development Corporation [EDSC] …' (Jensen, 2002). As Caton (2012: 1915) notes, 'tourism scholarship that demonstrates the economic benefits of resort development generally takes a particular definition of "economic benefits" for granted'; similarly museum expansion is often unthinkingly assumed to confer benefits through more visitors consuming 'local' products. However, the working assumption that what was good for the Museum and its visitors was ultimately good for immigrants and for the neighborhood at large was being challenged. Therefore, the Museum asked Kevin Jackson, then head of the New York Historical Society, to explain why the EDSC's action indeed served the public and State interest. Jackson (2002) did so by alluding to the historic importance of the Lower East Side immigrant experience in acculturation, citizenship and civic life, stating: 'the museum, and its proposed expansion, also serves the larger needs of the state and the nation by clarifying how "the places we call home" shape our identities and participation in civic life.' The Museum also strongly stressed presumed benefits to local businesses and residents. Yet, its rationale as to providing local economic benefit was effectively undercut by the economic development agency that had invoked the eminent domain. The EDSC's attorney stated: "'We see the [museum's] expansion as a worthwhile public objective," he said. "Economics is not the driving force. This is a civic project'" (Kates, 2002). In a critical turning point, the local Business Improvement District (BID) agreed that the Museum's actions did not provide sufficient local economic benefit to justify the use of eminent domain and voted against it (Silva and Wong, 2007: 34).

   Locally, the Museum's claim to represent the interests of newer immigrants and migrants seemed further vitiated by its lack of direct representation for residents belonging to groups who arrived in the neighborhood post 1935. Particularly galling, since the building's residents were mainly from Europe, 97 Orchard Street had no earlier historic 'Chinese' apartments.[4] In the midst of the fracas, the Museum suddenly announced it would commit to telling these stories: 'In 99 Orchard Street, the Museum will expand its interpretation to include stories of people in the neighborhood before and after those dates [1863–1935] including people from Africa, Latin America and Asia whose stories were not represented in 97 Orchard Street' (Abram, 2002).

A Pragmatic Morality?

Perhaps in response, the Fujianese community bolstered its opposition with yet another moral claim: that the Museum's actions would take away housing in an area which didn't have enough. Chinatown's existence and future growth have long been perceived as threatened by the impact of gentrification on affordable housing and business space (Lin, 1994, Lin, 1998, Kwong, 2009). Thus it was plausible to depict the Museum's proposed expansion as a reduction of Chinatown's housing stock. Meanwhile 99 Orchard Street's new upscale renters were described as neighborhood residents, and its owners, as local small business people. Locals, if only for the moment, were not landlords. Ultimately tenant rights became the issue politicians cited in withdrawing political support from the Museum. Here moral, normative lines were drawn by invoking both the need for state protection of tenants *and* for the protection of small businesses from the state.
   Seemingly few (except for the restaurant's waiters) can fully claim the moral high ground regarding the financial and real estate stakes of commodifying the past in a tourist, gentrifying present. All parties—the building's owners, its tenants, the Museum's founders, and the heritage tourists—are involved with gentrification typically as immigrants, migrants or someone who explicitly identifies as a descendant. Here the 'higher ground', seen in the expression of moral issues explicitly concerning the representation of a broader view of neighborhood residents and migration, gained a political outlet due to threats of eminent domain and job loss. Visible moral outrage can be fed and triggered by actions deemed decidedly ill-advised, particularly if community fallout seems to be predictable.
   The Museum clearly misread Chinatown's politics and its residents' sense that the Museum's stories of past Lower East Side life were primarily meant for

---

   4   Nineteenth-century and earlier twentieth century migration to Lower Manhattan mainly ensued from the Pearl River delta regions of China. New York's 'Chinatown' is considered the largest in any U.S. city, including San Francisco.

outside visitors. Its actions triggered the rare involvement of both documented and undocumented Fujianese workers with local organizations who worked through business and ethnic associations to bring in communal support from Queens and elsewhere. The coalitions that led these protests were ethnic and political, local and city-wide, and to a large degree reflected the increasing importance of New York's relatively new Fujianese community. The Museum which had not cultivated ties with the local Jewish community saw it siding in coalitions with Fujianese organizations as did almost every neighborhood organization. The Museum underestimated the Fujianese community's ability to rally neighborhood and city-wide allies, including the Community Board, the local Business Improvement District, numerous politicians, and the most unlikely of Lower East Side bedfellows: landlords and tenants groups (TenantNet, 2002).

Gazing Through a Past Prism

At historic 97 Orchard Street, residential apartments tell the very moving stories of selected Irish, German, Italian and Jewish tenants. Since its mission encouraged 'tolerance and historic perspective,' why did liberal Museum founders think that [heritage] audience(s) would find 'the experiences of today's newcomers' susceptible to empathetic responses when viewed through the filter of immigration from a prior era (Museum: The Lower East Side Tenement Museum, 2010a)? Its choice of an oblique gaze seems meant in part to draw attention to what the Museum viewed as similar harsh social processes of Americanization, even as it simultaneously pointed out future immigrant success.

In interpreting the Lower East Side as a 'gateway', the Museum emphasized the comparable circumstances of various groups in place. It saw the experiences of earlier groups as portraying the overcoming of shared hardship in achieving upward mobility. Director Ruth Abram (2004) remarked at a National Park Service Conference that 'the surrounding community is not terribly unchanged from the history told at the museum.' Difference diminished in stressing strong parallels between past and present, between similar ancestors and potentially successfully acculturated new immigrants. In 2001, a shrinking Jewish and Latino Lower East Side was proximate to a growing Chinese population facing seemingly familiar issues. While 9/11 caused a declining downtown garment trade to be further devastated and even as its issues with 99 Orchard escalated, in March of 2002, the Museum (2002, 2005) launched its *Piecing it Together* garment trade apartment tour. The Museum's tour outline prompts its guide to ask: 'By looking around, which immigrant groups currently live on the Lower East Side?' (2002, 2005: 2). The guide is then prompted to say 'The immigrant families we will be visiting today bare [sic] much in common with contemporary immigrant families in the garment industry on the Lower East Side' (Museum: The Lower East Side Tenement Museum, 2002, 2005: 5).

Heritage as Real Estate

For the Tenement Museum's primarily Jewish visitors, the Museum is a lieu de mémoire. In America's destination culture, it has become identified as a Jewish destination. Once known as the Great Ghetto, the densely settled Lower East Side was in 1911 the world's largest Jewish city, and the neighborhood figures prominently in the collective memory of the American Jewish past as a place of origin (Rischin, 1977, Kugelmass, 2000, Diner, 2000). This dynamic of memory is complex, not least in its relation to the disappearance of earlier European communities of origin, primarily through genocide. In describing the Museum's relation to Jewish heritage tourism, Diner (2000: 118) has written 'Indeed, tours organized by synagogues, Jewish community centers, and other Jewish groups … dominate the prearranged visits to the Museum. The largest number of 'off-the-street' visitors also happen to be Jews'.

A general commodification of heritage (and of protest) is manifest on the Lower East Side as it is increasingly hollowed out as a place of memory in connection to ethnicity. It can be seen in practices of seeming resistance and commemoration. Pocketbooks and T-shirts adorned with Puerto Rican flags are commodified along with Jewish books and humorous buttons. The Museum's garment trade tours tell visitors about the history of the Triangle Fire and ensuing street protests and rallies. Street art which uses a graffiti ethos brings visitors. Ethnic food is purveyed for local residents as well as for out-of-town visitors. The New York Times (Salkin, 2002: CY1) noted that 'even as the traditional [Jewish] neighborhood vanishes, interest in its place in Jewish heritage is exploding, evidenced by increased attendance at the Lower East Side Tenement Museum.' And the local is leaky here, especially since so many residents—such as NYU students—are unlikely to stay long or see themselves as living in an ethnic enclave.

But commodification is most salient where the stakes are highest: that is in real estate dealings. The Lower East Side's current ethnic communities all see their survival as dependent upon keeping and obtaining housing. Consumption and historic preservation are necessarily entwined in fund-raising and touring, as can be seen in staking out the moral ground as to what is in the public or state interest. Frank Sanchis, the then president of New York's Municipal Art Society, stated in advocating for the Museum.

> The uniqueness of this Museum lies in the authenticity and the integrity of its fabric, which merits, in fact demands, the highest degree of protection. The glory of the Museum is the brilliance of its programming and interpretation to the public, which is without parallel in our nation …. The justification I feel for the use of eminent domain in this case, lies in the immediately adjacent nature of the space provided by 99 Orchard St. Because of this adjacency, both of these issues-the core quality of the Museum, the protection of its fabric and the enhancement of its programming are served. (Sanchis, 2002: 1)

The irony that 99 Orchard Street was desirable precisely because it had been and could be further renovated may have been lost on the writer. Its fabric had no integrity so to speak, inasmuch as its extensive prior renovation meant it could never serve as a landmark building. Hence the Museum could do whatever it wanted to 99 Orchard, including making it handicapped accessible. Adjacency offered the hope of 99 Orchard Street sharing 97's perceived authenticity while removing the financial burdens and strictures incumbent with landmark preservation and renovation.[5] Not-for-profit institutions need visitors' money both as a direct funding source and as an inducement to institutional and governmental support. Although the Lower East Side in 2008 was listed by the National Trust for Historic Preservation as one of the 11 most endangered places in America, the big money has not come into the neighborhood for preservation, but rather to serve more visitors.

Meanwhile pressure on housing and small ethnic businesses increasingly makes it harder for those who are already there to remain in place. Gentrification is not just a question of Smith's (1996) revanchist city cleaning things up for the benefit of visitors. In the Lower East Side, it has its own particular aesthetic. Jason Hackworth (2002: 815) defines gentrification as 'the production of urban space for progressively more affluent users'. As Chris Mele (2000) has shown, the neighborhood's hip grunge ethos and the authenticity of its older tenement buildings and immigrant/migrant communities can form part of its attraction even as the neighborhood goes upscale—a process encapsulated in the story of 99 Orchard Street, to which I now return.

Conclusions: All's Well that Ends Well?

The Museum's behavior seems related to an institutional insistence that its formula in salvaging the past and attracting more outside visitors would translate into a growth in empathic moral thinking. Hence, its moral norms were not seen as simply self-interested but as engaging in a trade-off that valorized visitor sentiment for past immigrants over that of the livelihood and housing of local residents in whose name it ostensibly also spoke. As a sympathetic historical preservation report from a university graduate school of design program described it, 'The increasing number of visitors has led the museum to seek expansion, creating conflict with the community neighbors it seeks to represent' (Silva and Wong, 2007: 27).

---

5   The Museum's offer to purchase 99 Orchard at a relatively low price had already been turned down by the building's owners prior to its renovation. Once that renovation started, the Tenement Museum claimed that work on 99 Orchard Street had damaged 97 Orchard Street due to a shared 'party wall', thereby leaving it vulnerable to a careless neighbor. By the time however the eminent domain issue was in play, and renovation in 99 Orchard Street had finished which meant that imminent future construction damage to the Museum's fabric was unlikely.

In the Lower East Side's parlance, the Museum was termed a bad neighbor in a neighborhood in which neighborliness is a famously invoked value. Gendered neologisms such as '*di neksdorike*' (the next door neighbor, female) were coined locally in the past migration that the Museum depicts so as to describe a new type of relationship that crowded urban life valorized. As historian Paula Hyman (1991, 1998: 330) noted 'The historical experience of immigrant Jewish women embraced work and family, politics and social welfare, friendship groups and neighborhood.'. Being called a good neighbor is high praise indeed, an articulation of a sought after standard which inspires trust in promoting daily understandings of conviviality (Gilroy, 2004).

As an articulated ethos of the Lower East Side as a lived place and an imaginary, what should be expected of a good neighbor is important both to commemoration and daily life, and ultimately its consumption as a place of nostalgia. Hence, the wounding headline from the Jewish Daily Forward that said it all: 'Immigration Museum Called Bad Neighbor In Expansion Battle' (Keys, 2002). In promoting eminent domain against its own neighbor, the Museum lost moral credibility as well as support from inside and outside of the area. Its authenticity as a museum with attested institutional values of advocating for immigrants and for its neighborhood could be contested due to the 'un-neighborly' way in which the Museum violated publicly subscribed to norms.

But the Museum has come back. In 2002, the *Los Angeles Times* hinted that the Museum had other choices: 'While Abram insists she must have 99 Orchard St., others ask why the museum couldn't have looked for tenement property elsewhere.'(Getlin, 2002: A.14) Indeed, shortly after losing on 99 Orchard, the Museum bought two buildings on the block. By 2007, the Museum embarked on the quiet acquisition and renovation of a far more expensive corner building. Community opposition was negligible: it happened at a time which the block's gentrification seemed all but inevitable. The Sadie Samuelson Levy Immigrant Heritage Center at 103 Orchard opened in 2012. It marked another change as well: the aesthetic of the Center's building is not fully preservationist, in part because it incorporates a Museum shop and some remaining residential tenants. "The reality is it generates revenue for the museum," said David Eng, vice president of public affairs (Hedlund, 2011: 1). A visitor orientation movie now comfortably juxtaposes current Dominican and Cantonese immigrant stories with those of Jewish and Italian families.

Other changes, including new Museum management, have effectively improved relations with local groups. In becoming more responsive to the neighborhood's current ethnic mix, the Museum appears to be more explicit about the neighborhood's Jewish past even as its immigrant theme remains universalized. In another shift, the Museum's current website and outdoor tours sympathetically point out gentrification as a threat to the built environment and residents, with the Museum portrayed as a stakeholder interested in preserving that past and in protecting low-income residents. Yet at the same time, the Museum's visitor website information states: 'You can easily spend a morning, afternoon or evening on The Lower East Side. It's a thriving neighborhood, full of shops, restaurants and sites' (Museum: The Lower East Side Tenement Museum, 2010b). That this irony goes unremarked is also a sign of changed times.

From this story, we might pragmatically conclude that empathy, or tolerance, or anything touted as a moral benefit may need to be readily evident to its ostensible beneficiaries and to those in whose name it is articulated. A visitor sampling study conducted for the Museum by Randi Korn and Associates (2007), indeed offered advice as to whether the promotion of 'tolerance' would benefit from linking it to the representation of contemporary immigrants.

> Before visitors can be receptive to a message of tolerance, they must be introduced
> to contemporary immigrant experiences and perspectives .... Contemporary
> immigrant perspectives need to be personalized, too, to compete with the power
> of the historical stories and to elicit strong responses from visitors (viii)

I return then to my related, first moral question: How are living communities represented (or occluded) at 97 Orchard Street? I follow Sayer (2004) in viewing the resort to moral discourses by actors as claiming no ground higher than that of seeking to do the 'right' thing. In this view, 'the normative' is understood as dependent on existing webs of relationships and obligations. Moral norms are often articulated as though they were socially self-evident. Hence, the contextualized contestation of moral norms within economic dealings provides particular insight into the dynamics of the articulation of such norms. In becoming articulated and invoked precisely because contestation pushes such articulations to the fore, their potential use in shaping economic discourses comes into play in a heightened fashion. Nonetheless, when most everyone— including myself—is an actor in a drama called tourism and gentrification, an expected ambivalence in regard to consumption and production may very much be in order in attempting what Caton calls 'an analysis of the importance of value-engagement in our field with regard to the ideological and political-economic realities that characterize our location as workers in the tourism academy' (Caton, 2012: 1908).

Answers to such questions may hinge to a large degree on how contested moral norms get expressed and wielded locally and to what effect. Pragmatic outrage may provide both an effective and affective resort, particularly when calling institutions to task by pointing out contradictory aspects of their self-attested moral values. In this case, the issue of representation got raised to the foreground and its prioritization has remained an issue for the Museum. Here then are two answers supplied by the Museum concerning its plans. What the Museum did clearly understand by early 2002 was that given its oblique approach, its vulnerability touched on the question of who represented today's immigrants. Therefore, in a press interview and letter, Director Ruth Abram (2002: 2) promised that at 99 Orchard Street, the Tenement Museum would: 'Fully integrate the interpretation of immigrants past with that of contemporary immigrants and migrants.' In 2009 (under new management), the Museum's vice president stated that in the new building at 103 Orchard, 'we are going to consider telling the stories of immigrant groups that came to this country after 1935' (Lo-Down TV, 2009). I do think this will at long last happen in 103's new residential apartments, as well as in exhibits in 97 Orchard Street's commercial space ... that is once the Museum figures out where the money will come from.

References

Abram, R. (2002). *Statement Regarding the Planned Acquisition of 99 Orchard, Tenement Museum* [Online]. New York, Available at: <http://web.archive.org/web/20090106043110/http://tenement.org/statement.html> [Accessed 20 February, 2010].

Abram, R. (October 20, 2004). Harnessing the Power of History. In J. Ogline (ed.), Great Places, Great Debate: Opening Historic Sites to Civic Engagement, April 1–2, 2004, 2004 Center for Architecture New York. http://www.nps.gov/nero/greatplaces/openingkeynote.htm: National Park Service (NPS).

Brown, W. (2008). *Regulating Aversion: Tolerance in the Age of Identity and Empire*. Princeton, NJ: Princeton University Press.

Caton, K. (2012). Taking the Moral Turn in Tourism Studies. *Annals of Tourism Research* [Online], 39. Available: http://dx.doi.org/10.1016/j.annals.2012.05.021 [Accessed 1 July 2013].

Comment: Museums (2002). Tenement Museum. *Wall Street Journal*, January 9, 2002, p. A12, Available through: ProQuest <http://search.proquest.com.libproxy.lib.unc.edu/docview/398961384?> [Accessed 5 October 2010].

Diner, H. (2000). *Lower East Side Memories: A Jewish Place in America*. Princeton, NJ: Princeton University Press.

Getlin, J. (2002). Museum Plan Hits Too Close to Home. *Los Angeles Times*, April 18 2002. Available through: <http://articles.latimes.com/2002/apr/18/news/mn-38572 > [Accessed 12 February 2010].

Gilroy, P. (2004). *After Empire: Melancholia or Convivial Culture?* Abingdon, Oxfordshire, UK: Routledge.

Haberman, C. (2002). Your Tired, Your Poor, Your Building?: A Museum is Out of Space; Its Neighbor is Out of Patience. *The New York Times*, February 13 2002, p. B1, Available through: <http://www.nytimes.com/2002/02/13/nyregion/nyc-your-tired-your-poor-your-building.html> [Accessed 12 February 2010].

Hackworth, J. (2002). Postrecession Gentrification in New York City. *Urban Affairs Review*, 37(6), 815–843, Available: http://uar.sagepub.com/content/37/6/815.

Hedlund, P. (2011). *Lower East Side Tenement Museum to Open New Visitors' Center* [Online]. New York: DNAinfo.com, Available at: <http://www.dnainfo.

com/20110302/lower-east-side-east-village/lower-east-side-tenement-museum-open-new-visitors-center> [Accessed 6 June 2011].

Hyman, P. (1998). Gender and the Immigrant Jewish Experience in the United States. In J. Baskin (ed.), *Jewish Women in Historical Perspective*, 2nd edn. Detroit: Wayne State University Press.

Jackson, K. (2002). Letter of Support to ESDC. New York: The Lower East Side Tenement Museum.

Jensen, J. (2002). State Seeks Building To Expand Tenement Museum. *The Villager*, January 3 2002, Available through: <http://www.tenant.net/pipermail/nytenants-online/2002-January/000131.html> [Accessed 9 March 2010].

Kates, B. (2002). Immigrants Museum vs. Locals, Lower East Side Divided. *The New York Daily News*, April 28 2002, Available through: <http://www.nydailynews.com/archives/news/immigrants-museum-locals-east-side-divided-article-1.488936> [Accessed 12 February 2010].

Keys, L. (2002). Immigration Museum Called Bad Neighbor In Expansion Battle. *The Jewish Daily Forward*, February 6 2002. Available through: <http://www.highbeam.com/doc/1P1-79273071.html> [Accessed 12 February 2010].

Kugelmass, J. (ed.) (2000). Turfing the Slum: New York City's Tenement Museum and the Politics of Heritage. In H. R. Diner, J. Shandler, and B. S. Wenger (eds.), *Remembering the Lower East Side: American Jewish Reflections*. Bloomington and Indianapolis: Indiana University Press.

Kwong, P. (2009). Ask About the Gentrification of Chinatown. *The New York Times*, 14 September 2009, Available through: <http://cityroom.blogs.nytimes.com/2009/09/14/ask-about-the-gentrification-of-chinatown/> [Accessed 12 February 2010].

Lehmann, J. (2002). Museum in Bizarre Bid to Wreck Building. *New York Post*, 4 January 2002, Available through: <http://www.nypost.com/p/news/museum_in_bizarre_bid_to_wreck_building_yjCXV2QsELKlV5QOpvrmoM> [Accessed 12 February 2010].

Lin, J. (1998). *Reconstructing Chinatown: Ethnic Enclave, Global Change*, Minneapolis and London: University of Minnesota Press.

Lin, J. C. (ed.) (1994). *The Changing Economy of the Lower East Side*. Cambridge: Blackwell.

Lo-Down TV (2009). Tenement Museum's Visitor Center Renovation, Interview with Barry Roseman. In *Lower East Side Tenement Museum 103 Orchard Street Video* (ed.). New York: http://www.thelodownny.com.

Mele, C. (2000). *Selling the Lower East Side: Culture, Real Estate and Resistance in New York City*. Minnesota: University of Minnesota Press.

Museum: The Lower East Side Tenement Museum (1994). *Mission* [Online]. New York: Lower East Side Tenement Museum, Available at: Internet Archive <http://web.archive.org/web/20020609195435/http://tenement.org/about.html> [Accessed 4 October 2010].

Museum: The Lower East Side Tenement Museum (2002, 2005). Piecing It Together: Immigrant Families in the Garment Industry. New York: Lower East Side Tenement Museum.

Museum: The Lower East Side Tenement Museum (2010a). Blog: About Us. Available from: http://tenement-museum.blogspot.com [Accessed 19 November 2010].

Museum: The Lower East Side Tenement Museum (2010b). *Visit: Explore the Lower East Side* [Online]. New York: Lower East Side Tenement Museum, Available at: <http://web.archive.org/web/20101128165026/http://tenement.org/guider.html> [Accessed 28 October 2010].

Pine II, B. Joseph, and Gilmore, James H. (2007). Museums and Authenticity. *American Association of Museums: Museum News* (May/June), p. 7, Available: http://aamftp.aam-us.org/pubs/mn/authenticity.cfm?renderforprint=1.

Randi Korn and Associates (2007). Audience Research: Telephone Interviews with Visitors Prepared for the Lower East Side Tenement Museum. *Museum Visitor Studies, Evaluation & Audience Research*. Alexandria, VA: Randi Korn and Associates, Inc.

Rischin, M. (1977). *The Promised City: New York's Jews, 1870–1914*. Cambridge, MA: Harvard University Press.

Salkin, A. (2002). Fading Into History. *The New York Times*, 20 October 2002 p. CY1, Available through: <http://www.nytimes.com/2002/10/20/nyregion/fading-into-history.html?pagewanted=1> [Accessed 12 February 2010].

Sanchis, F. (2002). Letter of Support to ESDC. In Museum, T. (ed.), *About Us*. Letter of Support to ESDC.

Sayer, A. (2004). Moral Economy. *Department of Sociology* [Online]. Available: http://www.comp.lancs.ac.uk/sociology/papers/sayer-moral-economy.pdf [Accessed 26 December, 2011].

Sayrafiezadeh, S. (2003). The Fight Over 99 Orchard Street. In T. Beller (ed.), *Mr. Beller's Neighborhood*.

Silva, C., and Wong, K. (2007). *Memory: Lower East Side Tenement Museum, New York, NY*. Philadelphia: University of Pennsylvania, School of Design.

Smith, N. (1996). *The New Urban Frontier: Gentrification and the Revanchist City.* London, Routledge.

TenantNet (2002). Sunday Rally to Support LES Tenants—Oppose Eminent Domain Abuse. *NYTenants Online/TenantNet*, 4/28/02, Available through: <http://tenant.net/pipermail/nytenants-online/2002-April/000141.html> [Accessed 9 March 2010].

SECTION 3
Environmental Tourism Moralities

Chapter 10

On Decommodifying Ecotourism's Social Value: Neoliberal Reformism or the New Environmental Morality?

Stephen Wearing and Michael Wearing

Introduction

Ecotourism has caught the imagination of many local communities, governments, international organizations and the tourism industry. There is growing interest in the potential of ecotourism particularly by the tourism industry. For while ecotourism is increasingly being seen as a way to promote sustainable tourism, it is also believed to provide valuable income to local communities. Wearing and Neil (1999, 2009) and Wearing and Wearing (1999, 2006) have previously outlined the need for new approaches, in which decommodification principles and practices must take place to ensure sustainable and valued ecotourism. There are many definitions of ecotourism (Fennell, 2001). Despite these varied definition, it is widely agreed that it incorporates conservation of the natural environment, economic benefits for local communities and recreational, as well as environmental learning activities for visitors (this stems from the original definition by Ceballos-Lascurain, cited in Boo, 1990, see also Cater, 2006, Butcher, 2008, Biggs et al., 2012). We would suggest that one component of this debate is around the two traditionally 'competitive' forces of environmentalism and economy (cf. Stamou and Paraskevopoulos, 2004). It is this tension between environmentalism and the economy that is the focus of our discussion in this chapter.

   A clear ideological basis for ecotourism is at best vague, and difficult to reconcile as a reality in tourist practice (Butcher, 2007). Nonetheless, it is often suggested that the economic aspect of ecotourism has overridden environmental considerations (Buckley, 2001; Wight, 1993). Attempts to reconcile the economics of the capitalist market with environmental imperatives are many and attempts to reconcile economy and environment almost invariably leave the assumption of market or neoclassical economics intact. The dominance of the market model means that it is the ecological and social values of local communities that requires adjustment (Hay, 2002). The context for change is underwritten by supposedly irrefutable and unmovable laws of neoclassical economics and the rule of capitalist markets particularly linked to economic globalization in the last few decades. The resultant privatization strategies and policies, intense emphasis on anti-collectivism and individualism and the reduction of a person's merit to that of their 'market capacity' is seen by neoliberal reformers as the panacea to social and economic problems such as extreme poverty and inequality, violence and the loss of languages and cultures.

The modalities and technologies of neoliberal reformism have spread sometimes insidiously and unevenly into social and economic policy (Ong, 2007, Brenner et al., 2010). The general picture that emerges is that by degree neoliberal ideology and rationalities spread in and across national borders with an increasing pace and in many ways unconstrained by the challenge of alternative models and social actors who take on these models. Often in the Third World it is actors such as NGOs, The international Monetary Fund (IMF) and the World Bank that determine the extent of neoliberal reformism with little acceptance of the determent of such reform to communities through government policy and intervention in domestic politics. The central answer for development change in developing economies is economic growth and becoming more competitive in global markets or at least exporting goods, services and cheap labour for these global markets. There are of course exceptions and countries such as Vietnam have shown a considerable resilience in resisting American interference and multinational overdevelopment of their tourist industry (Wearing and Wearing, 2014).

We examine the need for a paradigm shift in the cultural recognition and decolonization of host communities in framing the operations of ecotourism. At the centre of our discussion is an underlying manifesto for moral cultural encounters or a more moral mode of encounter. In order for an alternative model of tourism to develop there is a need for a considerable shift in power from Western globalizing ideals to ones based on the frameworks and voice of both national and local communities. This we argue requires alternative paradigms, strategies and practice in the delivery of ecotourism. For such strategic and policy shifts to occur in local communities and stakeholder networks there is a need to challenge and move beyond neoliberal reformism. Such reform is too often imposed by governments and multinational for profit travel companies as the model of 'progress' and change. Can the 'grass roots' communities and significant tourist stakeholders including tour operators provide a new environmental morality that challenges the economizing imperatives of a global neoliberalism and market oriented reform, is the question we now turn our attention to.

Against Neoliberal Reformism

Butcher (2008) argues that ecotourism has developed as a conspicuous form of life politics—the growth in demand for ecotourism not only reflects a certain sensibility amongst western tourists, but also an attempt to 'make a difference' to the societies visited. As such it is closely linked to people's aspirations to improve the socio-economic status of other people and to promote sustainable development. This outlook, we argue, may limit human agency. We maintain that for a shift in power relations this 'new environmental morality' requires ecotourism to overcome the economic imperative central in neoliberal reformism. Thus, we argue that changes in places where 'moral ecotourism' is allegedly practiced will have to come 'from below' to challenge thinking at the centres of power in core institutions of global governance of the West and increasingly Asia.

Neoliberalist ecotourism appears as one emergent planning option which fits the sustainable development regime that has adapted itself and modernized over the last couple of decades to become the dominant and almost exclusive approach to reform in the development of economies and societies. With this dominance comes the intensifying intrusion of capital into the realm of nature, creating greater instrumental management, commodification, and marginalization of the peoples and environments of developing countries (e.g., Boo, 1990; Berle, 1990; Cater, 1993, 1994). Neoliberal regime change also brings the cultural systems and neocolonization of the West that has the capacity to popularize nature, politicize consumption, and make tourism a, if not the, predominant mode of spectacularized and global consumer culture (Cater, 2006). Cater (2006), points out that much of the literature on ecotourism is Western-centric, in that it is embedded in Western cultural, economic and political processes, pointing out that within the range of definitions the most common denominator is that it is nature-based going on to stress using Macnaghten and Urry (1998: 95) that "there is no single 'nature' only natures."

From this we can see the opportunity and problem in that nature can be variously constructed by different societies and therefore that there can be a range of ecotourisms. In the dominant global movement against this we have witnessed in neoliberal reformism the globalization of nature and therefore ecotourism with the predominance of, as Cater (2006) suggests, a Western 'classical conservationist' approach. We maintain that with a shift in the discourse to the local and indigenous as we have done elsewhere (cf. Wearing and Wearing, 1999) and a more critical directive there are opportunities to decommodify ecotourism in ways that will allow it to serve it original purpose (cf. Wearing and Neil, 1999, 2009). This reconfiguration creates space for what we call the 'new environmental morality' that moves beyond green consumerism to the imperative of sustainability and a position that addresses the inequalities of neoliberal reformism.

As with Bscher et al.'s (2012) work in biodiversity conservation we aim here to provide a synthesized critique of neoliberal reformism as a mechanism to illustrate why decommodification is an essential element for moral forms of ecotourism. This also facilitates the production of discourses that facilitate space for a new environmental morality within local cultures and enables the capacity of communities to resist and protest relentless if uneven commodification from the Global North (Brenner, 2010; Horowitz, 2012). This requires a strong counter-discourse and strategy to bring about a shift in the power base that de-legitimizes neoliberalism so eco-social natural realms are not constantly transformed through and for capital accumulation. Several critical authors have argued the case for a strong decolonizing and decommodifying of local tourist markets is resistance to neoliberal imperatives. For example, there are various references to; "the politics of transforming and governing nature under neoliberalism" (McCarthy and Prudham, 2004: 279); "the ongoing commodification of natural things" (Heynen and Robbins, 2005: 6); and the "global neoliberal imperative to 'stretch' and 'deepen' … the reach of commodity circulation rely on the re-working of environmental governance and on entrenching the commodification of nature, and vice versa" (Heynen et al., 2007: 3 quoted in Bscher et al., 2012: 4). The next step then is to move away from this ideology and develop a new morality as is apparent in the call for justice tourism (Higgins-Desbiolles, 2008). Such tourism requires alternative forms of globalization and local control over cultural and social processes due to the negative impacts of capitalist or economic globalization we suggest there is a need to chart a path to a more just global order through tourist development.

We suggest that neoliberal reformism will reform and yet facilitate global capitalism so that global markets predominate and dictate how nature is used in and through the expansion of capitalism. A new environmental morality is designed to more directly engage with cultural and social realities through the lens of the local and local communities' exchanges with nature, government and NGOs stakeholder interventions.

How are 'Moral Encounters' Possible?

In many ways, the everyday exchanges and encounters between tourist and locals are based on cultural illusions and a lack of authenticity of self. This lack of authenticity is created by the hegemony of a global tourism industry. The tourist encounter itself has a complexity of interaction that perhaps unlike similar exchanges brings extremes of identity together and shares each parties'—host and tourist—sense of the local and their belonging. Such an encounter can commonly involve postcolonial and gender-'race' features that in particular make communication and asymmetrical power relations difficult (Wearing and Wearing, 1999). Ecotourism is a difficult term to define in the critical tourism literature in that conservation, the natural environment and care and wellbeing of individuals and host communities are core values in this industry. Like international standards and obligations associated with universal human rights, these values challenge the economic and marketized agendas extant in national and international agendas for development. Questions remain as to which countries will adopt such agendas and standards given that they require compliance in countries of the Global South where there is often extreme poverty and inequality, notably in those 'out of the way' destinations that encourage ecotourist endeavours and tourist-host encounters. Such challenges and resultant questions are made more apparent when international standards and obligations are considered in terms of ecotourism morality.

This section will assess how moral encounters can be possible in an atmosphere of highly marketized interactions and exchanges between host and tourist. Feminist postcolonial analysis allows a broad lens on the inequalities and intersections of gender, race and socioeconomic positions (defined by social class and status) along with location and colonialism to be included in an analysis that shows the social order to be male, heterosexual and white in terms of dominance, normalization and subordination of the Other of whom women and children remain the most vulnerable. This theoretical positioning allows us to recognize both the vulnerability of host communities particularly when women and children are involved and the need to decolonize interactions which we have addressed before in sociological terms (Wearing and Wearing, 2006). A critical ethical framework on the moral encounters that we tentatively propose can be briefly summed up as one that at the very least decolonize moral encounters and redress the imbalance of power relations with full engagement and participation of the host communities in ecotourism planning and policy (Bhabha, 1983, 1994; Smith, 1999; Hollinshead, 1999, 2007; Wearing and Darcy, 2011). This agenda could encompass holistically the two pronged strategy of: a) the use of explicit principled ethical standards including meeting international human rights, fair trade and labour standards and obligations and, b) the development of practice-based ethics for tourist encounters with hosts in regards to tourist and tour operators in specific cultures and locations. All stakeholders in tourism need to be encouraged to set the agenda and pre-conditions for moral encounters.

An understanding of the experiential micro-politics and morals of tourism will assist an ethical framework that creates a critical awareness amongst tourists and hosts. Developing an alternative subjugated knowledge to that of the Western paradigms in development can counteract both the ethical and economic governmentality and colonization of 'host others'. Governmentality is defined both as the micro-politics of social control in any discursive context and struggle and more broadly as the relations of domination that form macro-social control (following Foucault, 1991). The social governing of the colonized 'other' by ecotourist practices should be understood critically within alternative codes and moral frames to that of dominant neoliberalism. These moral frames would facilitate compassion and a sense of urgency to act on behalf of the oppressed 'other as host' as well as understand and create awareness around the role of tourist subjectivities in the perpetuation of particular relations of power (Foucault, 1991, Wearing, Wearing and MacDonald, 2010, Law, Harrington and Wearing, 2012). This alternative critical awareness can focus on the social and ecological costs of purely 'profit oriented' tourism legitimized by neoliberal ideology. In this consciousness there is a need to ensure that the construction of social value is not pre-determined so that the Western view of nature—what has been largely a neocolonial legacy of several hundred years of exploiting primary and natural resources for the benefit of Empire—is not imposed on the local cultural 'other' in the tourism process as can be the case with rural and isolated communities. Host community input and participation is essential to this process in that language and power provide barriers to the potential clarity of the two way communication process or cultural dialogue of policy and governance in tourism.

An important aspect of redressing power inequalities is continued participation of host communities in their local economy. The tourism literature suggests that success for local communities is more likely if they are able to participate in the tourism decision-making process (Baud-Bovy, 1982; Dowling, 1993; Getz, 1986, 1987; Getz and Jamal, 1994; Gunn and Var, 2002; Jamal and Getz, 1995; Prentice, 1993; Simmons, 1994). The tourism industry is increasingly conscious of the fact that it must engage with the views of all people and not simply those with a formal connection to tourism projects (Hall and Testoni, 2004; Inskeep, 1998). The nexus of social and ecological values embodied in ethical codes for ecotourism draw attention to place as a social gestalt by linking these values to the community in which they are embedded. Johnston (1992: 10) notes that social values are "a collective attachment to places that embody meanings important to a community." Hay (1988: 31) adds that social values are "the foundation of our identity as individuals and members of a community" serving as an irreplaceable centre of significance. This is not simply a process of belonging to specific socio-cultural categories even for those at the margins of the global economy.

Importantly, this analysis points to new understandings of the 'intersectionality' of oppression in both developing and developed countries. Yuval-Davis (2011: 8) makes her claim for interactional contestations based on the national and global boundaries of the degree and forms of community 'belonging' i.e. 'intersectional analysis should not be limited only to those who are on the multiple margins of society, but rather that the boundaries of intersectional analysis should encompass all members of society'. Yuval-Davis's (2011) work and postcolonial feminists such as bell hooks (2009) on non-White identities, community, intersectional contestations and 'belonging' make the case for the complex interaction and intersections of social divisions such as gender, class, race and location as informing the power relations and the knowledge-planning dividing such encounters (see also Aitken and An, 2012). In exploring her own sense of place, in rural Kentucky USA, bell hooks (2009) demonstrates how the intersections of one's identity arrive from growing up with a culture of belonging that can be divided by the identities of race, class, gender and location, amongst other social divisions. Such 'intersectionality' applies to oppressors and the privileged as well as minorities and oppressed people across the globe. The host self as part of their community is located within both a sense of place and a sense of belonging that requires certainty and sustainability irrespective of the criss-crossed socio-cultural divisions that might be involved in local contexts. Sustainability being both about care of resources in these environments and 'also about the creation of meaning— the making of lives that we feel are worth living' (hooks, 2009: 1.). Belonging to a local or host community can therefore involve hybrid self-identification and inter socio-cultural category identity. Assessing the cultural significance of belonging and place involves the articulation of values and meanings, both past and present, through a process of community endorsement of these values.

Locating or embedding an environmental 'ethics' within the local community provides such an opportunity. Johnston (1992) made a distinction between social and cultural values based upon temporal location, holding that social values are primarily contemporary in nature. Social and cultural values are viewed here as a dynamic continuum of embedded values and meanings, bonded together within a contemporary framework and comprising the cultural landscape. Explicit moral agendas for change in ecotourism's impact on local cultures are commonly made by International NGOs (INGOs) engaged in development issues. Such organizations have helped to embed a 'new ethics' of care in the encounters between tourists and hosts notably in any trade or monetary exchange for local goods and services. INGO's such as The Fair Trade Federation have specific codes of conduct in Third World economies. These guidelines influence international moral agendas for destinations and tour and hotel operators as well as national government agendas. One of their key values is 'Trade as a Force for Positive Change' stated as:

> Trade should promote fair compensation, safe and healthy conditions, direct and long-term relationships, transparent business practices, and workplaces free from discrimination and forced child labor. When trade encompasses these practices, the lives of all people and their communities improve (Fair Trade Federation, 2012).

When ecotourism is conceived as 'a trade' exchange it can encompass these equalizing, non-exploitative, community-oriented, and sustainability principles. Additional moral values and practice that interlock with the fair trade ideas on moral tourism consumption include: respectful partnerships, community, sustainable practice; fullest commitment and consumer knowledge. In combination, these values provide a forceful alternative commitment to non-market ethical principles. Little assessment, however, of the compliance of tour operators in practice has been done to test the degree to which such principles are adhered to.

Postcolonial Moral Encounters and Contested Intersections

This contemporary framework for a new cultural morality and local economic practice redresses the spread of neoliberalism and its economizing and totalizing views of a market driven moral order in ecotourism in several ways. For example, Escobar (1995) refers to the 'post-development framework' where a more fluid understanding of "host-guest" interactions and identity can exist side by side with or in resistance to the constraints of globalizing forces and neoliberal reform agendas. As an example, Aitken and An (2012) observe how the most critical issue in China's Fanjingshan National Nature Reserve relates to the resource-use relations between local farmers and an endangered snub-nosed monkey species, *Rhinopithecus brelichi*. The use of Deleuze and Guattari's (1987) work to help understand the complexity of affective ecologies, while Escobar's work is useful in connecting local activism, ecotourism, and community networks. This framework on tourist practices helps to contest globalized hegemonic discourses that do not necessarily support sustainability at the local level. The locating of environmental morality within this landscape allows for the actions of local farmers that are variously connected to, and emotionally charged around, sustainability and the preservation of the snub-nosed monkey to become a prevalent part of the discourse. The rural farmer, the village wife and children and the extended kinship networks all need to be re-conceived in an 'ethics of the other' that gives preference to their cultural and social worlds in tourist enterprise (Wearing and Darcy, 2011).

This new conceptualization of morality can be found in other areas, for example Biggs, Hall and Stoeckl's (2012) research into levels of resilience of formal and informal reef tourism enterprises and the factors associated with the enterprise resilience in Phuket, Thailand following the 2004 Indian Ocean tsunami and the 2008 political crisis in Thailand. They find that informal enterprises reported better financial condition in a crisis scenario and higher levels of social capital in the form of government, family and community support than formal enterprises. Formal and informal enterprises both enjoy high lifestyle benefits from reef tourism, which supports resilience. Most formal enterprises had part foreign ownership/management (61%); no informal enterprise had any foreign ownership or management. Management policies supporting reef tourism should consider local nuances and the importance of lifestyle benefits for both formal and informal enterprises, and take steps to enable enterprise flexibility and cost-cutting during crises. The grass roots creation of a morality of encounter is not a simplistic matter. In many cases ecotourism has extended and deepened the geographies of neoliberalism by targeting and opening up new frontiers of nature (Duffy and Moore, 2010).

Neoliberalism and the Moral Silence of Ecotourism

The examples above suggest that the uneven spread of neoliberalism in tourism means that it needs to be understood in specific modalities and technologies at local levels. One significant local effect on host cultures is the extent to which the voices of citizen and stakeholder dissent are silenced. Silences on the advance of neoliberal reform remain in various forms of ecotourism over often blatant exploitation of land, the natural environment and the 'skimming off' of tourist profits by large tour operators, hotels and other key industry players such as airlines and tourist transport companies. Tiers of Government can be highly complicit in such silence in that trade off increases in local employment and industry for such exploitation. A level of political and moral silence is the result of the hegemony of market tourism in that price and quality in relation to profits from 'customers' are the major drivers in the 'industry'. This is what we name as an emerging moral silence about 'the real' social costs and benefits of a global and market-driven ecotourism. This is not to forget that "hosts and guests" embody autonomy and social agency and can make choices about what moral agendas they employ in encounters (Wearing and Wearing, 1999).

What can ecotour organizations and related communities do that represents or embody the missions of a social valuing of ecotourism? The traditional 'top down' method that is still emerging in the industry is to challenge ethical silence and thereby help to reshape ecotourist encounters and ecotour operation. The International Ecotourism Society (TIES) based in the USA has a broad three pronged code of conduct for its members of practice and promotion of principles, support of and participation of TIES in playing a role at local, national and international levels; and through implementation of their code of conduct play a role in educating about sustainable ecotourism as a TIES member. Similarly, the large multinational tour operator *Contiki Tour* partners in their tours with the Oceanic Society which has developed an ecotourism code of ethics. The Oceanic Society's code focuses on protection of wildlife and habitat for animals and a Third World code of adventure travel. The setting of these traditional codes and standards at this stage is in early development and is variable in impact depending on how ecotourism is defined and utilized by stakeholders. Nonetheless, at the core of these explicit ethical agendas is a new 'morality of care' offered in these principled approaches by some stakeholders for both communities and animal welfare. The moral turn as canvassed by the geography of care arguments give strong intellectual backing to such arguments (Smith, 1997, Barnett et al., 2005, Lawson, 2007).

There is also a need for what we call a 'bottom up' community development and participation approach to moral encounters that can empower local communities who participate in ecotourism development. Local and grass roots struggles and contestation over the socio-cultural costs and benefits of ecotourism 'trade' and implementation of eco-tourist policy and ethics can help to determine more equal ground rules for the moral encounter. The constant threat of marketization and globalized neoliberalism has heavily influences both the form and outcome of 'new morality' debates in ecotourism. Nonetheless, those who suggest such agendas need to guard against becoming apologist or handmaidens for neoliberal imperatives of creating new markets as a 'quick fix' to economic inequality in particular such as privatization and the individualism of 'consumer/tourist choice' and governance over markets.

Critics of the impact of neoliberalism have questioned the role of tourist mass markets and the potential for ecotourism to make a difference in terms of social justice for poor people and indigenous communities in these developing countries. Higgins-Desbiolles (2006) suggests a broader vision of tourism's transformative social power and outcomes is needed to move away from the dominance of market fundamentalisms of neoliberal tourism. She asserts that it is the minority world that has access to both mass tourism and also alternative tourism such as volunteer tourism, peace tourism and justice and reconciliation tourism. Ecotourism can be position across mass and alternative tourism in this way while not forgetting the majority of the world who do not travel because of poverty, disability and other reasons. While we are in sympathy with the critique of neoliberalism we argued for practical ways forward that have the potential for grass roots and decommodified forms of community based ecotourism. There is some flexibility and choice in how a country develops its local economy and resources and governments have made a difference in fending off the worst excessive of neoliberal agendas and free market ideas.

Mapping Cultural Alternatives for Ecotourism

In summary, the important connection has been established in this chapter between local communities and stakeholders. Questions remain about 'the transformative capacity' of ecotourism in making moral encounters for tourists and hosts (Higgins-Desbiolles, 2006, 2008). Central to our agenda for alternatives is to engage with and protect not only these communities but also nature's eco-systems. For example diving or swimming with the local sea life such as whales, seals, dolphins, turtles or on coral reefs means that communities are involved in providing transport, food, accommodation and labour to facilitate access to these sites. Public policy analysing helps us locate modes of alternative ecotourism within a network of actors and the development of a sustainable and economically viable ecotourism for local economies (Wearing, MacDonald and Wearing, 2010). These developments need to be seen in terms of broader social movements and activism that resists and establishes indigenous and local tourism markets and community involvement in these markets.

Alternative ecotourism can be separated out from mass tourism strategies and commercialized ventures of 'nature based tourism' by specifying the local costs and benefits, and the values added to community belonging, social integration and a just distribution of resources from this form of tourism (Higgins-Desbiolles, 2008). The inclusion of indigenous communities as hosts in profit making and sharing is paramount to the local social economy and therefore the morality and 'fair trade' of the ecotour encounter. Social justice as both cultural identity recognition and redistribution of resources for local communities cannot take place without recognition of their identity and cultures. This can be achieved most notably from challenging the oppressive intersections of power relations and encouraging through explicit promotion the 'becomings' of social, cultural and personal identity in these contexts (Probyn, 1996; Taylor, 2010; Yuval-Davis, 2011; Wearing et al., 2011; Law, Harrington and Wearing, 2012).

Conclusions

What we have sought to do in this chapter is to start new conversations around ecotourism development that take seriously a decolonizing model of community participation. Such models are commonly also used with Indigenous communities in areas such as mining land use or in determining social welfare concerns that can also have an impact on ecotourist agendas, community resistance and local community 'life worlds' (Smith, 1999; Yuval-Davis, 2011; Butcher, 2008; Walter, 2010; Escobar, 2012). Mixing the ethical and political agendas of appropriate cultural ecotourism with justice ecotourism and poverty alleviation ecotourism can make a significant difference to these communities (Nowaczek, Moran-Cahusac and Fennell, 2006; Hollinshead, 2007, Higgins-Desbiolles, 2006, 2008; Duffy and Moore, 2010, McCabe, Minnaert and Diekmann, 2011). This chapter has contributed to the framing of a new agenda for moral encounters in ecotourism by offering an alternate development model. It suggests realizing this model will require a radical shift from neoliberal 'profit oriented' tourism towards a new environmental morality.

References

Aitken, S. C. and An, L. (2012). Figured Worlds: Environmental Complexity and Affective Ecologies in Fanjingshan, China. *Ecological Modelling*, 229(24), 5–15.

Barnett, C., Cloke, P., Clarke, N., and Malpass, A. (2005). Consuming Ethics: Articulating the Subjects and Spaces of Ethical Consumption. *Antipode*, 37(1), 23–45.

Baud-Bovy, M. (1982). New Concepts in Planning for Tourism and Recreation. *Tourism Management*, 3(4), 308–319.

Beck, U. (1992). *The Risk Society*. London: Routledge.

Berle, P. (1990). Two Faces of Ecotourism. *Audubon* 92(2), 6.

Bhabha, H. K. (1983). The Other Question—The Stereotype and Colonial Discourse. *Screen* 24, November/December, 18–36.

Bhabha, H. K. (1994). *The Location of Culture*. London: Routledge.

Biggs, D., Hall, C. M., and Stoeckl, N. (2012). The Resilience of Formal and Informal Tourism Enterprises to Disasters: Reef Tourism in Phuket, Thailand. *Journal of Sustainable Tourism*, 20(5), 645–665.

Boo, E. (1990). *Ecotourism: The Potentials and Pitfalls*, Vol. 1. Washington, DC: World Wildlife Fund.

Brenner, N., Peck, J., and Theodore, N. (2010). Variegated Neoliberization: Geographies, Modalities, Pathway. *Global Networks*, 10(2), 182–222.

Bscher, B., Sullivan, S., Neves, K., Igoe, J., and Brockington, D. (2012). Towards a Synthesized Critique of Neoliberal Biodiversity Conservation. *Capitalism, Nature, Socialism*, 23(2), 4–30.

Buckley, R. (2001). Major Issues in Eco-labelling. In X. Font and R. Buckley (eds.), *Tourism Eco-labelling: Certification and Promotion of Sustainable Management*, pp. 19–26. Wallingford: CABI Publishing.

Butcher, J. (2007). *Ecotourism, NGOs and Development: A Critical Analysis*. London: Routledge.

Butcher, J. (2008). Ecotourism as Life Politics. *Journal of Sustainable Tourism*, 16(3), 315–326.

Cater, E. (1993). *Ecotourism in Belize and Dominica.* Discussion Paper No. 16, Department of Geography, University of Reading, United Kingdom.

Cater, E. (2006). Ecotourism as a Western construct. *Journal of Ecotourism,* 5(1–2), 23–39.

Deleuze, G., and Guattari, F. (1987). *A Thousand Plateaus: Capitalism and Schizophrenia.* Minneapolis: University of Minnesota Press.

D'Hauteserre, A. M. (2010). Government Policies and Indigenous Tourism in New Caledonia. *Asia Pacific Journal of Tourism Research,* 15(3), 285–303.

Diesendorf, M. (2000). Sustainability and Sustainable Development. In D. Dunphy, J. Benveniste, A. Griffiths, and P. Sutton (eds.), *Sustainability: The Corporate Challenge of the 21st Century,* pp. 9–37. Sydney: Allen & Unwin.

Dolnicar, S., and Leisch, F. (2008). Selective Marketing for Environmentally Sustainable Tourism. *Tourism Management,* 29(4), 672–680.

Domosh, M. (2004). Cultural Landscape in Environmental Studies. In N. Smelser and P. Bates (eds.), *International Encyclopaedia of the Social and Behavioural Sciences,* pp. 3081–3086. New York: Elsevier.

Dowling, R. (1993). An Environmentally-based Planning Model for Regional Tourism Development. *Journal of Sustainable Tourism,* 1(1), 17–37.

Duffy, R., and Moore, L. (2010). Neoliberalising Nature? Elephant-back Tourism in Thailand and Botswana. *Antipode,* 42(3), 742–766.

Escobar, A. (2012 [1995]). *Ecountering Development: The Making and Unmaking of the Third World.* Princeton, NJ: Princeton University Press.

Fennell, D. A. (2001). A Content Analysis of Ecotourism Definitions. *Current Issues in Tourism,* 4(5), 401–421.

Foucault, M. (1991). Governmentality. In G. Burchell (ed.), *The Foucault Effect: Studies in Governmentality,* pp. 81–104. London: Harvester Wheatsheaf.

Geddes, M. (2005). Neoliberalism and Local Governance—Cross National Perspectives and Speculations. *Policy Studies,* 26(3–4), 359–377.

Getz, D. (1986). Models in Tourism Planning: Towards Integration of Theory and Practice. *Tourism Management,* 7(1), 21–32.

Getz, D. (1987). *Tourism Planning and Research: Traditions, Models and Futures.* Paper presented at the Australian Travel Workshop, Bunbury, Western Australia.

Getz, D., and Jamal, T. (1994). The Environment–Community Symbiosis: A Case for Collaborative Tourism Planning. *Journal of Sustainable Tourism,* 2(3), 152–173.

Gunn, C. A., and Var, T. (2002). *Tourism Planning: Basic Concepts and Cases,* 4th edn. London: Routledge.

Hall, C. M., and Tucker, H. (eds.) (2004). *Tourism and Postcolonialism: Contested Discourses, Identities and Representations.* London: Routledge.

Hall, N., and Testoni, L. (2004). *Steps to Sustainable Tourism: Planning a Sustainable Future for Tourism, Heritage and the Environment.* Canberra: Commonwealth of Australia.

Harvey, D. (2005). *A Brief History of Neoliberalism.* New York: Oxford University Press.

Hay, P. (1988). Place and Literature. *Island Magazine*, 34/35, 31–36.

Hay, P. (2002). *Main Currents in Western Environmental Thought*. Bloomington: Indiana University Press.

Higgins-Desbiolles, F. (2006). More than an 'Industry': The Forgotten Power of Tourism as a Social Force. *Tourism Management*, 27(6), 1192–1208.

Higgins-Desbiolles, F. (2008). Justice Tourism and Alternative Globalisation. *Journal of Sustainable Tourism*, 16(3), 345–364.

Hollinshead, K. (1999). Surveillance of the Worlds of Tourism: Foucault and the Eye-of-power, *Tourism Management*, 20(1), 7–23.

Hollinshead, K. (2007). Indigenous Australian in the Bittersweet World. In R. Butler and T. Hinch (eds.), *Tourism and Indigenous Peoples: Issues and Implications*. Amsterdam: Butterworth Heinemann.

hooks, b. (2009). *Belonging: A Culture of Place*. London: Routledge.

Horowitz, L. S. (2012). Power, Profit, Protest: Grassroots Resistance to Industry in the Global North. *Capitalism Nature Socialism*, 23(3), 20–34.

Inskeep, E. (1991). *Tourism Planning: An Integrated Sustainable Development Approach*. New York: Van Nostrand Reinhold.

Inskeep, E. (1998). *Guide for Local Authorities on Developing Sustainable Tourism*. Madrid: World Tourism Organization.

Jamal, T., and Getz, D. (1995). Collaboration Theory and Community Tourism Planning. *Annals of Tourism Research*, 22(1), 186–204.

Janoski, T., Alford, R., Hicks, A., and Schwartz, M. A. (eds.) (2010). *The Handbook of Political Sociology*. New York: Cambridge University Press.

Johnston, C. (1992). *A Social Value: A Discussion Paper* (Vol. 26). Canberra: Australian Government Publishing Service.

Keiner, M. (2006). Rethinking Sustainability. In M. Keiner (ed.), *The Future of Sustainability*. Amsterdam: Springer.

Law, A., Harrington, M., and Wearing, M. (2012). Out of Work, Out of Leisure, Out of Place: Moral Regulation, Citizenship and Volunteering in the Rural 'Idyll'. *The Greek Review of Social Research*, 136(3), 63–78.

Lawson, V. (2007). Geographies of Care and Responsibility. *Annals of the Association of American Geographers*, 97(1), 1–11.

Macnaghten, P., and Urry, J. (1998). *Contested Natures*. London: Sage.

McCabe, S., Minnaert, L., and Diekmann, A. (eds.) (2011). *Social Tourism in Europe: Theory and Practice*. Clevedon: Channel View.

McCarthy, J., and Prudham, S. (2004). Neoliberal Nature and the Nature of Neoliberalism, *Geoforum*, 35(3), 275–283.

McGrew, D., and Held, A. (2000). The Great Globalization Debate: An Introduction. In D. Held and A. McGrew (eds.), *The Global Transformations Reader*. Cambridge: Polity Press.

National Asian Pacific American Women's Forum (NAPAWF) (2008) *Rights to Survival and Mobility: An Anti-trafficking Activist's Agenda*, Takoma Park www.napawwf.org.

Nowaczek, A. M., Moran-Cahusac, C., and Fennell, D. A. (2006). Against the Current: Striving for Ethical Ecotourism. In J. Higham (ed.), *Critical Issues in Ecotourism: Understanding a Complex Tourism Phenomenon*, pp. 136–157. Oxford: Butterworth-Heinemann.

Ong, A. (2007). Neoliberalism as a Mobile Technology. *Transactions of the Institute of British Geographers*, 32, 3–8.

Prentice, R. (1993). Community-driven Tourism Planning and Residents' Preferences. *Tourism Management*, 14(3), 218–227.

Probyn, E. (1996). *Outside Belongings*. London: Routledge.

Probyn, E. (2005). *Blush. Faces of Shame*. Minneapolis: University of Minnesota Press.

Simmons, D. (1994). Community Participation in Tourism Planning. *Tourism Management*, 15(2), 98–108.

Smith, D. (1997). Geography and Ethics: A Moral Turn? *Progress in Human Geography*, 21(4), 583–590.

Smith, D. (1998). How Far Should We Care? On the Spatial Scope of Beneficence. *Progress in Human Geography*, 22(1), 15–38.

Smith, L. T. (1999). *Decolonizing Methodologies: Research and Indigenous People*. London: Zed.

Stamou, A. G., and Paraskevopoulos, S. (2004). Images of Nature by Tourism and Environmentalist Discourses in Visitors Books: A Critical Analysis of Ecotourism. *Discourse and Society*, 15(1), 105–129.

Steinert, H., and Pilgram, A. (eds.) (2007). *Welfare Policy from Below: Struggles Against Social Exclusion in Europe*. Ashgate: Aldershot.

Stenning, A., Smith, A., and Willis, K. (2008). *Social Justice and Neoliberalism: Global Perspectives*. London: Zed.

Taylor, G. (2010). *The New Political Sociology*. London: Palgrave.

Tipton, F. B. (2009). Southeast Asian Capitalism: History, Institutions, States, and Firms. *Asia Pacific Journal of Management*, 26, 401–434.

Valentine, G. (2005). Geography and Ethics: Moral Geographies? *Progress in Human Geography*, 29(4), 483–487.

Walter, M. (2010). Market Forces and Indigenous Resistance Paradigms. *Social Movement Studies*, 9(2), 121–137.

Wearing, B., and Wearing, S. (1996). Refocussing the Tourist Experience: The Flaneur and the Choraster. *Leisure Studies*, 15(3), 229–243.

Wearing, M. (ed.) (2011). *Social Identity*. New York: Nova.

Wearing, S., and Darcy, S. (2011). Inclusion of the 'Othered' in Tourism. *Cosmopolitan Civil Societies Journal*, 3(2), 18–34.

Wearing, S., and Neil, J. (1999). *Ecotourism: Impacts, Potential and Possibilities*. Oxford: Butterworth-Heinemann.

Wearing, S., and Wearing, M. (1999). Decommodifying Ecotourism: Rethinking Global-local Interactions with Host Communities. *Leisure and Society* (*Losier et Societe*), 22(1), 39–70.

Wearing, S., and Wearing, M. (2006). Rereading the 'Subjugating Tourist' in Neoliberalism: Postcolonial Otherness and the Tourist Experience. *Tourism Analysis*, 11(2), 143–165.

Wearing, S., and Wearing, M. (2014). Decommodifying Grass Roots Struggles against Neoliberalism: Imagining a Just, Local and Sustainable Eco-tourism. In J. Mosedale (ed.), *Current Developments in the Geographies of Tourism*. Farnham: Ashgate.

Wearing, S., Wearing, M., and MacDonald, M. (2010). Understanding Local Power and Interactional Processes in Sustainable Tourism: Exploring Village–Tour Operator Relations on the Kokoda Track, Papua New Guinea. *Journal of Sustainable Tourism*, 18(1), 61–67.

Wight, P. (1993). Ecotourism: Ethics or Eco-Sell? *Journal of Travel Research*, 3, 3–9.

Yuval-Davis, N. (2011). *The Politics of Belonging: Intersectional Contestations*. London: Sage.

Chapter 11

The Moralization of Flying: Cocktails in Seat 33G, Famine and Pestilence Below

Brent Lovelock

Introduction

As I begin to write this chapter, I reflect upon an article that I read in a newspaper over the weekend –"CO_2 levels head into unknown territory." For the first time since measurements began, the concentration of carbon dioxide in the atmosphere has surpassed 400 parts per million, breaching a threshold not seen for three million years (Sunday Star Times, 2013). It was not only this article that piqued my interest, but also the material carried on the bottom quarter of the same newspaper page: "Holiday Clearance! Fiji $869, Los Angeles $1599 and Phuket $1739 book now!" The juxtaposition of this report—on arguably the worst environmental and humanitarian catastrophe that the world has ever faced—with advertisements to carry on flying, appealed to my sense of irony.

Yet, some commentators fail to see any humour in the situation. Writer and environmental activist George Monbiot (2006) has told us that "We are all killers until we stop flying." His comment refers to the impacts of the extreme weather events (drought, starvation, flooding) and sea level rise associated with global warming. Monbiot asserts that "… if we want to stop the planet from cooking" we have to stop flying. Yet, while we (or most of us anyway—e.g. 70% of Americans believe in global warming (Leiserowitz et al., 2012)) understand this to be the case, it has little impact upon our behaviour. As Monbiot (2006) notes, "[w]hen I challenge my friends about their planned weekend in Rome or their holiday in Florida, they respond with the strange, distant smile and avert their eyes. They just want to enjoy themselves."

Is such behaviour immoral? Sitting in seat 33G, sipping my duty free chardonnay, peering out at the Pacific atolls far below (soon to disappear with climate-induced sea level rise), should I and my fellow passengers feel morally inferior? And if so, why do we keep on flying? First, we must establish that the question about whether or not to fly, for our next holiday, is above all a moral problem (for a fuller discussion see Lovelock and Lovelock, 2013). A moral problem, simply speaking, is one in which the actions of the moral agent have implications for others. And a *responsible* or *conscientious* moral agent is someone who is concerned with the interests of everyone affected by what he or she does (Rachels and Rachels, 2010). It is argued that most passenger air travel represents unnecessary luxury consumption, which responsible moral agents should willingly reduce in order to mitigate global climate change (Cafaro, 2013). In this chapter I examine why very few of us act as conscientious moral agents when it comes to the question of touristic flying—and why we experience moral dissonance or 'selective moral disengagement' (Bandura, 2007). I put forward a number of reasons for why this may be the case. First, the larger problem of climate change (and thus, the smaller question about flying) has certain characteristics that make it difficult for us to recognize as a typical or 'paradigm moral problem' (Jamieson, 2010). Not only are there complexities around the impacts (and benefits) of our flying, that add to the confusion, but we can also argue that our flying is inconsequential in the overall scale of humankind's carbon emissions, and thus to anthropogenic climate change. A number of these factors come together in what Gardiner (2006) describes as a 'perfect moral storm', a storm that allows us to excuse ourselves from taking moral action (and cancelling that flight). In this chapter, I argue that central to the problem of our carbon behaviour is the issue of agency. Agency, within the touristic setting is complicated by the liminality of the touristic act, and the dictates of the neoliberal context that provide a structure in which immoral behaviour is both expected and rewarded. The larger issue at work here is whether or not, in the face of global calamity, we can rise above ourselves as individuals, or as a society, to stop flying (and other carbon-unfriendly acts) and help address climate change.

Climate Change—A Problematic Moral Problem?

There are various paradigms for what constitutes a moral problem: an individual acting intentionally harms another individual; individual harms are clearly identifiable; cause and effect are closely related in time and space. Jamieson (2010) explains that if we vary any of these dimensions, the case for a problem being a *moral* problem weakens, and that this is at the root of problems around dealing with the climate change problem—and associated problems such as whether or not to fly for our touristic purposes.

To illustrate these challenges, and how they impact upon moral problems, Jamieson (2010) asks us to consider the example of 'Jack' intentionally stealing 'Jill's' bicycle: the individual acting intentionally has harmed another individual, the individuals and the harm are clearly identifiable, and they are closely related in time and space. He then asks us to consider some further examples.

> In Example 2, Jack is part of an unacquainted group of strangers, each of which, acting independently, takes one part of Jill's bike, resulting in the bike's disappearance. In Example 3, Jack takes one part from each of a large number of bikes, one of which belongs to Jill. In Example 4, Jack and Jill live on different continents, and the loss of Jill's bike is the consequence of a causal chain that begins with Jack ordering a used bike at a shop. In Example 5, Jack

lives many centuries before Jill, and consumes materials that are essential to bike manufacturing; as a result, it will not be possible for Jill to have a bicycle (Jamieson, 2010: 436).

While it may still seem that moral considerations are at stake in each of these cases, this is less clear than in Example 1. Jamieson (2010) likens the climate change to his Example 6: acting independently, Jack and a large number of unacquainted people set in motion a chain of events that causes a large number of future people who will live in another part of the world from ever having bikes. He argues that in this case it is difficult to identify the agents and the victims or the "causal nexus" between them and "for the network of moral concepts (for example, responsibility, blame, and so forth) to gain traction" (Jamieson, 2010: 436). Thus the climate change problem does not have the characteristics of a "paradigm moral problem," where harm causation has a central position in modern moral philosophy. He argues that to view climate change as a problem of individual moral responsibility "requires a revision of everyday understandings of moral responsibility" (Jamieson, 2010: 438).

Yet, an inability to see the links between behaviours that are spatially or temporally separated and the collective or total sum of the moral issue that results may not be because humans are unable to, but simply maybe because it suits them not to. For example, when it comes time to wash the dishes in our house, there is a general scampering away from the kitchen sink, with our teenage children leading this charge. They use all sorts of excuses to get out of the job—e.g. they did not eat much that day and therefore did not contribute much to the general pile of dishes; those dishes are not mine—they are dad's, mum's, brother's or sister's; or they were away staying at a friend's house so why should they have to contribute to the dishwashing etc. Yet clearly, as a family member, and living under one roof, there is an individual and collective responsibility to do the dishes.

Ignorance, a refusal to engage, looking the other way, are rational strategies that people engage with when they seek to absolve themselves of moral responsibility and to realize their own ends. So perhaps Jamieson's description of the problem underestimates our cognitive capacities, and our capacity to recognize our own responsibility. And perhaps we are also guilty of exploiting (or feigning) ignorance and an inability to connect the fact that by flying somewhere, we will cause (eventually … somewhere) harm to others.

Moral Dissonance and the Complexities of Climate Change

The gap between intention and behaviour is addressed by the term 'cognitive dissonance'. *Moral* dissonance occurs when a person's behaviour or general cognitions are in conflict with his/her moral values i.e. moral dissonance is cognitive dissonance, only with a moral dimension (Lowell 2012). Dissonance is well illustrated in studies which consistently show a gap between attitude and behaviour. For example, Jamieson (2006) reports on a 2005 poll undertaken in

Britain, where 89% of participants were 'deeply concerned' about climate change; yet the majority of participants opposed higher taxes on air travel.

In explaining this moral dissonance, disconnect, or gap between "high minded words and low-down behaviour" in relation to personal carbon consumption and climate change, Jamieson (2006: 98) identifies a number of causal factors. Firstly, it is linked to 'cognitive deficiencies', outcomes of the complexity of the science of climate change and of the associated social and political complexity. Secondly, and coupled with this are the 'cognitive illusions' involved in understanding climate change, for example, a cold winter may make it hard for us to believe in climate change—or even make us welcome it (Jamieson, 2006). And, thirdly, climate change may not register on many people's personal radars as a topic worthy of much attention or action. This has been attributed to the very nature of climate change which is incremental and where impacts can be indirect. As Jamieson (1991: 323) notes, "[w]hile climate change may kill millions, it will be on the death certificate of no one."

Complexities—And the Immorality of Not Flying

Just as there are complexities around the outcomes of carbon consumption and climate change, so too are there complexities around the touristic outcomes of flying or not flying. A complication for Joe/Jill tourist is the potential negative social and economic impact that *not flying* may have on both travel generating regions and destinations. Indeed, a convincing argument is that it may be immoral NOT to fly—especially to developing country destinations where foreign exchange from tourism is much needed to battle poverty (Gössling, 2013; Hall et al., 2009). Acknowledging, however, that citizens within developing country destinations are ironically probably more vulnerable to the impacts of climate change than those in developed generating regions, Gössling (2013: 260) notes that "the paradoxical conclusion may be drawn that while tourism lifts a share of humanity out of poverty, it simultaneously jeopardizes the living conditions of another share of humanity through its contribution to climate change."

Urry (2002) however, considers corporeal travel necessary and beneficial for society, and outlines a set of obligations that may entail physical 'co-presence'. For Urry (2002: 270), a "good society would seek to extend possibilities of co-presence [from travel] to every social group and regard infringements of this as involving undesirable social exclusion." This begs the question of how a 'good society' may foster travel for its citizens yet protect its citizens and non-citizens from the profound impacts of climate change? (see also Urry, 2011, 2012).

Selective Moral Disengagement

Similar in ways to moral dissonance, in trying to explain why people (and consequently, organizations too) don't always behave in ways that a sensible, collective morality may indicate, Bandura (2007: 8) employs the notion of 'selective moral disengagement'. He describes this phenomenon as "[d]isengagement of moral self-sanctions [that] enables people to pursue detrimental practices freed from the restraint of self-censure." He goes on to identify such disengagement as an important impediment to the collective action needed for large scale social and environmental problems—for example action to address climate change.

In developing moral agency (the ability to make moral judgments) individuals construct standards of right and wrong that serve as guides or deterrents for harmful practices: "[i]t is through the ongoing exercise of evaluative self-sanctions that moral conduct is motivated and regulated" (Bandura, 2007: 9). However, moral standards do not create a fail proof moral control system, and as Bandura (2007: 9) notes, "there are many psychosocial measures by which moral self-sanctions can be selectively disengaged for harmful practices." There are a variety of reasons why individuals adopt a 'foreshortened perspective' when it comes to environmental practices: the "[b]ountiful immediate rewards of consumptive lifestyles" not the least, especially if the negative impacts of such are slowly cumulative, unanticipated and irreversible (Bandura, 2007: 10). Bandura (2007) identifies eight psychosocial mechanisms for selective moral disengagement, and these operate at both the individual and social system levels:

1. Moral justification
2. Exonerative comparison
3. Euphemistic labeling
4. Minimizing, ignoring or misconstruing the consequences
5. Dehumanization
6. Attribution of blame
7. Displacement of responsibility
8. Diffusion of responsibility

These mechanisms operate at four loci—behaviour, agency, outcome and recipient. We observe most of these mechanisms operating with respect to the question of touristic flights. For example, we morally justify our flights to developing countries because of the 'good' we can bring through our expenditure there; we compare the carbon output from flying to other more harmful industries; we talk about 'global warming' which "conveys the image of a mildly pleasant condition" (Bandura, 2007: 19); we blame the tourist 'industry' and the airlines (Low cost carriers! Cheap fares!) rather than ourselves as individuals; we downplay the actual harm of aviation in terms of its contribution to greenhouse gases (only 5%!); we distrust the messengers—those 'greenies'—as radicals who are scaremongering; and we ignore the impacts on a distant (unknown and uncared for?) poor.

Importantly, this moral disengagement occurs at the individual and collective levels, although as Bandura notes, the latter requires a network of participants vindicating harmful practices. Bandura (2007: 12) refers to the example of tobacco, and the network of agriculturalists, biotech researchers, scientists, movie actors, advertisers, chemists, investors and shareholders, lawyers and legislators, governments, tobacco companies and consumers that collectively comprise the social system—"a huge cast of moral disengagers"—that fosters the continuity of the harmful practice of smoking. A similar cast of moral disengagers could readily be identified for the practice of touristic flying.

Gardiner (2006: 397) argues that climate change involves a convergence of a set of global, intergenerational and theoretical problems, or a 'perfect moral storm' that makes us "extremely vulnerable to moral corruption"—or makes it difficult for us to act morally around climate change. The perfect storm is generated by a range of mechanisms through which we fool ourselves and others about the issue: distraction, complacency, unreasonable doubt, selective attention, delusion, pandering, false witness and hypocrisy (Gardiner, 2006: 407–408).

Liminality and Morality

But what is it about tourism and travel that makes moral disengagement easier perhaps, than in other aspects of our lives? Research, for example, points to people making 'correct' moral decisions regarding their choice of transport to travel to work or to go to do their shopping. But this morality does not seem to translate across into touristic activities—or at least into decisions re whether to fly or not to fly. Despite the contradiction that it is the world's largest industry, Ryan and Kindler (1996) describe holidaying as a marginal or 'liminal' activity. Liminality is a term first used in 1909 by Van Gennep to describe the transition from adolescence to adulthood (Preston-Whyte, 2004). Turner (1974: 47) extended liminality to other spheres of social functioning, defining it as "any condition outside or on the peripheries of everyday life." Since then, the concept has been adopted by some tourism researchers to describe the aberrant behaviours of tourists e.g. sex tourists (e.g. Ryan and Kinder, 1996). While liminality has been used in a variety of contexts, it generally refers to a transitional state, space or place. In defining liminal space, Preston-Whyte (2004: 350) refers to "escape from the daily grind of social responsibilities" and being "beyond normal social and cultural constraints." Individuals engaging in tourism become "… freed from the constraints of responsibilities to employers and social roles they normally occupy … answerable to no-one but him or herself" (Ryan and Kinder, 1996: 510). Thus tourists become liminal people, "between places, times and conventions" (Pritchard and Morgan, 2006: 764).

Just as liminality has proved a useful concept for explaining how individuals may justify their choice of sexual partner, or other behaviours within tourism settings, it has value in helping to explain decisions around touristic carbon consumption. Turner (1996) noted that

> People who find themselves in liminal space are temporarily beyond the normative structure. In other words, they enter a sort of limbo, and experience

the tension between the existence of established rules and the limitations of those rules. (Cited in Cunha and Cabral-Cardoso, 2006: 214).

It has been argued that a liminality perspective allows us to develop a better understanding of organizational ethics and decision-making, and why we may observe the suspension of general or universalistic rules (Cunha and Cabral-Cardoso, 2006).

So, for the issue of flying and touristic carbon consumption, the liminality of the act of tourism mitigates against the moral agent (the tourist) arriving at a decision that could objectively be considered moral, in terms of the potential harms arising from that decision. Thus selective moral disengagement is easier within this liminal setting, where the decision itself is made within a temporal and existential space (a liminal space) that is not conducive to 'staying within the rules'—the liminal space where we are free to ignore any moral script that may be provided by wider society. Wider society in this case also fails to provide much guidance.

Limits to Liminality and the Role of Agency

While I implicate liminality here, it should be noted that some believe that there are limitations to liminality as an explicating concept. Franklin considers that liminality "assumes that tourists are unthinking, unfeeling and unchanging 'intellectually challenged' dolts who let the experience wash over them in a homogenous wave of escape or relaxation" (Franklin, 2003 cited in Yarnal and Kerstetter, 2005: 370). I tend to sympathize with Franklin's view, that liminality doesn't automatically presume a restriction on agency.

Agency and the fragmentation of agency (Gardiner, 2006) is key to understanding our actions with respect to carbon consumption and flying. Agency is the conscious and deliberate ability to act and implicitly no person (at least those considering travelling) is without 'agency'. Agency is a critical factor in individuals developing 'carbon capability'—"the skills, situated knowledge, motivation and capacity to cut carbon" (Whitmarsh et al., 2011: 63). A social practices model of sustainable consumption centralizes the complex agency-structure dialectic that determines the social practices through which carbon capability is formed (Whitmarsh et al., 2011). Thus in trying to identify strategies for engaging the public in climate change mitigation, Butler (2010: 18) argues that we need to "… to address the problematics of agency"—something we have failed to do. She believes that we need to understand relations of agency so that spaces for the "enactment of change" might be found, allowing us to act in 'morally' correct ways. So, a more profound understanding of agency may help us to become better moral agents?

Gardiner (2006) argues that the problems around acting morally with regard to carbon consumption and climate change arise from the dispersion of causes and effects, and the fragmentation of agency. Thus, it becomes possible to not take ownership of the consequences of our actions—as they either came before or came from somewhere else. Here agency is revealed to be a concept that is directly linked to individual consciousness (and conscience) and action. But agency might also be used to refer to the collective, if individuals are prepared to take ownership of other peoples' actions and make moral choices and change behaviour in response. It is the apparent refusal to take responsibility for the actions of others (an expression of individual agency) that enables people to continue to fly in the face of climate change. It is individualized agency which denies responsibility for the past and current actions of others and minimizes the "impact" their action will have on the now and the future.

We might hear for example somebody say "Well I am not responsible for the damage caused during industrialization and I am not rich and famous and do not fly around the world every-day, I am taking one trip to Fiji." Thus, my agency is not the primary or original cause of the problem and my contribution is so minor that it remains "not my fault" and further why should I be penalized because of the actions of others?

Inconsequentialism: My Flight Will Make No Difference

The diffusion or abdication of responsibility, revealed by travellers who argue that that their emissions from flying will 'make no difference' is referred to as inconsequentialism (Sandberg, 2011). "If the actions I perform as an individual only have an inconsequential effect on climate change, then it cannot be wrong from me to perform that action" (Sandberg, 2011: 229). Sandberg (2011: 232) discusses a hypothetical flight from Stockholm to Paris return, producing 35 tonnes of CO_2,

> ... the choices of a single individual very seldom influence whether a particular flight takes place or not i.e. whether there will be a flight from Stockholm to Paris on any given day will not depend on whether *I* go on that flight ... my behaviour actually has *no* marginal effect here. Just as much carbon dioxide will be emitted irrespective of whether I go to Paris.

Sandberg notes the appeal of this (lack of) marginal effects argument but that intuitively we know that there is something wrong with the inconsequentialist position, a position that has been described as 'ethical solipsism' (Kutz, 2000 cited in Sandberg, 2011) where individual action is also 'imperceptible harm' (Parfit, 1984 cited in Sandberg, 2011).[1]

---

1   Parfit (1984, cited in Sandberg, 2011) asks us to consider a case in which a thousand torturers have a thousand victims. The torturers have an ingenious way of avoiding individual responsibility. Rather than torturing one victim each, each torturer presses a

While the inconsequentialism argument may be morally correct, it fails if we consider increased risk as harm and/or if "my flying causes others to fly, more often, when I could have done something else instead to make others stop flying" (Sandberg, 2011: 247). The use of the inconsequentialism argument for environmental inaction displays what Sandberg (2011: 248) believes to be a "reproachable character trait." Aristotelian virtue ethics takes virtue and vice to be at least as basic as moral duty and that the issue of what character traits we *ought* to have is morally important. Sandberg (2011: 248) also argues that we are all under a *collective* obligation to reduce carbon emissions, and that "While it may not typically be [morally] wrong of me to drive or fly, then, it may be wrong for *us* to do so ..."

So if this is the case, why does the collective obligation get lost? What agency determines this? We need to consider that agency is shaped by the broader social and political environment within which choices are being made. The industry that supports 'flight' (Bandura's 'huge cast of moral disengagers' (2007)) is compelling and acts in the service of global capitalism. All of the marketing that surrounds this part of the industry stresses individual agency, freedom, choice, power, empowerment—the key elements of what makes a successful individual within a neoliberal frame. We observe a morality born of neoliberalism, which has led to the rise of the individual and the demise of communalism or collective social responsibility.

Making Individuals Act in the Interests of All and Others

That climate change is a moral issue with harmful consequences is beyond doubt. That flying and climate change are clearly interlinked is also beyond doubt. That we (all human individuals) have a collective moral obligation to do something about our flying and thus its contribution to climate change is, however, challenging in the least. Caney (2005) argues for an individualist approach (c.f. collective) to the issue of responsibility for climate change, while Sandberg (2011) notes our collective responsibility. Ironically, it is our ability to separate in this way, the individual on the one hand and the collective on the other that enables moral abdication. Yet, as Harris (2008) points out, international negotiations and efforts with respect to climate change have 'failed'. Indeed, this could be said to particularly apply to touristic aviation, where our collective heads have been in the collective sand (because of the collective benefits of capitalism). Thus, arguably,

---

button which inflicts only a thousandth of some electrical current on all of the victims. The result is that all one thousand of the victims feel severe pain but none of the torturers makes any victims' pain perceptibly worse (2011: 233). Parfit asks if this an acceptable way of avoiding moral responsibility? He concludes that inflicting a thousandth severe pain on a thousand victims is morally equivalent to inflicting sever pain on one victim directly (in Sandberg, 2011: 233).

there is a clear need to focus on our individual responsibilities, but bearing in mind that maybe this will only work (to address carbon-related behaviour) if we remarry the individual to the collective and that punitive measures might be the only way to realize this.

In the travelling public, research points to confusion over whose responsibility it is. Asthana and McKie's (2005 cited in Holden, 2009: 382) research with the public revealed the perspective that "Flights are so unrealistically cheap. It makes it difficult for people to say no to them. The government should take that decision away from people" (presumably through increased taxation and charges). The role of low cost carriers has been cited as contributing to this phenomenon (e.g. Lovelock and Lovelock, 2013). In support of this position i.e. that governments should regulate and legislate to save us from ourselves and our base desires to engage in such activities as flying, governments *have* identified harm from *other* activities (e.g. smoking, drinking alcohol) and have attempted to remove that choice for consumers, or at least reduce demand—e.g. through aggressive taxes on tobacco and alcohol. Yet, as noted above, higher taxes on flights are rejected by would be travellers (just as they are by drinkers and smokers), even if these are clearly focused on ameliorating the impacts of climate change. So, failing this approach, can we rely upon the suppliers of this evil drug, travelling, to take action to reduce our consumption? Mark Ellingham, founder of the *Rough Guides* series of travel guides compares the tourism industry (again, Bandura's 'huge cast of moral disengagers') to the tobacco industry, in its denial of its true impact, particularly the effects carbon emissions from flying are having on global warming (in Barkham, 2006 cited in Holden, 2009: 382). However, just as we haven't seen the tobacco industry exactly cosying up to governments and health agencies in trying to reduce the consumption of tobacco, how likely is it that we will see airlines rushing to warn the public about the dangers of consuming airline travel? While the moral failure of big business and government to address flying's contribution to climate change is inexcusable, their turpitude does lead us back to the individual.

Solutions? The Morality of Carbon Offsetting and Rationing

Having established that it may be immoral to fly, are there any actions that individuals can take to correct the 'moral balance sheet'? Luckily, the airlines have offered us a salve for our (and their?) moral consciousnesses—carbon offsetting. I am happily ensconced in my window seat, far above those fading atolls and their inhabitants (soon to vanish off our maps ...), do I have any right to feel morally superior to the passenger seated beside me? I have paid my carbon offsetting and she hasn't! Based upon consequentialist arguments, the consequences of emitting and offsetting are the same as not emitting—thus the two are morally equivalent (Hyams and Fawcett, 2013). But this raises the bigger question of whether the assessment of what is a moral action (or not) should involve more than just a consideration of consequences i.e. whether issues of rights, justice, fairness and duty come into play? And of course we need to bear in mind that whether or not we offset our flights, both actions are morally worse than not flying (emitting) in the first place!

The morality of offsetting is complex and needs to take into account a range of factors. A utilitarian argument for example (see Dhanda and Hartman, 2011) would need to consider the value of human or other lives lost, the land permanently degraded, and the air and water polluted etc. Added to this is the debate about the credibility of many offsetting schemes, Harvey and Fidler (2007: n.p.) arguing that there are "widespread instances of people and organizations buying worthless credits that do not yield any reductions in carbon emissions." Dhanda and Hartman (2011: 136) further warn that

> As long as the purchaser of carbon credits remains naïve about the process, uniformed about standards, confused by conflicting standards and overwhelmed by choice, she or he shall not fully comprehend the eventual consequences of their actions (on themselves or on other stakeholders).

Given the arguable morality and dodgy outcomes of offsetting, and considering that it is highly unlikely that tourism's air travel emissions will be addressed through individual choice and consequent behavioural change (there is no indication from a range of studies [e.g. Becken, 2007; Cohen and Higham, 2011; Cohen et al., 2011] that individuals are prepared to modify their flying behaviours), what options does this leave us? Randles and Mander (2009) believe that 'deep interventions' such as formal regulation and fiscal means may be necessary—a sort of 'enforced morality'.

Rationing is an approach that has been advocated, based upon the premise that every person shares in a common property right to the Earth's atmosphere. This is the moral basis for the claim that every person has an equal entitlement to emit CO_2 and that "emissions beyond one's share of the threshold violate the natural property rights of humanity, whose members own the atmosphere in common" (Moellendorf, 2011: 107). While we can't expect rationing to be wildly popular with the travelling public, such procedures have been put in place before, e.g. during and after WWII, when fuel was rationed. Some even envisage a future where "... countries might decide that [global climate change] is important enough to demand sacrifices from all their citizens, even rich ones, and strictly limit the number of allowable discretionary flights per person" (Cafaro, 2011: 203). However, taking this a step further, others advocate for a tradable system of Personal Carbon Allowances (e.g. Hyams, 2009)—the morality of neoliberalism strikes again; those who can afford to pay, can pollute.

It is encouraging, though, to observe the rise of voluntary citizen action to reduce emissions. Groups known as CRAGs (Carbon Rationing Action Groups) have emerged in some countries (e.g. in the UK, USA and Canada), where members pledge to one another to live low carbon lives (Krakoff, 2011). Such lives, however, would largely preclude air travel because of the huge carbon sacrifices that would have to be made in other spheres of life.

Conclusions

Transportation (and by implication travel) choices are moral choices, suitably captured in the campaign title of the Evangelical Climate Initiative "What would Jesus drive?" (Krakoff, 2011). And while we all would like to be seen as moral, virtuous beings (like Jesus!), this is somewhat easier at the abstract level (Bandura, 1999). In reality, a range of complicating factors come together around the climate change problem, and likewise the flying problem, as illustrated by Gardiner's (2006) 'perfect moral storm'. A further complication is that little moral guidance is advanced by society as a whole: as Jamieson (2010: 438) points out "Although all human societies have moral rules about food and sex [etc], none has a moral rule about atmospheric chemistry."

These factors and the liminal state in which travel is anticipated and enacted, make it more difficult for us to behave morally around the issue of holiday flying. Or, conversely, selective moral disengagement (Bandura, 2007) around the issue is so much easier. By flying, the modern tourist is simply utilizing "... the [tourism] infrastructure which has subjected time and space to ecologically destructive forms of control in order to enjoy elements of the liminal experience of the pre-modern pilgrim" (Northcott, 2007: 227). While liminality may 'confuse' morality, however, there may be limitations to the extent that we can draw upon liminality as an alibi for ecologically and socially destructive behaviours such as flying.

A similar question arises around the issue of agency. We have identified issues around agency—in terms of individuals developing 'carbon capability'—their cognitive and behavioural capability to make, ultimately, what are moral decisions around their carbon use. While arguments around the complexity of (carbon-climate) cause and effect, and its fragmenting and compromising impact upon agency, are understandable ... I can't help but feel that such questions around agency may be side stepping personal moral responsibility. I suspect that this is only the case if we consider the individual to be outside of the collective. Of course, it is not. And it is only when we conceptualize the individual and society, the individual and the collective as separate entities that we can morally disengage and not take responsibility for our personal actions around climate change and touristic flying.

Ultimately, the trouble with morality is that "... it opposes the regular inclinations, and in an uncompromising way, without offering anything in return" (Gardiner, 2011: 306). Deciding to be a conscientious moral agent and turning down the next opportunity of jetting away to Majorca may at best only offer a sense of satisfaction that you are doing the 'right' thing—that you are indeed behaving morally. This internal reward—being a virtuous person—is for some people, reward enough. Failing that, I guess it's nice to feel that you're doing your bit to look after the Earth ... and those on the atolls far below.

References

Bandura, A. (1999). Moral Disengagement in the Perpetration of Inhumanities. *Personality and Social Psychology Review*, 3(3), 193–209.

Bandura, A. (2007). Impeding Ecological Sustainability through Selective Moral Disengagement. *International Journal of Innovation and Sustainable Development*, 2(1), 8–35.

Barkham, P. (2006). Oops, We Helped Ruin the Planet. *The Guardian*, June 2, 2013, p. 6.

Becken, S. (2007). Tourists' Perception of International Air Travel's Impact on the Global Climate and Potential Climate Change Policies. *Journal of Sustainable Tourism*, 15(4), 351–368.

Butler, C. (2010). Morality and Climate Change: Is Leaving Your TV on Standby a Risky Behaviour? *Environmental Values*, 19(2), 169–192.

Cafaro, P. (2011). *Beyond Business as Usual: Alternative Wedges to Avoid Catastrophic Climate Change and Create Sustainable Societies*. In D. G. Arnold (ed.), *The Ethics of Global Climate Change*, pp. 192–215. Cambridge: Cambridge University Press.

Cafaro, P. (2013). Reducing Consumption to Avert Catastrophic Global Climate Change: The Case of Aviation. *Natural Science*, 5(1A), pp. 99–105. DOI: 10.4236/ns.2013.51A016.

Caney, S. (2005). Cosmopolitan Justice, Responsibility, and Global Climate Change. *Leiden Journal of International Law*, 18(4), 747–775.

Cohen, S. A., and Higham, J. E. S. (2011). Eyes Wide Shut? UK Consumer Perceptions on Aviation Climate Impacts and Travel Decisions to New Zealand. *Current Issues in Tourism*, 14(4), 232–235.

Cohen, S., Higham, J., and Cavaliere, C. (2011). Binge Flying: Behavioural Addiction and Climate Change. *Annals of Tourism Research*, 38(3), 1070–1089.

Cunha, M. P. E., and Cabral-Cardoso, C. (2006). Shades of Gray: A Liminal Interpretation of Organizational Legality–Illegality. *International Public Management Journal*, 9(3), 209–225.

Dhanda, K. K., and Hartman, L. P. (2011). The Ethics of Carbon Neutrality: A Critical Examination of Voluntary Carbon Offset Providers. *Journal of Business Ethics*, 100(1), 119–149.

Gardiner, S. M. (2006). A Perfect Moral Storm: Climate Change, Intergenerational Ethics and the Problem of Moral Corruption. *Environmental Values*, 15(3), 397–413.

Gardiner, S. M. (2011). *A Perfect Moral Storm: The Ethical Tragedy of Climate Change*. Oxford: Oxford University Press.

Gössling, S. (2013). Climate Change and Tourism Development. In B. Lovelock and K. M. Lovelock, *The Ethics of Tourism: Critical and Applied Perspectives*, pp. 258–261. London: Routledge.

Hall, C. M., Scott, D., and Gössling, S. (2009). Tourism, Development and Climate Change. In C. D'Mello, S. Minninger, and J. McKeown (eds.), *Disaster Prevention in Tourism—Climate Justice and Tourism*, pp. 136–161. Chiang Mai: Ecumenical Coalition on Tourism and German Church Development Service (EED).

Harris, P. G. (2008). Climate Change and Global Citizenship. *Law & Policy*, 30(4), 481–501.

Harvey, F., and Fiddler, S. (2007). Industry Caught in Carbon 'Smokescreen'. *Financial Times*, April 25, 2007.

Holden, A. (2009). The Environment–Tourism Nexus: Influence of Market Ethics. *Annals of Tourism Research*, 36(3), 373–389.

Hyams, K. (2009). A Just Response to Climate Change: Personal Carbon Allowances and the Normal-functioning Approach. *The Journal of Social Philosophy*, 40(2), 237–256.

Hyams, K., and Fawcett, T. (2013). The Ethics of Carbon Offsetting. *WIREs Climate Change*, 4, 91–98. DOI: 10.1002/wcc.207.

Jamieson, D. (1991). The Epistemology of Climate Change: Some Morals for Managers. *Society and Natural Resources*, 4(4), 319–329.

Jamieson, D. (2006). An American Paradox. *Climatic Change*, 77(1–2), 97–102.

Jamieson, D. (2010). Climate Change, Responsibility, and Justice. *Science and Engineering Ethics*, 16(3), 431–445.

Krakoff, S. (2011). Parenting the Planet. In D. G. Arnold (ed.), *The Ethics of Global Climate Change*, pp. 145–169. Cambridge: Cambridge University Press.

Leiserowitz, A., Maibach, E., Roser-Renouf, C., Feinberg, G., and Howe, P. (2012). *Climate Change in the American Mind: Americans' Global Warming Beliefs and Attitudes in September 2012*. Yale University and George Mason University. New Haven, CT: Yale Project on Climate Change Communication. http://environment.yale.edu/climate/files/Climate-Beliefs-September-2012.pdf.

Lovelock, B., and Lovelock, K. M. (2013). *The Ethics of Tourism: Critical and Applied Perspectives*. London: Routledge.

Lowell, J. (2012). Managers and Moral Dissonance: Self Justification as a Big Threat to Ethical Management? *Journal of Business Ethics*, 105(1), 17–25.

Moellendorf, D. (2011). Common Atmospheric Ownership and Equal Emissions. In D. G. Arnold (ed.), *The Ethics of Global Climate Change*, pp. 104–123. Cambridge: Cambridge University Press.

Monbiot, G. (2006). We are All Killers until We Stop Flying. *The Guardian*, February 28, 2006. http://www.monbiot.com/2006/02/28/we-are-all-killers/ (accessed 20/9/2013).

Northcott, M. S. (2007). *A Moral Climate: The Ethics of Global Warming*. London: Darton, Longman and Todd.

Preston-Whyte, R. (2004). The Beach as a Liminal Space. In A. Lew, C. M. Hall, and A. M. Williams (eds.), *The Blackwell's Tourism Companion*, pp. 249–259. Oxford: Blackwell.

Pritchard, A., and Morgan, N. (2006). Hotel Babylon? Exploring Hotels as Liminal Sites of Transition and Transgression. *Tourism Management*, 27(5), 762–772.

Rachels, J., and Rachels, S. (2010). *The Elements of Modern Philosophy*. New York: McGraw-Hill.

Randles, S., and Mander, S. (2009). Practice(s) and Ratchet(s): A Sociological Examination of Frequent Flying. In S. Gössling and P. Upham (eds.), *Climate Change and Aviation Issues, Challenges and Solutions*, pp. 245–271. London: Earthscan.

Ryan, C., and Kinder, R. (1996). Sex, Tourism and Sex Tourism: Fulfilling Similar Needs? *Tourism Management*, 17(7), 507–518.

Sandberg, J. (2011). "*My* Emissions make No Difference": Climate Change and the Argument from Inconsequentialism. *Environmental Ethics* 33(3), 229–248.

Sunday Star Times (2013). CO_2 *Levels Head into Unknown Territory*, May 12, 2013, p. 3.

Turner, V. (1974). *Dramas, Fields and Metaphors*. New York: Cornell University Press.

Urry, J. (2002). Mobility and Proximity. *Sociology*, 36(2), 255–277.

Urry, J. (2011). *Climate Change and Society*. Cambridge: Polity Press.

Urry, J. (2012). Social Networks, Mobile Lives and Social Inequalities. *Journal of Transport Geography*, 21, 24–30.

Whitmarsh, L., Seyfang, G., and O'Neill, S. (2011). Public Engagement with Carbon and Climate Change: To What extent is the Public 'Carbon Capable'? *Global Environmental Change*, 21(1), 56–65.

Yarnal, C. M., and Kerstetter, D. (2005). Casting Off: An Exploration of Cruise Ship Space, Group Tour Behaviour, and Social Interaction. *Journal of Travel Research*, 43(4), 368–379.

Chapter 12

A Plutonium Tourism Ode:
The Rocky Flats Cold War Museum

Lindsey A. Freeman

I begin your chant, openmouthed exhaling into spacious
sky over silent mills at Hanford, Savannah River,
Rocky Flats, Pantex, Burlington, Albuquerque
I yell thru Washington, South Carolina, Colorado,
Texas, Iowa, New Mexico,
Where nuclear reactors create a new Thing under the
Sun, where Rockwell war-plants fabricate this death
stuff trigger in nitrogen baths ...

Allen Ginsberg, "Plutonian Ode," 1978[1]

Introduction

Howled through the verses of "Plutonian Ode," a poem written by Allen Ginsberg in 1978 which begins this chapter is a cartography of the Cold War landscape of the United States of America.[2] In the post-nuclear era, much of the atomic geography produced in the twentieth century is in danger of being forgotten. The clandestine network of nuclear laboratories and factories of the last century often remain unseen or even unimaginable, much like radiation itself. Outside of their immediate geographical nexuses, nuclear sites are often amnesic spaces, blind spots and black outs in the national collective memory. Ginsberg's (1978) poem reminds us that nuclear industries were sited in and helped to build real communities; they did not exist in de-populated vacuums. The diverse ways in which these communities were (and are still being) affected by the Manhattan Project, the Cold War, and the nuclear industries that followed are still being discovered, uncovered, and debated.

---

1   In *Collected Poems 1947–1997* by Allen Ginsberg. Copyright © 2006 by The Allen Ginsberg Trust. Courtesy of HarperCollins Publishers and The Estate of Allen Ginsberg.

2   In 1978 when Ginsberg wrote this poem, he had been spending some time protesting by sitting on the railroad tracks that led into the Rocky Flats plant, where he was arrested for civil disobedience. See: Allen Ginsberg, *Plutonian Ode and Other Poems [1977–1980]* (San Francisco: City Lights, 2001).

One way that the historical legacy of the nuclear twentieth century is being presented and experienced is through the emergent practice of nuclear tourism. Rocky Flats, the site of one of the key nuclear nodes of the Atomic Age, located just sixteen miles northwest of Denver, Colorado, and the site of a new Cold War museum, is a prime example of both a space in danger of forgetting its nuclear complexity and a new site of nuclear tourism. For the duration of the twentieth century's chilly battle of nuclear proliferation (1952–1989), the plant churned out more than 60,000 plutonium pits for nuclear weapons, creating mountains of triggers for the United States' nuclear arsenal.[3] Filled with fissionable plutonium, the triggers were the vital centers, the exploding hearts, of the United States' nuclear and thermonuclear bombs; weapons infinitely more powerful than those used against Hiroshima and Nagasaki.

Rocky Flats was a sprawling industrial complex, almost a city unto itself. Its 800 structures and buildings spanned out across 6,551 acres of land, which if viewed from the air resembled the shape of a huge grenade, an appropriate contour for a place dedicated to the policy of Mutual Assured Destruction.[4] It is hard to fathom that such a huge place, both in terms of actual geographic space and of importance to the geo-political landscape of the last century, could be forgotten. Language plays a role here. And memory. After the plant was closed in 1992, a massive cleanup effort was enacted and the area was renamed Rocky Flats Environmental Technology Site. Then, it was renamed again, most remarkably, Rocky Flats Wildlife Refuge. Plutonium-239, the flavor of the element used in the triggers, has a half-life of 24,360 years, meaning that it emits radioactivity for 240,000 years.[5] The half-life of human memory is much, much shorter.

While the actual site of Rocky Flats is being erased and buried, or in the official language of the Department of Energy, 'decontaminated and decommissioned,' The Rocky Flats Cold War Museum is being constructed and curated. Funded in part by a congressional appropriation of $492,000, which was secured by then-senator Wayne Allardin in 2007 and other anonymous donations and volunteer labor, the museum has rented space, collected oral histories and assembled material objects

---

3   Rocky Flats received plutonium in the form of 'buttons' taken from spent fuel rods from the Hanford Nuclear Reservation in Washington State and the Savannah River Site in South Carolina. At Rocky Flats these buttons where then transformed into 'triggers,' which power nuclear warheads. The triggers then travelled by trucks along the highway to the Pantex nuclear weapons facility in Amarillo, Texas, where the weapons were assembled and finished.

4   Mutual Assured Destruction (MAD) is a military strategy and policy of national security, which uses the rhetoric of deterrence by threat of retaliation; wherein if one side made an attack, both sides would be completely obliterated, when the other side answered. This stance was employed by the United States and the USSR throughout the Cold War.

5   As one popular Rocky Flats protest song goes: "We'll all be glowing for a quarter of a million years." Anne Waldman, "Warring God Charnel Ground (Rocky Flats Chronicles)," *Vow to Poetry* (Saint Paul: Coffee House Press, 2001): 232.

from the nation's nuclear industry preservationists. The space will house artifacts donated from large bureaucratic offices, such as the Department of Energy, as well as memorabilia from the attics of individual Rocky Flats employees and anti-nuclear activists. Mothballed plutonium glove-boxes, dusty Geiger counters, and scribbled lines of anarchist poetry on yellowed paper will get a chance to live again through nuclear curation.

The museum, which is scheduled to open in 2013, has the stated agenda to address the multifaceted legacy of the nuclear factory: to "present all of the complex story of the Rocky Flats nuclear weapons plant through the voices of those who were directly involved—workers, protestors, scientists, community leaders, regulators, artists, and others" (Rocky Flats Cold War Museum Press Release, 31 August 2012). If Rocky Flats is able to pull this off it will be the first nuclear museum and the first site of nuclear tourism to do so. In the last several decades, not only Rocky Flats, but Cold War bunkers, former missile silos, sites of atomic testing, as well as the factories and laboratories of the Manhattan Project, have all become sites of interest for tourists (see for example: Freeman, 2010, 2013; Hodge and Weinberger, 2008; Vanderbilt, 2002).

At the intersection of tourism and history, these spaces, while important in battling the full erasure of atomic memory, bring their own sets of problems and challenges to ethical sightseeing and critical tourism.[6] In sites of nuclear tourism, the tensions between nuclear history and atomic nostalgia, anti-nuclear protest (which is often absent from these spaces) and patriotism can overlap to such a degree that they threaten to produce a muddled space, a cacophony of competing voices where nothing can be heard. As the United States continues to wrestle with its nuclear past, present, and future, nuclear touristic spaces should invite ethical, moral, and environmental concerns into their construction and reception. Thus far, nuclear museums have tended towards nationalism and scientism, favoring the rhetoric of the US military and industrial science (Freeman, 2010; Taylor, 2010; Wray, 2006; Zolberg, 1998). The Rocky Flats Cold War Museum promises a break in this celebratory stream. This chapter examines how sites of nuclear tourism, in general, and the

---

6   Critical tourism should be understood here as social practice where tourists enter sites with knowledge of their constructedness and with historical knowledge. The critical tourist is able to recognize that there is often a dissonance between what is displayed and narrated and what has been hidden from view. Critical tourism is a leisure practice, but should also be understood as a method of social inquiry, employed with the goal of recognizing, questioning, and exhuming the power dynamics behind touristic displays. Critical tourism was first described by Lucy R. Lippard in *On the Beaten Track: Tourism, Art, and Place* (New York: New Press, 1999). In this chapter my position as a researcher is also influenced by Dean MacCannell's figure of the 'tourist-ethnographer' as described in *The Tourist: A New Theory of the Leisure Class* (Berkeley, CA: University of California Press, 1999). I have also outlined this position further in, *Longing for the Bomb: Atomic Nostalgia in Post-Nuclear Landscape*. Forthcoming in 2014 from The University of North Carolina Press.

Rocky Flats Cold War Museum, in particular, struggle to define and interpret the American nuclear past, both in the local, as well as in the national and international contexts of the Cold War and beyond.

Rocky Flats During the Cold War (1952–1989)

On 23 March 1951, the *Denver Post* ran the following enthusiastic headline: "There's Good News Today. U.S. to Build $45 Million A-Plant Near Denver."[7] Even as the press trumpeted the benefits to the region in economic terms, Rocky Flats was beset with a lot of environmental challenges from the start. Initially, the Atomic Energy Commission (AEC) was concerned that the plant was located too close to Denver.[8] After the wind flow patterns were assessed, the AEC's fears were alleviated. This is because when the wind readings were taken, they were not measured at the Rocky Flats site, but rather twenty miles away at Denver's Stapleton Airport, where the prevailing winds arrive from the south (Lamm-Wirth Task Force on Rocky Flats, 1975, pp. 32–35). The winds from Rocky Flats typically blow east-southeast, right towards the center of metropolitan Denver. In addition, the powerful seasonal Chinook winds, which can gust up to 140 miles per hour, were not taken into consideration. It is not uncommon for these winds to ravish the Rocky Flats area, to snap telephone poles in half and flip over cars, effectively transforming Volkswagens into frustrated beetles with their wheels spinning uselessly in the air.

Beyond the initial wind miscalculation, operations at Rocky Flats were not always above board. Among the most egregious violations were two major fires where the seriousness of the danger of the events where kept secret from the public. The first blaze occurred in 1957, when a fire ignited in a processing line. There was a brief mention of the fire in an un-bylined article in the *Denver Post*, but no detailed report was ever filed and no journalist followed up after the initial story ran. Most remarkably the article did not mention that the fire started in a *plutonium* processing line (for more see Ackland, 2009, p. 257). The second fire, the so-called 'Mother's Day Fire of 1969' is now commonly referred to as 'The day we almost lost Denver.'[9] In addition to the fires, there were many other everyday practices at

---

7   In the early days, Rocky Flats was under the auspices of the Atomic Energy Commission (AEC), followed by the Department of Energy (DOE), after its creation in 1976. Day-to-day operations were run by a series of corporate contactors, first, Dow Chemical (1952–1975), then Rockwell International (1975–1992), and lastly, EG and G, a company that had its roots in the Manhattan Project.

8   It should be noted here that there is always a choice about which communities should be downwind, after all the wind has to blow somewhere. And when it blows past a nuclear weapons plant, it carries toxic substances with it.

9   For a detailed timeline of the fire, including oral histories from Rocky Flats workers and fire fighters who battled the plutonium fire, visit journalism professor Len Ackland's

the plant that were hazardous to workers, including the processing methods and storage practices of waste products. For example, plutonium in the air ducts and leaking barrels of radioactive waste were unacknowledged threats.

The plant was shuttered in 1989, after an FBI and EPA raid, code named "Operation Desert Glow," found multiple violations of environmental laws. At the time of the raid, Rocky Flats was under the control of the Department of Energy. This is the only instance in the history of the United States, where one federal agency conducted a raid on another federal agency. After the FBI's investigation, plutonium was found lodged in the ventilation ducts at the plant. Enough plutonium, in fact, that a 'criticality' episode or a spontaneous nuclear chain reaction was possible. After years of controversy surrounding the safety of the plant, in January of 1992, the DOE officially announced the plant would stop producing plutonium and began the lengthy process of decommissioning and decontamination of the site. In 1995, a Superfund cleanup began. In 2001, Congress passed the National Rocky Flats Wildlife Refuge Act, a stroke of legislation that would turn the site into a nature preserve—from Superfund site to Super fun site. Since 2007, the refuge has been under the stewardship of the U.S. Fish and Wildlife Service. At the time of the writing of this chapter the site is still deemed unsafe for human visitation, but is home to large populations of white deer, elk, and the endangered Preble's meadow jumping mouse, which has become a kind of mascot to the area.[10]

Filling all those warheads with plutonium hearts was messy business, leaving behind a horrific toxic landscape, invisible under the grassy Colorado mesa. Today, active debates about what to do with the land in the near proximity of Rocky Flats and what to do about the legacy of the plant divide the community. One attempt to discuss this history is being undertaken by the DOE's Office of Legacy Management, which unsurprisingly puts a very positive spin on Rocky Flats' role in the Cold War. Another is through the Rocky Flats Cold War Museum, which is still forming its message.

The Museum in the Making

Driving into the section of town where the up-and-coming museum will be located, I immediately notice the area's decidedly hometown feel. The Rocky Flats Cold War Museum is located in an old post office in a historic section of town, where visible from its door is a water tower proclaiming 'Olde Town Arvada'. This quaint

---

Rocky Flats Virtual Museum, www.colorado.edu/journalism/cej/exhibit/1969fire01-08. html; For a more in-depth history of the plant itself see: Ackland's *Making a Real Killing: Rocky Flats and the Nuclear West* (Albuquerque: University of New Mexico Press, 1999).

10   The Preble's meadow jumping mouse (Zapus hudsonius preblei) is an incredible tiny rodent that is capable of jumping three feet in the air. The mouse, which is currently listed under the Endangered Species Act, is endemic to the upland habitats of Colorado and Wyoming and is found nowhere else in the world.

scene, proudly rustic, can allow us to imagine what Arvada might have been like decades before Rocky Flats; before a gigantic town-sized factory complex was built to churn out plutonium triggers at a fevered pace for the Cold War weapon store.

Inside the developing museum dedicated to the dominant geo-political conflict of the twentieth century, an opposite, modern aesthetic is developing. Specimens of the hulking machinery used in the nuclear business occupy the corners and hug the walls, like shy middle schoolers at a dance; while, informational leaflets rest on every available surface, awaiting organization and display; and towards the door (exit through the gift shop) there is a nascent atomic store, which is already filled with nuclear texts and objects that lie in wait as future souvenirs. Among the objects are: glow-in-the dark cups, a jar of the most nuclear of all candies the cinnamon flavored Atomic Fireballs, buttons that whine: "I Think I'm Having a Melt Down," and a deck of unusual, informational cards that I cannot resist purchasing—"Repository: A typological guide to America's Ephemeral Nuclear Infrastructure"—that tell the story of US nuclear waste.[11]

The museum's director Connie Bogaard, an affable and sophisticated woman from The Netherlands with a background in museum creation and aesthetics working on her PhD, was kind enough to open up the museum for myself and the two colleagues I managed to drag along with me on a sunny summer Saturday afternoon. Bogaard explained in detail the plans for the museum, which will be organized spatially into six 'zones': (1) secrecy and security; (2) pride and protest; (3) decommission and decontamination; (4) half-life; (5) the hot zone; and (6) a potential last zone in the making that will include, in the words of the director "the debate of nukes in the world today." This last zone, being the most controversial might be placed in a separate room, where museum officials will have a "sit down with visitors." There is critical potential in this special room, but also risk. How this will be handled and who will dole out the information remains to be seen. The organization of these zones is a good reminder that museums and historical sites are, as Lippard (1999, p. 119) argues, "the battlegrounds in a life-and-death struggle between memory, denial, and repression." They play an intrinsic role in what the public sees and consumes with respect to nuclear history.

Nuclear Tourism: Historically, Presently

Nuclear tourism began in 1949 with the opening of the very first museum dedicated to the atom, The American Museum of Atomic Energy in the Manhattan Project city of Oak Ridge, Tennessee.[12] By the 1950s, nuclear tourism had reached a fevered pitch as visitors flocked to Las Vegas, not only to gamble, carouse, and

---

11 "Repository" is a project of Smudge Studio, 2012. For more see: www. smudgestudio.org.

12 The museum is now called the American Museum of Science and Energy.

ogle showgirls, but also to see mushroom clouds dance across the horizon in the nearby Nevada Test Site. The city of Las Vegas had a vigorous advertising campaign, rendering the viewing of a nuclear blast, as just one more glitzy display on offer, one more spectacular event to see in the sensational desert. Highrollers, lowrollers, lounge singers, cigarette girls, call girls, and vacationers of all stripes would stay up all night, often convening on the rooftops of hotels, drinking specialty themed atomic cocktails and watching the explosions. Since 1992, there has been a moratorium on testing, and it is the Cold War and its battered landscape, the after-effects, rather than the blasts themselves that have become tourist attractions.

In its early days, nuclear tourism was utopian, future oriented and sexy. By contrast, post-millennial nuclear tourism tends to be nostalgic or doom-tinged; either a celebration of an expired dream of a nuclear future we never quite reached, or an exhibition space of the Cassandra Complex, illustrating a dark future where we drown in our own nuclear waste. In the United States, sites of nuclear tourism have tended to favor the former. Elsewhere, such as the Chernobyl site in Ukraine, spaces of nuclear tourism have leaned more towards the later.

Both dark and nostalgic nuclear tourism have much in common with the practice of gazing at rusted industrial sites and failed industrial projects, sometimes called 'ruin porn.' This is fitting because after all, the nuclear industries, like many other modern industrial projects, have fallen on hard times. On the one hand, nuclear tourism offers a look at the hubris of nuclear industries, irradiated and in states of halted decay; it offers material reminders of what's left of atomic utopian dreams after the melt down and the fallout. On the other hand, sites of nuclear tourism, especially museums, often attempt to herald the 'success' of the Cold War. They can be seen as efforts to conjure a pastness of a previous formidable enemy, they are halls of patriotic and anti-Communist sentiment. Without exception, every American nuclear museum—the National Museum of Nuclear Science and History, the Atomic Testing Museum, the American Museum of Science and Technology, the Bradbury Science Museum, etc. has a display of nuclear workers decked out in full protective gear, looking like super heroes from a strange-seeming future. And like all spaces of nationalism, they justify and celebrate sacrifice to the nation; in this case any ill effects of radiation or other maladies caused by working as a Cold Warrior are seen as necessary and heroic. Here, the laboratory and the factory are displayed as surrogates for the battlefield.

The nuclear museums that have emerged in the decline of the Atomic Age are dominated by the themes of danger, secrecy, and atomic nostalgia. The rhetoric at these sites offers an experience similar to what an amusement park gives us, a chance to feel afraid, to be close to danger, but also to feel safe—we have faith that the apparatuses that we are enclosed in, the harness of an upside-down rollercoaster or the defense industry of the US has us—that ultimately we are secure. In these spaces, it is other countries, such as North Korea and Iran, who are shown as dangerous.

Nuclear sites are immensely productive spaces for creating imaginaries; they have an aura, a glow, all their own. Building on Walter Benjamin's argument that modernity brings with it the decline of the auratic, the sociologist John Urry argues that traditionally museums have been "premised upon the aura of the authentic historical artifact," but that with postmodernism there has been a shift from auratic display to nostalgic display (Benjamin, 2003; Urry, 2002; Edgar, 1987). In the nuclear context, aura and nostalgia are not oppositional but powerfully constitutive. In the Rocky Flats Cold War Museum, there is a glove-box on display, like one that nuclear plant workers used to handle plutonium and other toxic substances. I placed my arms inside. Even though I was told that this was not an actual Rocky Flats glove-box because of the worry over contamination, when I tucked my limbs into the thick rubber gloves I had a Karen Silkwood moment.[13] I tried (with little success I might add) to move small pegs around, all the while nervously sweating with Allen Ginsberg's (1978) line, "my voice resounds through robot glove boxes," repeating on loop in my head. It was a moment of nuclear vertigo. It was impossible not to feel fear of contamination, atomic anxiety, and the aura of the nuclear.

While it may seem strange to want to spend one's leisure time placing hands inside gloves built to handle some of the most toxic substances in the world, as Dean MacCannell (1999, p. 203) has pointed out "most things that are now attractions did not start out that way ... It is the 'you have got to see this,' or 'taste this,' or 'feel this' that is the originary moment in the touristic relation." In the context of the nuclear museum, this creates a "fetish of the work of others," which transforms nuclear labor, much of it mundane, into a spectacle to be consumed by others (MacCannell, 1999, p. 6.) You've got to put your arms into the glovebox! Imagine what its like to form a plutonium trigger!

Nuclear tourism engages not only with individual anxieties, but also with shared fears, collective pride, and the furtive history of former secret production regimes. This is part of its appeal. The anthropologist Hugh Gusterson (2004, p. 24) suggests that nuclear tourism "offers the promise of a glimpse into the sublime and the forbidden." Through visiting these sites, tourists encounter narratives of workers who were entrusted with matters of national security, sometimes with full knowledge of what they were doing, sometimes not. Typically, what the nuclear tourist confronts is an incomplete archive of information, blocked by state secrets, patriotism, and curatorial oversight.

Along with danger and secrecy, the nuclear tourist will rub up against the rhetoric of the victory culture of World War Two and atomic nostalgia (Freeman, forthcoming in 2014). Steinmetz (2008, p. 220) defines nostalgia as "the sense of having lost an entire sociohistorical context and the identification bound up with it ...

---

13   Karen Gay Silkwood (1946–1974) was a labor union activist and nuclear industry whistle blower who died in a car crash under mysterious circumstances. She worked for the Kerr-McGee Cimarron Fuel Fabrication Site plant near Crescent Oklahoma, making plutonium pellets for nuclear reactor fuel rods.

It is a fantasmic desire to re-experience a social past." Unsurprisingly, many who worked in the nuclear industries prefer to see themselves as atomic citizens doing their part for democracy, agents of peace, rather than part of an industrial army for war. The Journalist Len Ackland, who was a founding board member, but no longer active member of the Rocky Flats Cold War Museum, refers to this special brand of nukespeak as the 'Cold War Heroes' narrative, which "portrays plant managers and workers as having 'won' the Cold War by building nuclear weapons crucial to defending the nation against the Soviet Union, which then collapsed" (Ackland, 2009, p. 252). The danger is that the Cold War Hero narrative could be passed on, as nostalgia, from those who actually participated in the nuclear industries of the twentieth century to the next generation. As Steinmetz (2008, p. 220) reminds us, nostalgia most often "refers to a past that one has experienced oneself, but it also encompasses historical situations mediated by the descriptions of people with whom one identifies." To identify uncritically with the Cold War Hero narrative is to ensure selective remembrance in the future. Still, it should also be taken into consideration that nostalgia can also be a productive form of remembering; it can "be an anti-dote to the betrayal caused by forgetting" (Lippard, 1999, p. 158). An atomic nostalgia that is temporary, that looks not only towards what has been, but propels future thinking could be the first step in assessing the nuclear past, a first antidotal shot in the arm towards real critical thinking.

Conclusions

At the Rocky Flats Cold War Museum before its opening, I pick up a brochure the shape and size of a business envelope. The handout depicts a handsome layout of the enormous factory site of the former Plutonium Plant, stretched out like a small city across the plateau with the Rocky Mountains in the backdrop. Above the peaks, white quarter inch text spells out an abbreviated history of sentiments towards the place: "Rocky Flats—Some loved it. Some hated it. Some never knew it existed." Inside the brochure shows what remains of the built environment of Rocky Flats—nothing more than a series of scars in the landscape. This is not a nuclear ghost town, like Pripyat, Ukraine, the site of Chernobyl, where schools and homes were abandoned in a hurry, and structures can be seen with sagging foundations and rotting teddy bears or damaged dolls (those favorite images of photographic journalists of disaster). Rocky Flats, by contrast, appears empty with only faint impressions in the geography of what once was.

This lack of materiality produces a challenge for the future, both for the museum and for memory more generally. At the moment, barbed exchanges fill local coffee shops and newspaper columns over a proposal for a new highway system and plans to open the Nature Reserve. People are talking.[14] Environmentalists warn that

---

14   Among those still talking about Rocky Flats is the writer Kristen Iversen. See her personal and historical account of the individual and social costs of growing

building a highway would disturb the toxic and radioactive particles embedded in the soil, releasing them into the air. Pro-highway folks argue that the new road will help commerce and that the environmentalists are, like always, over reacting. Nearly as divisive are the conversations regarding the historical legacy of the plant: some see the former trigger factory as a triumphant warhorse, a necessary evil in the fight (for peace) against Communism; some decree Rocky Flats an environmental abomination; and others point to Rocky Flats as an example of the irrational rationality of Mutual Assured Destruction. The Rocky Flats Cold War Museum promises to address all these sides. But can a museum, which promises so much, actually be a public sphere for critical debate? And moreover, should it be?

A museum dedicated to Rocky Flats could produce a series of monologues, decorous and fractious by turns: a love letter to the nuclear weapons industry, a time capsule of Cold War production, a nod to mid-twentieth century counter culture protest, and a warning letter to the future. Historically, American museums devoted to nuclear endeavors have chosen to delight in the atomic, encouraging an implicit atomic nostalgia, a glorious pastness, rather than mourn the loss of nuclear innocence directly, which would involve a serious acknowledgement of the sacrifices of land and workers. Nuclear museums, when they have taken into account some of the negative aspects of the nuclear age, have done so with soft landings.

In the post-nuclear era, sites of nuclear weapons production and storage must be re-visited and studied in order to understand our current radioactive geography, or as the documentary filmmakers Don Argott and Sheena M. Joyce have so termed it: 'The Atomic States of America.' If the Rocky Flats Cold War Museum is able to deliver on its promise of telling the complex story of this important node in America's nuclear apparatus, then tourists should flock to this site. If not, then critical tourists should still visit the museum, although they should bring with them historical and contemporary knowledge about the space they visit. They should attempt to cut through what the philosopher Alain de Botton (2002, p. 14) has called "the distracting woolliness of the present."

As we enter into our seventh decade of nuclear tourism, we have new opportunities to re-evaluate our nuclear past and to visit these sites as critical tourists, not only as atomic utopians, curiosity seekers, or dark tourists. Armed with new knowledge about our nuclear past, we have the chance to pull apart narratives that seek to distill the complicated politics of the nuclear weapons industry and the communities they affect into the simplified columns of love, hate, and ignorance. The preservation of atomic artifacts and their display in museums provides at least the possibility that the public will have a space to contemplate the complex and contradictory legacy of the Cold War and the nation's nuclear weapons program.

---

up near and even working at the weapons factory in *Full Body Burden* (New York: Crown, 2012).

Acknowledgements

I would like to thank sociologist Monica Brannon for driving the car, anthropologist Linsey Ly for lending her ample navigating skills, and the museum's director Connie Bogaard for opening up the museum to us on a Saturday afternoon and sharing some of her insights into its planning and construction.

References

Ackland, L. (1999). *Making a Real Killing: Rocky Flats and the Nuclear West.* Albuquerque: University of New Mexico Press.

Ackland, L. (2009). Open Wound from a Tough Nuclear History: Forgetting How We Made Ourselves an Endangered Species. In Patricia Nelson Limerick, Andrew Cowell, and Sharon K. Collinge (eds.), *Remedies for a New West: Healing Landscapes, Histories, and Cultures*, pp. 248–261. Tucson: University of Arizona Press.

Argott, D., and Joyce, S. M. (Directors) (2012). *The Atomic States of America.* 9.14 Pictures. Film.

Benjamin, W. (2003). The Work of Art in the Age of Its Technological Reproducibility. *Selected Volumes, Volume 4, 1938–1940.* Cambridge: Belknap Press.

Blackwell, A. (2012). *Visit Sunny Chernobyl: And Other Adventures in the World's Most Polluted Places.* New York: Rodale.

De Botton, A. (2002). *The Art of Travel.* New York: Vintage.

Edgar, D. (1987). The New Nostalgia. *Marxism Today* (March): 30–35.

Englehardt, T. (1998). *The End of Victory Culture: Cold War America and the Disillusioning of a Generation.* Amherst, MA: University of Massachusetts Press.

Freeman, L. A. (2010). Happy Memories Under the Mushroom Cloud: Utopia and Memory in Oak Ridge, Tennessee. *Memory and the Future: Transnational Politics, Ethics and Society*, pp. 158–178. New York: Palgrave Macmillan.

Freeman, L. A. (forthcoming 2014). The Manhattan Project Time Machine: Atomic Tourism in Oak Ridge, Tennessee. In Brigitte Sion (ed.), *Death Tourism: Disaster Sites as Recreational Landscape.* London: Seagull Books.

Freeman, L. A. (forthcoming 2015). *Longing for the Bomb: Atomic Nostalgia in Post-Nuclear Landscape.* Chapel Hill: The University of North Carolina Press.

Ginsberg, A. (2001). [1978]. *Plutonian Ode & Other Poems [1977–1980].* San Francisco: City Lights.

Gusterson, H. (2004). Nuclear Tourism. *Journal for Cultural Research*, 8.1 (January): 23–31.

Hodge, N., and Weinberger, S. (2008). *A Nuclear Family Vacation: Travels in the World of Atomic Weaponry.* New York: Bloomsbury.

Iversen, K. (2012). *Full Body Burden.* New York: Crown.

Lamm-Wirth Task Force on Rocky Flats (1975). Final Report, October.

Lippard, L. R. (1999). *On the Beaten Track: Tourism, Art, and Place*. New York: New Press.

MacCannell, D. (1999). *The Tourist: A New Theory of the Leisure Class*. Berkeley: University of California Press.

Steinmetz, G. (2008). Harrowed Landscapes: White Ruingazers in Namibia and Detroit and the Cultivation of Memory. *Visual Studies*, 23(8): 211–237.

Taylor, B. C. (2010). Radioactive History: Rhetoric, Memory, and Place in the Post-Cold War Nuclear Museum. In Greg Dickinson (ed.), *Places of Public Memory: The Rhetoric of Museums and Memorials*, pp. 57–87. Tuscaloosa: University of Alabama Press.

Urry, J. (2002). *The Tourist Gaze*. London: Sage.

Vanderbilt, T. (2002). *Survival City: Adventures Among the Ruins of Atomic America*. Princeton, NJ: Princeton Architectural Press.

Waldman, A. (2001). Warring God Charnel Ground (Rocky Flats Chronicles). *Vow to Poetry*, pp. 229–238. Saint Paul, MN: Coffee House Press.

Wray, M. (2006). Blast from the Past: Preserving and Interpreting the Atomic Age, *American Quarterly*, 58: 467–483.

Zolberg, V. (1998). Contested Remembrance: The Hiroshima Exhibit Controversy. *Theory and Society*, 27: 565–590.

Chapter 13

Paying for Proximity:
Touching the Moral Economy of
Ecological Voluntourism

Gordon Waitt, Robert Melchior Figueroa and Tom Nagle

Introduction

John was walking up a path with other volunteers from the penguin viewing platform in the dark. The beam of light from the torch he carried picked-up out how we shared the path with penguins returning that evening to their burrows. He, like the other volunteers were very excited. John extended his hand and touched a penguin on the back. In one instantaneous movement, the penguin turned its head and immediately snapped back. Everyone fell silent. We all understood from working as volunteers in a nature reserve that touching penguins was forbidden. To break the silence, John started laughing. Later, talking over a hot drink before retiring for the day, he started to talk about his desire to touch the penguin as a way to become closer to nature. He told me that to his surprise and disappointment, the penguin was not soft to the touch, but felt course, like fish scales.

I met John in 2013 on a volunteer conservation tour to Montague Island, New South Wales, Australia. John, like many visitors to Montague Island described the location as a 'wilderness'. Working in collaboration with National Parks of New South Wales, I was working as part of a team project exploring the social transformations brought about by volunteer nature tourism. Within the three years of this project, from 2010–2013, we have had the chance to observe and talk to voluntourists, who pay around $580 each to participate in a 3-day itinerary on the island. Through open and semi-structured interviews with participants on the island, and follow-up interviews after their trip, we developed a richer understanding of volunteer tourism in the flow of life. Having observed nature voluntourist practices we became particularly interested in the role of touch in how people engage with sets of ideas about nature and nature conservation on Montague Island. John was not the only voluntourist who felt the need to touch in the moment of encounter with penguins. This chapter explores touch as a mechanism to disclose the moral compass of voluntourists in places were human touch is unwanted (see Figure 13.1).

Figure 13.1   Montague Island Nature Reserve: Landing prohibited.
               Source: author

Touch and the Moral Economy of Voluntourism

Moral encounter is the defining concept for this collection. In this chapter we deploy touch to explore volunteer tourists' 'moral compass' at moments of encounter with penguins. Touch, we argue, provides insights to the moral and political accountability of the subject through affective registers and emotional ties triggered by contact between bodies, both human and non-human. Since affect, emotion, and reason have long-interconnected relationship in moral theory, our emphasis on researching touch and imagination in tourist experiences is well-positioned for assessing moral tourism; in particular, the moral positions in nature voluntourism. In our account, touch can provide important clues for investigating the dynamic nexus between self, place, practices, morals, ideas and experiences in a globally connected world. In doing so, this chapter builds upon research investigating the intersections between bodily materiality, embodied encounter, environmentalism, humanitarianism and affective and emotional relations in moral tourism (Crouch, 2002; Gibson, 2010; Mathers, 2010; Swain, 2004; Tucker, 2009).

We extend the sense and meaning of touch beyond simply registering contact conveyed through sensory receptors and nerve endings on the skin as temperature, texture and pressure. Although we agree with thinkers like Sedgwick (2003: 15) who point out that regarding "the sense of touch, texture itself is not coextensive with any single sense, but rather tends to be liminally registered on the border between touch and vision, this fails to reach the fuller holistic extension of touch. We are more inspired by feminist commentators like Haraway (1997), Probyn

(2000) and Braidotti (2006) who rethink the body away from any universalisms. We align our study on the grounding that bodily touch provides insights to moral environmental encounters. This feminist approach we assume in our work resists the binaries of outside or inside the body-self and the idea that experience flows through discrete senses, whereby touch privileges textural qualities without integrating holistic sensory experience with smell, sight, taste or sound.

Respecting the holistic and relational approach to touch, our feminist influences are conceptually part of the same phenomenological philosophical tradition of the body-self as the philosopher Merleau-Ponty (1962) initiated. Through investigations of the body-self Merleau-Ponty (1962) persuades us to reject the Cartesian legacies of a universal body divided materially by sensory experiences which also distinguish between subject and object, mind and body, and inner and outer worlds. These feminist scholars share a great deal of Merleau-Ponty's premises about the body-self, but they also draw our attention further to the workings of contemporary power relations. Two points about the feminist political phenomenological contributions are important here. First is the politics of location. Tourists are part of the uneven power geometries that are inclusive of the global economy. The tourist is a moral agent always located within these power geometries that shape social worlds. The second, and related point, is that power is a dynamic web of interconnections. Probyn argues that the subject-object, us-them, human-nature divides are underpinned by colonial, patriarchal, heterosexual narratives. Drawing on Deleuze and Guattari's notions of assemblage and affect (1998), Probyn (2000) mobilizes affective registers and emotional ties to rethink our individual agency and collective relationships as an assemblage of flows, forces or intensities stable enough to help make sense of space and time and political embodiment. Affective registers and emotions, alongside representations, are understood to have a key role in shaping the intensive and dynamic entity embodied simultaneously as 'individual' self and 'collective' relationships. In short, as agents participating in the dynamics that shape social worlds tourists are socially located within existing power geometries and also inherit the ability to the shape and reshape these dynamics.

Our entry point at the global level of collective relationships taps the neoliberal incentives and ambitions for ecotourism. As discussed by Mowforth et al. (2008), green consumption is the new activism; although increasingly mainstreamed by neoliberal principles. The moral economy in which environmental consumption has flourished in the Western world is within the political-economy of the global marketplace driven by neoliberalism—in which the primary role of the state is to protect and expand an unregulated market on a quest to privatize social services. In nature voluntourism, environmental issues are adopted, adapted and sold in the global market as products within the broader moral economy. Even as alternative tourism or simply moral tourism, the neoliberal market is an overarching domain within which the moral economy of tourism of any kind is devised.

Voluntourism is one example of civic engagement pertaining to narratives that promote moral modes of consumption in a wide-range of social arenas such as, fair trade consumerism (Goodman, 2004), the 'slow food' movement (Guthman, 2003) and 'green' purchasing of household products (Gibson et al., 2010). However, unlike these modes, voluntourism involves an industrial stream of travel (Campbell et al., 2008), and is more available to explore insights through touch as we have extended its meaning to account for intimate encounters of an embodied, relational morality. Moreover, in the global economy, voluntourism is valued at an estimated US$1.6 billion (Wearing, 2001; TRAM, 2008). Furthermore, voluntourism in its ecotourism incarnation, is one example of the fastest growing tourist markets in the broader tourism industry which is the second global industry behind oil/gas industry (Brown, 2005: Tomazos and Butler, 2010). Nearly a century after the explicit consumerist model of national parks was well in play, we can still find in 2002, the International Union for the Conservation of Nature (IUCN) echoing with a call for nature tourism within national parks and protected areas to be accepted as an effective tool for the support of conservation and management (see Eagles et al., 2002). According to Eagles et al. (2002: xv): "Protected areas need tourism, and tourism needs protected areas. Though the relationship is complex and sometimes adversarial, tourism is always a critical component to consider in the establishment and management of protected areas." Advocates of neoliberalism hold that increased tourist numbers within protected areas can be used as a tool to build a unifying objective for park visitors to appreciate a compassion for nature. While advocates for sustainability within the global economy herald ecotourism for its influence in increasing protected areas, fostering viable alternatives for local economies, and preserving cultural heritage (Campbell et al., 2008; IES, 2006).

In response to the growth of voluntourism, the research agenda includes geographical imaginaries (Mostafanezhad, 2013), motivations (Brown and Lehto, 2005; Campbell and Smith, 2006; Coghlan, 2006, 2007; Sin, 2009), encounters (Cousins et al., 2009; McIntosh and Zahra, 2007; Sin, 2010), and implications for the moral ambitions of volunteering on behalf of broadening global justice (Gray and Campbell, 2007; McGehee and Norman, 2001; McGehee and Santos, 2005; Pezzullo, 2007; Conran 2011). Our chapter adds to these works on voluntourism by investigating what we term the pedagogy of touch; that is the role of affective and emotional relationships triggered by the intimate practices and personal experiences of touch, understood within the context of power geometries that shape ecotourism. Our objective is to provide insights to the role of the most intimate encounter, that of touch, in both sustaining and challenging the moral economy of ecotourism.

Our Entry Point: The Power Geometries that Shape Voluntourism on Montague Island

> Each stay provides the opportunity for you to **participate** in hands-on Nest Box Penguin Surveys and contribute to the long term protection of the Island's Little Penguin Colony. Participation is optional and no prior experience is required. (Montague Island NSW http://www.montagueisland.com.au/ Accessed 11/10/2010.)

The environmental authority in New South Wales, the National Parks and Wildlife Service, designate Nature Reserves with the highest moral capital. General public purposes and access to all Nature Reserves are highly limited and restricted. Montague Island became catalogued and territorialized as a nature reserve in 1990. For many environmental scientists this is a place for nature, not mass tourism, as a key breeding site for seabirds, including little penguins (*Eudyptula minor*).

The classification as a 'Nature Reserve', under New South Wales National Parks and Wildlife Service legislation, is just one example of the whitened cultural history of this island that extends into current voluntourism management. For Yuin people, the Australian Indigenous peoples of this place, access to this island is restricted to their men and is known as *Baranguba* (NSW National Parks and Wildlife Service 2008). But, for British and European Australians this place became known as Montague Island, following the construction of a lighthouse station in the early 1880s (Pacey 1991). In 1953, bureaucratic division put the buildings under the jurisdiction of the Commonwealth Government, and the flora and fauna under the jurisdiction of the National Trust of Australia. Today, the lighthouse station buildings are legitimated by their listing in the Register of the National Estate, managed by the National Parks and Wildlife Service under the Heritage Act 1977. How could people be accommodated as tourists on Montague Island without sacrificing ecological preservation?

In a Nature Reserve, where public purposes and access are highly restricted for preservationist morality, possibilities for voluntourism may at first appear surprising. However, because tourism permits a moral economy of environmentalism to coexist with dominant economic discourses the expansion of voluntourism organized by a non-government organization (NGO) in a protected area is neither unexpected nor unusual. In keeping with a neoliberal agenda within the New South Wales National Parks and Wildlife Service, the *Montague Island Nature Reserve Plan of Management* (1995) makes clear that ecotourism should be encouraged for the benefit of the local economy; and stipulates public access for: "encouragement of scientific and educational inquiry into environmental features and processes" (Montague Island Nature Reserve Plan of Management, 1995: 34).

Initially tourists were permitted access to only a small portion of the Island for only a few hours until they are chartered back by boat as part of an educational day-tour or to observe the evening penguin parade. Underpinning the appeal of Montague Conservation Tours (the NGO) within the moral economy of environmentalism is the island's remoteness from metropolitan centres and the unique birdlife, particularly a colony of little penguins (*Eudyptula minor*) that are specific to the Australian East Coast. Unsurprisingly, penguins have enormous market appeal within the moral economy of nature tourism. Throughout the twentieth and current century, we have witnessed penguins, along with polar bears, dolphins, seal pups, kangaroos and whales, adopted by environmental organizations to symbolize pristine regions (often synonymous with the idea of "wilderness") threatened by the encroachment of human settlement and industries. Moreover, penguins are easily anthropomorphized by their flightless upright stature, social behaviours, such as the 'penguin parades,' their depiction in the popular imaginary from tuxedo wearing characterizations that continue down to their arm-like flippers, their formal marching behaviour and on to now-common images of fun-loving sledding folk. However, their very appeal could be the perfect ingredient to ensure the destruction of their habitat.

To negotiate the conflicting moral economies of penguin appeal, tourism revenue, and preservation, the educational virtues of ecotourism inspired scientific voluntourism to be permissible by amendments to the Plan of Management. This allow up to 12 paying volunteers (A$580/night) to stay only two nights accommodated in the former lightkeeper's quarters under the condition that they are engaged in research. Tourism numbers stay down by the two-night limit, conditions of voluntourism in the name of research, and costs restricting the island to the economically privileged (almost exclusively white), discerning nature volunteer. These voluntourists are invited, they are not obligated despite the condition of research, to participate in two related conservation management programs: the 'Seabird Habitat Restoration Project' to help remove the non-native kikuyu grass (*Pennisetum clandestinum*) and revegetate the island with native plant species, such as mat-rush (*Lmoandra longifiolia*), conducive to seabird nesting; and the 'Little Penguin Monitoring Program' to help count the number of breeding pairs and chicks which assists scientifically investigating the suitability of their nesting boxes (see Figure 13.2). Over 350 nesting boxes were initially introduced as an interim measure to facilitate breeding in places devoid of nesting sites in borrows, and below vegetation cover. Since, 2006, around 200 people each year have paid to volunteer their labour as part of Montague Island Conservation Tour.

Figure 13.2   Little penguins in a nesting box. Source: author

Montague Island Nature Tours are therefore one manifestation of how neoliberalism is present in environmental management organizations through fostering collaboration with NGOs (in this case Conservation Volunteers Australia). Montague Island Nature Tours illustrates a pioneering effort to set up connection the culture of contemporary environmental sciences and that of tourism; what we call *science ecotourism*. In science ecotourism tourists engage in basic research, data collection and labour to promote these science and educational objectives as part of their experience and to assist the experts who work at the higher levels of conservation, research, and data collection as full-time occupations. Science ecotourism is complicated by that fact that the very notion of a 'nature reserve' is destabilized by the somewhat contradictory decision of inviting voluntourists to participate in hands-on scientific touring activities in a protected area that is established to exclude human influence and public infringement upon the island's ecosystem. Montague Island provides an illustration of a moral economy forged at the nexus of a neoliberal economic vision serving individual consumers who can afford to pay, conservationist environmental science, and a willingness to contribute individual human labour for the greater ecological and human good. At the same time, this moral economy destabilizes problematic dominant narratives. The consumer's labour and purchasing power generates a pseudo citizen science that tarnishes the elitism of science as an experts-only domain. Ironically, the ecotourism within this globalized moral economy also destabilizes the preservationist purism and socially constructed wilderness ideal that nature exists apart from of human interactions, impacts, and values.

Little Penguins, Touching Encounters and Moral Compasses

In this section we draw on participants' narratives and sense of the 'Little Penguin Monitoring Program' to explore the moral pedagogy of touch; specifically in regards to performing their sense of moral responsibility to penguins in a protected area. To emphasize the role of participants as embodied agents acting within the moral economy we rely upon a spatial analysis at the juncture of three key themes.

1. Expectations and the sense of nature: This theme introduces the spatial framing of Montague Island as 'wilderness', pointing to the synonymy between penguins and wilderness, while noting wilderness up close is less commercialized and *more* realistically natural.
2. Participation in the moral and epistemic authority of science practices: This theme concentrates on becoming a scientific researcher and the permissible spatial proximity that privileges science tourism.
3. Perceptions of economic privileges and entitlements: This theme addresses touching as a form of consumer entitlement. Despite moral codes upon

touch, some people purposefully sought out penguins to touch as a way to draw together their embodied experience of this place with their status as *paying* voluntourists.

Wilderness

Reading entries in the park's Visitor's Book confirms that for many visitors, close encounters with penguins is the highlight of visiting Montague Island. These encounters are spatially-contingent, and help (re)territorialize Montague Island as wilderness that both relies upon the modernist colonial human/nature binary as a unique destination where tourists come closer to nature. For example, one entry reads: "I loved the penguin surveys, counting chicks and eggs! Beautiful environment." Participating in the restoration work serves to reconfigure the constructed boundary between humans (here) and nature (out there). The ecological voluntourism subverts the commoditization of nature as a spectacle that typifies the distancing mechanism in mass nature tourism. As Sandra, a retired professional in her sixties from Sydney, who has returned to Montague Island for the third time tells:

> We have been to Philip Island down in Victoria but we didn't really like that very much, it was just ah, very commercialised. You had to pay so much to go this far and so much more to go any further. Whereas, out here [at] Montague the penguins are just right. Here it's much more natural. The penguins don't care. They just go and do their thing.

Sandra's moral sentiment expresses that commodification demoralizes both nature and the consumer which makes paying for proximity at Montague Island a greater moral purchase that brings humans closer to nature, despite the fact that ecotourism is product within the neoliberal global economy. As her quotation intimate, the pleasures that Montague Island Conservation tours provide arise in part from the less-commercialized encounter with little penguins than anywhere elsewhere in Australia. For Sandra, encountering penguins on Montague Island feels morally good as the tour is sensitive to the penguins because they are less affected by the human presence. Again, the visceral affects of Montague Island are documented in the Visitor's Book as 'beautiful', 'peaceful', 'paradise' and 'wilderness', that defy the kind of sentiment Sandra expresses for Philip Island. The excitement and pleasure of paying to visit, then volunteering labour on, Montague Island centres on the possibilities of 'feel good' politics and as Campbell et al. (2008: 212) remind us, alternative consumerism like ecotourism "makes capitalism nicer."

Adrienne, a professional worker in her forties from Sydney, on her third conservation tour reflects upon the moral alternative offered at Montague Island:

> it was good to be doing something 'useful' in adverted commas and also something that was unique to the Island like that. Something that can't be done

elsewhere … most other places they won't let you anywhere near them [little penguins]! This is obviously controlled conditions; there only ten of us, but it's very unique to the Island.

Montague Island Conservation tours trade on a feel good politics that aligns a robust and enduring synonymy between wilderness, environmental science, penguins and the restricted presence of humans. The once-in-a-lifetime opportunity to experience an encounter with a little penguin marks out time spent on the island as not only 'extraordinary' but also the knowledge of participating in a good cause—a defining distinction of alternative tourism.

Privileged Proximity of Scientific Voluntourism

In this section, we draw attention to how touch is highly restricted in the face of a greater environmental morality towards species preservation. Restriction against touch makes sight eclipse as the dominant sense in *doing* scientific voluntourism and encountering penguins. Moreover, the visitor's experience of the little penguin survey is more performatively aware than most activities on the island because of the purposeful directive of scientific voluntourism. To encounter penguins in close proximity, the performative repertories of volunteer tourist require moving through bushes within a designated restoration zone, touching and being touched by bushes and grass, sighting penguins, as well as recording observations about the age and numbers of penguins. Crucial to the privilege of touching the surrounding terrains is the holistic touch of basic scientific instruments, such as a table, clipboard, etc., that legitimate the voluntourists' presence and defines the moral spatial relations that permit these privileged embodied agents to engage the penguins (without touching) and to move beyond from ordinary touristic restrictions.

For example, David, a semi-retired journalist in his sixties from Newcastle, New South Wales, explains how the map to help locate nesting boxes allowed him to effect an order and narrative to his purpose as a voluntourist:

> So, I was like, look I'm out here to find these penguins so I'm going to traipse through this bush like good solider Kurt and find these penguin boxes, mark them off on the map, check if there's a penguin and yeah it wasn't that hard. … yes I did, I found it quite scientific and also very exciting, and I've never seen a penguin at such close range before. So it was great, very rewarding.

Interpreting David's survey work in the discursive regime of scientific voluntourism, the task has an authoritative quality of the soldier following orders. The performative objective that directs David renders one impression of his sense of self as the 'good soldier'. At the same time, the bush is traipsed and not marched because of the level of difficulty and endangerment to human life. David engages the bush for a purpose other than walking/hiking or what typical tourism renders. In David's case, leaving domestic responsibilities for those of the unpaid labour of voluntourism based upon the scientific objective induced positive affects, narrated as 'exciting', 'great' and 'very rewarding'. David illustrates how proximity to penguins facilitated by the scientific objective of the survey supplanted most voluntourists enjoyment of the bush. The moral condition of the voluntourist is following the guidance of the parks official, the abstract directive of the map, the privileges of scientific knowledge production, and the tactile engagement that combines to produce the positive affection through the embodied exposure to the penguins in close proximity.

Yet, the voluntary labour also induced anxiety amongst some participants. Impediments to voluntourism are produced by tensions within the penguin monitoring research project, and the value of volunteer labour for scientific objectives. Consider Adrienne responding to this dual-dynamic. She describes the tensions concerning voluntary labour: the moral idea of volunteering as helping and concomitant marginalization of volunteer efforts under the authoritative lens of scientific use-value:

> yeah. It [monitoring penguins] was good, but I've got no idea how useful the data we collected is going to be, especially when the guide stuffed up the plan and then changed his mind a hundred thousand times … that's not really going to work out well. He had no idea! You don't tell someone who's volunteering that you're going to throw away their data.

Adrienne is obviously displeased to the point of insult at the thought that her labour is worthless for the scientific performative objective. For her, like all those for whom assisting, helping, contributing, and working is an embodied practice that defines their selves as voluntourists. The cultural discourses of scientific objectivity by measurement and accurate data collection threaten to undermine their sense moral worth; specifically their sense of responsibility, experience of pleasure by moral action and self-worth as a volunteer. These moral feelings get aggravated in contexts where those embodying scientific authority administrating the survey and directing the moral actions of the voluntourists seemingly lack scientific objectivity. Science is infused with values and judgements, but the voluntourists increase their proximity to the terrain, surrounds, penguins *through* scientific practice. All of these factors are messy in themselves and none of them are designed specifically for touristic satisfaction. Thus, in scientific voluntourism, proximity to data collection as well as the subject of study produces frustrations that reshape purposes of physical labour, moral energy and the constructed ideals of scientific research.

Touch and Entitlement

This third theme, underscores that despite the discursive regime that prohibits touching penguins, both park officials and voluntourists cross the moral terrain by reaching out and touching the penguins. In a hesitant manner, Adrienne talked about one such occasion where a guide allowed visitors to handle a penguin chick. Even National Park officers, who advocate and police a 'do not touch' ethos, extends alternative moral license allowing volunteers to touch penguins during nesting box surveys.

> Well a national park officer has let us have a little chick out of the boxes when we were out there and kind of unofficially held one and passed it around a little.

Adrienne's comments illustrate both the way in which nesting penguin's embodied space is disrupted and the way that the preservationist ethos can be violated in small amounts for the right kind of public. We already presume officials touch penguins when necessary for preservation, so the moral restriction is inherently flexible for environmental science. The question is how the voluntourists understand their role with this moral allowance and their embodied relationship to scientific authority? For the voluntourist the rare opportunity of a touching engagement with the penguin also calls forth moral reflexivity between the voluntourist body-self and the penguin. The body language and hesitation in the voice of everyone we spoke to suggests that touching penguins was understood as morally conflicting.

Yet, our observations suggest some people purposefully sought out penguins to touch as a way to draw together their embodied experience of the place and their status as *paying* voluntourists. A different pedagogy of touch is grafted onto the encounter with penguins when touch is fused to the entitlement of consumerism. When we asked people if they had touched the chicks in the nesting boxes, those who admitted to touching them usually talked about how these small, fluffy, downed animals embodied cuteness. This is not a scientific touch-term of a biologist, so the moral allowance is drawn to the visceral, good-touch and the entitlement that calls for greater intimacy with nature. As argued by Rodaway (1994: 149), when people are hesitant to trust their sight, they resort to touch 'so verifying the truth like doubting Thomas'. However, as we state from the onset of this chapter, the touch is part of a larger social location and a holistic embodied sensory experience. Achieving the truth of the penguin cuteness with this holistic socially located experience also means achieving the truth of entitlement of the voluntourist and the truth that science constantly uses to reaffirm its authority to touch and investigate anything in nature.

Despite preservation ideologies linking touch to damage and contamination, touching the soft down of penguin chicks became a source of sensuous pleasure often understood as a moral benefit derived from the good voluntourism labour and consumer reward. For example, David implies volunteer labour inscribes a sense of ownership rights over penguins' bodies.

> This is the first penguin seen, this was the first box we opened and bang! There was a penguin and that was very exciting! It was either the first or the second anyway. There's our little penguin in there and you can see that's it's barely

moulted, well, actually it could be fully moulted or those feathers on the floor have come from another penguin who used the box earlier.

"Our little penguin" can be protectionist, investigative and/or expressive of entitlement. However, the underlying point of this section is that paying voluntourist is given a sense of entitlement. Touch becomes a consumer prerogative that bends the principles of preservationist morality. Penguins are no longer positioned with the relationships that sustain voluntourism as untouchable.

Finishing Touches

This chapter has drawn concepts of embodiment to conceptualize moral encounters of tourism that demands thinking about a pedagogy of touch that pays attention to the materiality of bodies, affective capacities, situated knowledge and the context of uneven power geometries that shape social and cultural worlds. We argued touch provides clues to the moral compass of encounters that are always embodied and registered in narratives. The pedagogy of touch requires engaging with the lessons learned from the fact that different bodies have different affective capacities; that is, the encounters of tourism are always lived and felt through embodied histories and yearning for particular futures. Our interpretation points to the different ways that the affective registers and emotional relations triggered by touch configures the agent's moral compass by reconfiguring and dissolving social and spatial borders. We demonstrated that science and neoliberal privatization agendas are two critical forms of privilege in the moral economy of ecotourism. We revealed how scientific voluntourism is performed, represented and negotiated via touch and how the moral compass built on a narrative to separate humans from nature gets reoriented. The performance of the penguin monitoring as part of restorative and preservation work legitimizes understandings of this place as pristine and often enhances the pleasure of being on this island as a volunteer; hence increasing the tourist value of the island in a global tourist industry. The intimate mechanics of the penguin survey dovetailed within an anthropomorphic cultural matrix means that many visitors must confront an affective intensity to reach out and touch penguins. Visitors often understand this tactile intensity as unwanted, but that only brings them to the moral complexity where competing values and embodied contexts make simple preservationist principles, such as "do not touch," the subject of moral dilemmas. The performatives of the survey vary in results, but we discovered that often a sense of ownership over the penguins opened voluntourist bodies to touch, draping entitlement over conversation science principles. We encourage future research to attend to the embodied geographies and pedagogy of touch to investigate if and how encounters within the moral economy of ecotourism make and remake difference.

Acknowledgements

Our thanks to Michael Adams, David Clifton and Nora Ward who were integral in helping us frame our argument; to those that facilitated the project particularly Preston Cope, DECC NPWS Area Manager (Central) Far South Coast and Mark Westwood DECC NPWS Discovery Coordinator (Montague Island Tours) and everyone who participated in this project.

References

Braidotti, R. (2006). Posthuman, All Too Human: Towards a New Process Ontology. *Theory, Culture & Society*, 23(7–8), 197–208.

Brown, S., and Lehto, X. (2005). Travelling with a Purpose: Understanding the Motives and Benefits of Volunteer Vacationers. *Current Issues in Tourism*, 8(6), 479–496.

Campbell, L. and Smith, C. (2006). What Makes Them Pay? Values of Volunteer Tourists Working for Sea Turtle Conservation. *Environmental Management*, 38(1), 89–98.

Campbell, L., Gray, M., Gray, N. J., and Meletis, Z. A. (2008). Political Ecology Perspectives on Ecotourism to Parks and Protected Areas. In K. S. Hanna, D. A. Clark, and D. S. Siocombe (eds.), *Transforming Parks and Protected Areas Policy and Governance in a Changing World*, pp. 200–221. New York: Routledge.

Coghlan, A. (2006). Volunteer Tourism as an Emerging Trend or an Expansion of Ecotourism? A Look at Potential Clients' Perceptions of Volunteer Tourism Organizations. *International Journal of Nonprofit and Voluntary Sector Marketing*, 11(3), 225–237.

Coghlan, A. (2007). Towards an Integrated Image-based Typology of Volunteer Tourism Organisations. *Journal of Sustainable Tourism*, 15(3): 267–287.

Conran, M. (2011). They Really Love Me! Intimacy in Volunteer Tourism. *Annals of Tourism Research*, 38(4) 1454–1473.

Cousins, J. A., Evans, J., and Sadler, J. P. (2009). 'I've Paid to Observe Lions, Not Map Roads!'—An Emotional Journey with Conservation Volunteers in South Africa. *Geoforum*, 40(6), 1069–1080.

Crouch, D. (2002). Surrounded by Place: Embodied Encounters. In S. Coleman and M. Crang (eds.), *Tourism: Between Place and Performance*. Oxford: Berghahn Books.

Deleuze, G., and Guattari, F. (1998). *A Thousand Plateaus: Capitalism and Schizophrenia*. Translation by Brian Massumi. Minneapolis: University of Minnesota Press.

Eagles, P. F., McCool, S. F., and Haynes, C. D. (2002). *Sustainable Tourism in Protected Areas: Guidelines for Planning and Management*. IUCN

(International Union for Conservation of Nature), Thanet Press, Cambridge, Available Online: http://data.iucn.org/dbtw-wpd/edocs/PAG-008.pdf.

Gibson, C. (2010). Geographies of Tourism: (Un)ethical Encounters. *Progress in Human Geography*, 34(4), 521–527.

Gibson, C., Waitt, G., Head, L., and Gill, N. (2010). Is It Easy Being Green? On the Dilemmas of Material Cultures of Household Sustainability. In R. Lane and A Gorman-Murray (eds.), *Material Geographies of Household Sustainability*, pp. 19–33. London: Ashgate.

Goodman, M. (2004). Reading Fair Trade: Political Ecological Imaginary and the Moral Economy of Fair Trade Foods. *Political Geography*, 23(7), 891–915.

Gray, N. J., and Campbell, L. M. (2007). *Journal of Sustainable Tourism*, 15(5), 463–482.

Guthman, J. (2003). Fast Food/Organic Food: Reflexive Tastes and the Making of "Yuppie Chow." *Social & Cultural Geography*, 4(1), 46–58.

Haraway, D. (1997). *Modest_Witness@Second_Millennium. FemaleMan©_ Meets_OncomouseTM*. London: Routledge.

International Ecotourism Society (IES) (2006). *Global Ecotourism Fact Sheet*. https://ibgeography-lancaster.wikispaces.com/file/view/TIES+GLOBAL+EC OTOURISM+FACT+SHEET.PDF (accessed 30 May 2013).

Mathers, K. (2010). *Travel, Humanitarianism, and Becoming American in Africa*. New York: Palgrave Macmillan.

McGehee, N. G., and Norman, W. C. (2001). Alternative Tourism as Impetus for Consciousness Raising. *Tourism Analysis*, 6(3–4), 239–251.

McGehee, N. G., and Santos, C. A. (2005). Social Change, Discourse and Volunteer Tourism. *Annals of Tourism Research*, 32(3), 760–779.

McIntosh, A., and Zahra, A. (2007). A Cultural Encounter through Volunteer Tourism: Towards the Ideals of Sustainable Tourism? *Journal of Sustainable Tourism*, 15(5), 541–556.

Merleau-Ponty, M. (1962). *The Phenomenology of Perception*. Translation by Colin Smith. London: Routledge & Kegan Paul.

Mostafanezhad, M. (2013). The Geography of Compassion in Volunteer Tourism. *Tourism Geographies*, 15(2) 318–337.

Mowforth, M., Charlton, C., and Munt, I. (2008). *Tourism and Responsibility: Perspectives from Latin American and the Caribbean*. New York: Routledge.

New South Wales National Parks and Wildlife Service (1995). *Montague Island Nature Reserve Plan of Management*. New South Wales National Parks and Wildlife Service. Available online: http://www.environment.nsw.gov.au/ resources/parks/pomfinalmontague.pdf.

NSW National Parks and Wildlife Service (2008). *Montague Island Seabird Habitat Restoration Project, Proceedings of Shared Island Management Workshop, Narooma, New South Wales, November 2008*. National Parks and Wildlife Service, New South Wales Environmental Trust, New South Wales Department of Environment and Climate Change Available online: http:// www.montagueisland.com.au/download/proceedings_for_web.pdf.

Pacey, L. (1991). *The Lure of Montague*. Narooma, NSW: Laurelle Pacey, Narooma.

Pezzullo, P. (2007). *Toxic Tours: Rhetorics of Pollution, Travel and Environmental Justice*. Tuscaloosa: The University of Alabama Press.

Probyn, E. (2000). *Carnal Appetites: Food Sex Identities*. New York: Routledge.

Rodaway, P. (1994). *Sensuous Geographies: Body, Sense and Place*. London: Routledge.

Sedgwick, E. (2003). *Touching Feeling: Affect, Pedagogy, Performativity*. Durham, NC: Duke University Press.

Sin, H. L. (2009). Volunteer Tourism—Involve Me and I Will Learn? *Annals of Tourism Research*, 36(3), 480–501.

Sin, H. L. (2010). Who Are We Responsible To? Locals' Tales of Volunteer Tourism. *Geoforum*, 41(6), 983–992.

Swain, M. (2004). (Dis)embodied Experience and Power. In J. Phillimore and L. Goodson (eds.), *Qualitative Research in Tourism: Ontologies, Epistemologies, Methodologies*. New York: Routledge.

Tomazos, K., and Butler, R. (2010). The Volunteer Tourist as 'Hero'. *Current Issues in Tourism*, 13(4), 363–380.

Tucker, H. (2009). Recognizing Emotion and its Postcolonial Potentialities: Discomfort and Shame in a Tourism Encounter in Turkey. *Tourism Geographies*, 11(4), 444–461.

TRAM (2008). *Volunteer Tourism: A Global Analysis*. Arnhem: ATLAS.

Wearing, S. (2001). *Volunteer Tourism: Experiences That Make a Difference*. Cambridge: CAB International.

SECTION 4
Moral Methodologies

Chapter 14
Humanism and Tourism:
A Moral Encounter

Kellee Caton

Introduction

Does tourism need moral philosophy? Surely tourism is an activity with vast moral implications. Tourism education sometimes proceeds as though sales of airline tickets and hotel beds, satisfaction of tourists with site visits and hospitality services—indeed the successful packaging and delivery of "experience" as a phenomenon—were the whole of the enterprise (Inui, Wheeler, and Lankford, 2006; Ring, Dickinger, and Wöber, 2009), but tourism is clearly about more than these things. It is no less than a practice through which different individuals with different biographies from different cultures and life-spaces collide. Much thought has been given to tourism's 'impacts'; indeed, investigations of tourism's role in various environmental and social processes, such as climate change (e.g., Hall and Higham, 2005), political economy (e.g., Su, Wang, and Wen, in press), cultural power dynamics (e.g., Jeong and Santos, 2003), and ideological production (e.g., Echtner and Prasad, 2003), constitute some of the most critical intellectual output of our field. However, until recently, tourism has rarely been considered overtly as a space of moral encounter.

In his pioneering work on philosophy's application to tourism, Tribe (2009) notes that philosophy as a discipline has not tended much to influence the canon of tourism knowledge, nor have tourism scholars been quick to engage with key philosophical questions—for example, those involving the perennial issues of truth, beauty, and virtue—despite their obvious relevance to the tourism world. As I have argued elsewhere (Caton, 2012), virtue in tourism is a particularly important question to take up and not an easy one at that as its complexity is profound. As an activity historically associated with leisure and pleasure, the figure of the Self looms large in tourism. The tourist wishes to relax and escape, or alternatively to push her own boundaries and experience a sense of triumphant overcoming, or to simply disappear into a foreign environment where she can temporarily become somebody else besides her usual self. But there is always an Other in tourism as well: someone—or a whole community of people—who must facilitate the Self's quest, and yet that someone is a subject in his own right, with his own dreams and desires.

Fortunately, recent years have seen a surge of interest in moral matters in the tourism domain (as cogently summarized in the introductory chapter of this volume), partly because, as a field, tourism studies is finally freeing itself of the chains of positivism as the dominant mode of knowledge production going, and thus finding a wealth of research issues formerly ruled out of bounds that are now open for exploration, and partly because the over-privileged parts of the world (from which many tourism scholars write) finally appear to be crawling out of the stupor of materialism, consumerism, and Eurocentric and colonialist ideology and seeing the writing on the wall regarding the damage we've done to our planet and our failure to build adequate relationships with our fellow human beings to face the global social challenges that currently confront us. This chapter explores the philosophy of humanism, a perspective which has increasingly come to influence tourism studies in its process of moral awakening. The following two sections present an overview of this philosophical movement and a discussion of some of the key criticisms and controversies it has provoked. The remainder of the chapter then explores humanism's increasing presence in tourism scholarly concerns, as well as the potential that taking a humanistic turn holds for enlarging and deepening the epistemological and pedagogical expanse of tourism studies. It concludes with thoughts on the potential vistas for understanding that unfold, inviting our research attention, once we open the door to humanistic moral philosophy in tourism.

What is Humanism?

Humanism is a philosophical movement that emphasizes the moral capacity of human beings and our responsibility to use this capacity in service of the greater good. Humanism rejects religion, the traditional basis for morality in human societies, as being necessary for fulfilling that role, arguing that humans need not look to the supernatural realm for moral justification. Instead, humanity naturally and internally contains all the capacity it needs to negotiate the moral realm— to live lives of good we need look no further than ourselves. Those identifying with the humanist outlook view morality as being rooted in the human capacity for compassion. This capacity, an evolutionary product of our need for social cooperation, is seen as requiring no further justification beyond itself. Humanism is, at its core, pragmatic. Richard Rorty (1989), one of the twentieth century's most famous voices in humanist philosophy, describes the figure of the humanist-pragmatist as the "liberal ironist"—with the label of "liberal" referring to "one who believes that cruelty is the worst thing we do," and the notion of "ironist" referring to an acceptance of the irony that there are no secure foundations of truth for even our most deeply held beliefs—including those about the worth of compassion and the horrors of cruelty. In true pragmatist form, ends and processes are judged as good or bad based on their outcomes: specifically, on whether or not they increase the happiness and decrease the suffering of human beings and other living creatures, including future generations. Thus, consequences trump truth as humanism's central concern. We do not need epistemological criteria (i.e., truth foundations) to *prove* that happiness is good and suffering is bad; instead, we can easily make these judgments simply based on the outcomes of shared human experience (although certainly not everyone's definition of pleasure and pain will be the same). Humanism's pragmatic orientation naturally leads its affiliates to emphasize contextual reasoning and situation-based judgments, rather than blanket rules, for moral choices and behaviors, and this is another reason that the movement often asserts itself as existing in opposition to religious-based forms of morality, when the latter are generalized as constituting codified systems of relatively inflexible rules.

It is probably most accurate to say that humanism as we know it in the modern sense only arose after the mid-eighteenth century with the Enlightenment, but tracing the intellectual and cultural roots of this movement is a more complex undertaking, not least for the reason that the term has been used in many senses, in many times and places in recorded history, and these various connotations are not unrelated to the present philosophical movement under discussion. During the Renaissance, humanism was associated with valuing the intellectual and artistic contributions of the humanities—literature, music, visual art, and philosophy, for example—and the term was adopted in a curricular sense in higher education after that time to indicate a stance promoting the liberal arts. The term has also been used to connote a love or appreciation for that which is human, a position which casts an optimistic gaze on our species and its works and potential. Similarly, the specific ideas embraced by humanist philosophy, as noted above, in particular its emphasis on compassion-based morality that derives from human beings without need of being undergirded by supernatural forces and on the human call to moral responsibility, also have deep roots regardless of whether the word "humanism" was used to describe this way of thinking or not. In this sense, humanistic reasoning can be traced to Renaissance thought, as well as to much earlier traditions as diverse as Buddhism, Confucianism, and ancient Greek and Medieval Islamic thought. These traditions all emphasized one or more central humanist principles, such as tolerance; the call to "do unto others"; the value of reason, science, and other forms of scholarship in serving as a basis for understanding the world and forming sound decisions; the importance of individual free thought; and the need to work in service of social progress and the greater good.

In the modern era, humanism began to find more formal and institutionalized expression in the "ethical culture movement" that arose in the UK and the US. Early ethical societies in London were generally affiliated with liberal religious traditions like Unitarianism and were central hubs for championing social reforms in areas such as women's equality, worker's rights, and public health (Law, 2011). Their American counterparts would take another hundred years, until the end of the nineteenth century, to spring up, and when they did, under the leadership of fallen-away rabbi-in-training turned university professor Felix Adler, they took the movement further on its trajectory away from religious affiliations and toward establishing its own independent identity. The ethical societies formed under Adler's vision emphasized the possibility of (indeed the *need* for) morality to exist independent of theology; the responsibility of human beings to engage in philanthropic activities and work for social progress; the need to continuously strive for self-improvement (in keeping with the transcendentalist sentiments so *en vogue* in the American Northeast at that time); and the importance of judging others based on their actions rather than on ascribed characteristics like gender or religion ('deed not creed') (Radest, 1969). Humanism had much to show for itself in the nineteenth and twentieth centuries, serving as a driving force behind a variety of successful progressive social causes, including slavery abolition, labour rights, women's suffrage, civil rights for racial and ethnic minority groups, disease eradication, and universal education for children in many parts of the world. As these activities evidence, key to the philosophy of humanism is the belief that human beings have the power—through scholarly inquiry, logical reasoning, empathy, communication, and many other important capacities—to improve our own lives and the lives of those around us: the *status quo* is not inevitable.

Controversies and Criticisms

It is perhaps the destiny, especially in our current "information age," of all loose coalitions of ideas, in philosophy or elsewhere, to eventually become more codified than many of their adherents might prefer. Certainly, this is the case with humanistic thinking, which as noted above, has incredibly diverse roots and is united only by a handful of very simple principles, such as a belief in the moral capacity of human beings; a view that theology is not necessary as a basis for morality and that human compassion is instead the best starting place; the placing of a high value on free thought, reason, and scholarly inquiry as tools for social improvement; and the belief that human beings hold a duty to improve themselves and their societies. Indeed, if the publishing industry is any indication with its spate of humanism 'guides' and 'handbooks' (e.g., Hancock, 2011; Herrick, 2005; Cave, 2009), this philosophical perspective is faring no better than any other in escaping the ossification process. Such a reality makes discussion of the scholarly and political criticisms and controversies surrounding humanism difficult, as it is easy to generally assume a sort of standard, garden-variety version of the thing, when of course there are many strands of humanism and much internal disagreement about the particulars. Thus, any given criticism may be applicable to some conceptualizations of humanism but not others. The discussion in this section will therefore proceed holding the 'popular guidebook' version of humanism at hand, while also recognizing that many self-declared humanists (of both the professional and armchair philosopher sort) have already wrestled with the issues outlined here and created their own modifications to mainstream popular humanist thought, which serve them in their own thinkings and doings.

From the get-go, humanism has faced a battery of criticisms, the most popular of which tend to be perhaps the least well-founded (and conversely, the most well-founded of which tend to be perhaps the least frequently considered). The philosophy's emphasis on secularism has unsurprisingly rendered it a target for conservative religious groups, and in the United States for the political right, which has become increasingly aligned with such groups (Jelen, 1994; Baumgartner, Francia, and Morris, 2008). Those in the Religious Right tend to equate humanism with moral relativism. This critique misses the mark, because although humanism advocates a flexible and contextual approach to moral reasoning, recognizing as it does that life's inevitable complexity often presents in the form of dilemmas for which there are no easy solutions, it holds certain fundamental principles about human dignity and care for others to have irrefutable value and to be at the core of moral decision-making; thus, it is anything but relativistic.

Humanism is also not synonymous with Romanticism, although it is often confused as such. Romanticism was a movement that arose predominantly in the first half of the nineteenth century in Europe, in response to and critique of the Industrial Revolution and its concomitant rationalization of many aspects of modern life. The Romantic Movement held the figure of the individual in high regard, as well as the notions of free artistic expression and emotional indulgence. Nature loomed large in the world of Romanticism, and Romantics were often suspicious of the synthetic human world, viewing human life to be perhaps at its most authentic when individuals were able to contemplate the natural world in solitude. Thus, although Romanticism shares with humanism a positive view of the capabilities of humankind and a belief that humans should aspire to greatness, the former lacks the profoundly social character of the latter, as well as the latter's admiration of science and modernity. In humanism, it is not primarily the individual's quest for experience of the world, but rather his or her capacity to grow, improve, and contribute to social good, that is defining. Humanism is also not romantic in the sense of naïvely believing that there are easy answers to the moral conundrums any individual will inevitably face in his or her life course. To act with compassion is the goal, but just how to best exercise compassion in any given situation is a perennial question in any human life, and many times an easy answer is not forthcoming. Humanism does not seek to gloss this reality, but rather holds it directly at heart.

A closer critical analysis of mainstream humanism, as captured in the popular literature, actually points to other issues that constitute more important grounds for critique. The first of these has to do with humanism's position on religion. Mainstream humanism is characterized in the popular literature as being almost antagonistic to religion, in the sense of framing religion as not only an unnecessary bedrock for morality, but actually as a dangerous one. Although the classic caveats are noted—"many religious people often pursue the same goals as humanists," "every day there are instances of humanists and religious adherents working alongside each other for positive social change," et cetera—religion tends to be characterized as a dogmatic worldview with an unyielding set of rules that predetermine the moral stance one can take on any given issue. This is a reductionistic and grossly over-generalizing take on religion. Given that much of the popular literature on humanism has come out of the United Kingdom and the United States, where Christianity is the dominant religious tradition, Christianity is often used in this literature as an example of a dogmatic religious system that is not easily reconciled to humanist philosophy, and so I, too, will draw on it as an example in this critique, with the understanding that any of the world's religious traditions could likely serve just as well.

Christianity comes in many forms, from Roman Catholicism, with its hierarchical structure of leadership in matters of both theological interpretation and church operations; to evangelical Protestantism, with its much looser organizational structure of small churches, occasionally led by pastors without formal seminary training; to separatist traditions like the Amish and Mennonites; to Unitarian Universalism, which draws on the Christian tradition as only one of many religions orientations that undergird its approach. Even within a single denomination of Christianity—United Methodism, for example—there are various theological schools of thought which individual clergy and parishioners may subscribe to, such as liberation theology, which links faith directly to political responsibility, or process theology, which holds God as being in a continuous relationship with his creation, an interaction which causes him to change over time, just as those he has created change over time as a result of their unfolding relationship with him. Given the incredible diversity of conceptualizations of Christianity alone (both in a formal theological sense and in the actual lives of practitioners of *any* given strand)—indeed conceptualizations ranging all the way from the conviction that humans are bound by a set of laws laid down by God from the time of earthly creation to views which hold that the whole process is forever in negotiation, with God and humans figuring out their relationship together as they go along—it seems odd to say that religion and humanism are *de facto* in opposition to one another because religion is *de facto* dogmatic. Instead, it seems that the core of humanism's point in this regard is that deities and theology aren't *necessary* for morality. One may agree with this idea while still holding faith in the existence of deities and still participating in the practices of a particular religious tradition.

This critique may seem an arcane matter, unfit for inclusion in a book that is predominately about tourism (and in a chapter that is about humanism and its relationship to tourism), but in fact it is highly pertinent. Religion and tourism are related in many ways, including that religion serves as one motivation for tourism (for instance, in the case of pilgrims or religious music festival attendees) and that religious sites are a part of the larger cultural field that is commodified by tourism. Tourism is also a key component of the contemporary culture-leisure apparatus through which people seek to connect with the metaphysical, in an era when fewer people than ever before in the western world adhere to the religious convictions of their forebears, instead seeking to carry out their own individualized quests for life meaning (think New Age and the popularization of mystic offshoots of religious traditions like Kabbalah and Sufism). Thus, if humanism is conceived in limited terms, as a movement whose orientation can only be truly shared by the non-religious (i.e., not the traditionally religious nor the postmodern seekers who forge their own path), then its ability to serve as a philosophical perspective that reaches across lines of difference to unite various actors in our tourism world is inevitably stunted.

The other major critique I would offer of mainstream humanism of the 'guidebook variety' is that it can ring a bit too celebratory of science as a means to knowledge and social improvement, to the point of expressing the kind of blind faith that many in academia have come to see as *scientism*. Again, humanism will be of limited applicability in our tourism community if it is conceived as embracing science naïvely and at the expense of other ways of knowing. As noted below, tourism studies is finally beginning to move decisively beyond positivism only thinking, to embrace hermeneutic and critical perspectives on knowledge production, while also still entertaining the traditional, received scientific position. As optimists who hold a deep belief in the human capacity for creating ideas and materialities that improve our collective condition, humanists should be the first to realize, after Feyerabend (2010), that creativity is an inherent part of even the most 'hard science' pursuits, and that all knowledge production is, at best, a truly human creation, with all the 'imperfections' this reality implies. Thus, humanism will only grow to have more internal coherence as its mainstream advocates begin to take more of a pragmatist turn (Dewey, 2005) and come to embrace human creativity as part and parcel of the knowledge production process. It will also come nearer to its principle of advancing compassion if it takes the more inclusive position of recognizing multiple paths to knowledge, rather than promoting a hegemonic Western approach at the expense of other cultural epistemological systems (Feyerabend, 2010). Humanism need not hinge on blind faith in science, and it will surely serve our tourism world better as a moral philosophy if it is open to the diverse knowledge-pathways and meaning-narratives of the various actors—of all ethnicities, nationalities, faiths, genders, sexualities, ages, and bodily conditions—who share the tourism stage.

Exploring Humanism's Applicability to Tourism

Tourism is an activity that is at once both profoundly social and individualistic. Popular culture is most aware of it in the latter sense. The practice of tourism tends to be viewed as one of freedom, relaxation, and escape—a chance to indulge in fantasy and experience exotic and invigorating sensations that provide a contrast from the stressors, routines, and ennui that often characterize regular workaday life. It is also an opportunity for individual identity-building, as travel experiences become part of a person's biography and contribute to the way she makes sense of herself and her own history. Furthermore, if Maffesoli (1996) is correct, and we are now living in "the time of the tribes," a postmodern era in which identity is increasingly organized around affinity with lifestyle groups that share aesthetic and experiential sensibilities (including those packaged by the commercial market and constituting the "culture industry"), then tourism is one more site where such "emotional communities" spring up to constitute individual identity in terms of leisure-lifestyle group affiliation (think backpackers or festival attendees), as opposed to in terms of, say, occupational or political affiliation—the sorts of identity containers that had more purchase during modernity.

Through this lens of individual freedom, pleasure, and identity-articulation, it becomes harder to see tourism as part of the public sphere—as a domain in which the types of issues moral philosophy likes to press are applicable. Eagleton (2007) explores this idea in a broader sense, in his historical tracing of what has happened to the notion of the "meaning of life" in western culture. Without desiring to romanticize history, Eagleton argues that questions about the meaning of life arose rather less frequently before modernity, as their answers often felt readily apparent, being tied strongly as they were to the domains of religion, love and sexuality, and culture. Although we often forget it today, these domains were firmly located in the public sphere before modernity, a reality that had both benefits and drawbacks. With the quest for freedom from the absolute rule of church and state, and with the rise of positivist science, however, "fact and value seemed to split apart, leaving the former a public affair and the latter a private one," and the major domains of life meaning named above increasingly became the province of the private sphere (Eagleton, 2007, p. 21). Capitalist modernity, with its instrumentalist economic system, also entered the picture. As Eagleton (2007, p. 22) notes, "[i]t was a way of life dedicated to power, profit, and the business of material survival, rather than fostering the values of human sharing and solidarity. The political realm [became] more a question of management and manipulation than of communal shaping of a common life." Thus, although the shared anchors of life-meaning—culture, religion, and intimate relationships— had shifted out of the public sphere, people continued to cling to them as tightly as ever because the public sphere failed to replace them with anything that could command respect as a source of deep communal meaning. The symbolic realm related to culture, religion, and intimate relationships became more important than ever—and capitalism found a way to market it (Bauman, 2007; Eagleton, 2007). Modern tourism is, in many ways, part of this process of commodification of that which is basic to human life-meaning—culture, religion, art, physical wellness, hospitality, bonds with intimates and bonds with strangers, and so forth. Modern tourism practice is part of the process through which these anchors of life-meaning have been smuggled from the public into the private, individualistic sphere.

It has thus been difficult to imagine tourism in collectivist terms and therefore to really grapple with it as a moral domain (unless we take morality in an individualistic, Foucauldian [1998] sense, as "care of the self"). Capitalism keeps us on the treadmill, seeking our meager breathing space where we can get it—which means often in the arms of a tourism industry all too ready to profit from our craving for escape and release—and little imaginative energy is left to see things a different way. Humanistically inclined tourism scholars are increasingly trying to combat this challenge and to redirect the focus away from tourism as an instrumental economic activity and toward tourism as a profoundly social space where fundamental issues of Self and Other appear in stark relief, within the terms constituted by capitalist modernity (see Caton, 2013). They thus concern themselves with the ways in which tourism thwarts human happiness and well-being, and with its potential to do otherwise, and their work generally falls under the banner of the "critical turn" in tourism studies (Ateljevic, Pritchard, and Morgan 2007). Like humanists in general, tourism scholars who are humanistically inclined typically hold optimism that tourism practice can be improved and brought to better serve the interests of social justice, equality, and human flourishing, a position captured in Pritchard, Morgan, and Ateljevic's (2011) notion of the "Academy of Hope," but they do not hold naïve optimism in this regard. As noted, humanism is not romanticism. There is an acceptance that, on a fundamental level, the tension between Self and Other, individual good and social good, is powerful (Rorty, 1999). Much effort is thus spent attempting to understand the constraints that thwart human flourishing in tourism and to devise strategies that take into account the full reality of these constraints, while trying to move actors in our tourism world closer to the philosophical position on happiness advocated by Aristotle: that we are at our individual best when we live in harmony with our fellows and help them, among other ways, to create space for fulfilling their individual desires and projects, just as they help us to do the same in return (Fennell, 2006; Eagleton, 2007; Rorty, 1999; Wright, 2000). Such a humanistic approach is helpful in addressing moral concerns in tourism because tourism is inevitably a huge domain, involving actors from a variety of cultural and subcultural traditions, who vary greatly in their goals, dreams, and desires, and so a compassion-based approach emphasizing inherent human dignity and responsibility to one's fellows is a useful starting place, as we go forward to tackle the complexities of how the varied understandings and desires of the subjects of tourism intersect. Humanism cannot singlehandedly solve these complexities, but its relentless pursuit of the win-win over the zero-sum generates a praxis of moral creativity that can push us in the right direction without encouraging us to become starry-eyed in our expectations. We need not imagine that a perfect tourism world can ever be created: only a better one.

Hand-in-Hand: Humanism and the Humanities

Are there ways that tourism epistemology and pedagogy could better serve as sites for addressing moral concerns? In his groundbreaking article "The Truth about Tourism," Tribe (2006) argues that although tourism scholars may wish to see ourselves as lions forging through the untrammeled jungles of the phenomenon that is tourism, in search of the truth about our field, we may actually be more akin to lions in a circus cage, walled in by constraints so transparent that we easily fail to notice them, our knowledge production efforts unwittingly taking the shape of the cage. Tribe identifies five key realities that impinge on our knowledge production processes, one of which is "rules": a shorthand term he uses to refer to such issues as "disciplinarity, paradigms, postmodernity, traditions, discourse, and methodology" (p. 365). Drawing on others' analyses as well as his own, Tribe notes that tourism studies has traditionally been dominated by the discipline of economics, with social research disciplines like sociology, geography, and anthropology falling in behind, and he argues (again in line with a long tradition of scholars like Aronowitz and Giroux [1991]) that disciplines tend to shape the kinds of questions that can be asked through scholarship and the kinds of philosophical approaches and methods that can be used to answer them.

I have observed elsewhere (Caton, 2012) that moral matters have been slow to be taken up by tourism studies in part because the key disciplines behind tourism's investigation have historically been heavily under the sway of positivism and have also tended to be inclined to economic reductionism, in terms of the types of tourism concerns they have addressed. Although it is dangerous to generalize too fully about what kinds of disciplinary approaches have the capacity to lead to which types of understanding, it is not a stretch to imagine that a greater infusion of content and perspective from the humanities into tourism epistemology and pedagogy would render our field better equipped to engage with moral issues, as humanistically inclined tourism scholars are calling it to do.

I am far from the first to note the value of the humanities for tourism knowledge production. Tribe has written extensively on the relevance of both philosophy (2009) and visual art (2008) to tourism understanding; Rydzik, Pritchard, Morgan, and Sedgley (2013) have undertaken arts-based empirical work in tourism; and there is a distinguished tradition of advocacy for taking arts-based approaches toward social research pursuits more broadly (e.g., Barone, 1995; Knowles and Cole, 2008). As Eisner (2008) argues, the arts are valuable to social research because they help us access and express the human condition in ways that regular language doesn't allow for. They thus expand the realm of what can be understood about any given human phenomenon (including tourism) by helping us to explore portions of it that can't be conveyed representationally through verbal language. The arts are also valuable in helping us confront complexity and destabilize taken-for-granted ideas about the phenomena we study (Barone, 1995), which is important because those taken-for-granted ideas sometimes ride atop ideological agendas that may not be in the interests of social justice (Hollinshead, Ivanova, and Caton, in press). Nonetheless, despite their potential for platforming moral engagement, very little tourism research to date has actually drawn on the humanities in its knowledge production process.

Similarly, the humanities—particularly philosophy, visual art, music, dance, literature, and drama—are seldom drawn on in the tourism curriculum. In a forthcoming chapter in Dredge, Airey and Gross's *Handbook of Tourism and*

Hospitality Education, I outline five key benefits the humanities hold for tourism education (Caton, 2014). First, philosophy can help students build critical reasoning capacity through Socratic dialogue (see Nussbaum, 2010). Second, the historical realist and pragmatist strains of contemporary philosophy can help students learn to reason about the relationship between truth-pursuit and moral responsibility and to engage with life's big questions without losing sight of social complexity and contingency. Third, the arts are a valuable tool for cultivating flexible minds, which can see the possible beyond the actual (see Boyd, 2009). Fourth, the arts are stellar at fostering empathetic capacity and moral imagination (see Barone, 1995; Verducci, 2000). Fifth, as demonstrated by cognitive neuroscience, the arts are effective at engaging learners because they key into important brain functioning patterns that humans have needed to hone for evolutionary survival (see Boyd, 2009); they also allow us to reach our students on a deep level, engaging them in ways that go beyond the merely instrumental (see West, 2009; Rosales, 2012). Each of these strengths of the humanities is relevant for the cultivation of students as moral subjects who can think about tourism as a domain of moral engagement and responsibility and ultimately behave more competently in it. Neoliberalizing pressures in higher education, in general (Aronowitz, 2000; Giroux, 2007; Barnett, 1994) and specifically in tourism (Ayikoru, Tribe, and Airey, 2009; Dredge, Airey, and Gross, 2014), render it challenging to integrate humanities coursework into the curriculum space. Caving to such pressures as an academy, however, and allowing tourism education to continue down a trajectory that is almost exclusively vocationalist and managerialist, aids and abets the reproduction of tourism practice in its current form, as a domain in which the ideologies of capitalism, materialism, and performativity run wild, leaving precious little space for tourism to be conceived as a space of moral encounter. In this atmosphere of instrumentalist tourism education, it is difficult for today's students to hear the call of humanistic perspectives on tourism, which enjoin them to act in service to the greater good and hold faith that the world can be changed for the better, and then to deliver on this call as tomorrow's practitioners in the field.

It is perhaps intuitive that the humanities in many ways go hand-in-hand with humanism as a philosophy and a social movement. The humanities embrace the human creative subject—engaging characteristics unique to, or most fully developed within, her species, such as imagination, emotionality, empathy, representational capability, and aesthetic sensibility—to confront all that lies in the experience of being human. And core to that experience is the moral self, who, for better or for worse, must navigate the world bound relationally with other creatures. Thus, as elsewhere throughout the academic landscape, the humanities have much to offer in tourism studies, both from a scholarly and a pedagogical perspective, and taking them seriously as a component of both epistemology and curriculum can help to encourage the kind of moral reflection and capacity-building that humanism so powerfully advocates—and that our tourism world so desperately needs.

Conclusions

The moral agenda that lies before tourism studies is sweeping. As Tribe (2009) notes, moral issues in tourism have generally been interpolated through the notion of sustainability, and most commonly environmental sustainability, but the ground for exploration is broader than that. There are many 'big questions' we can ask. For instance, what does it mean to live a happy life, and how does tourism contribute to achieving this, for hosts and for guests? There is a rich literature in moral philosophy exploring different conceptions of happiness, and one can ask whether tourism tends to lead to a sort of infantilization of participants that provides immediate, base gratification, or whether it can help to facilitate deeper kinds of happiness. Or, what constitutes a just tourism world? Is it possible to outline general principles by which we should treat each other in tourism, in order to promote compassion and human dignity? Are there times, as Tucker (2013) and Mostafanezhad (2013) suggest, when even our most noble of capacities— empathy, for instance, or the desire to lend a helping hand—become imperialistic? What happens when individual and social good conflict? How do we balance the individual search for beauty in tourism with the more social notion of virtue?

The ground for moral exploration in tourism is indeed fertile. Travel is arguably a unique domain in the contemporary human experience, in that it is *the* mechanism in today's world through which we can have visceral experiences of spaces and customs beyond those of our own home, often under the liberating spell that comes with a mindset of leisure and play, but always with the sense of mystery that comes from being in a 'space apart,' not at home but not fully a member of the society we are visiting either. Thus, it is the dwelling place *par excellence* for explorations of our relationships to ourselves and others, and of the responsibilities we may hold on each front. By presenting a discussion of one strand of moral philosophy, humanism, and exploring its relevance to tourism and to the process of creating and conveying tourism understandings, I hope to encourage others to join the conversation and provide discussions of other aspects of, or traditions or movements within, moral philosophy that can help to illuminate the phenomenon we study. After so many centuries of Enlightenment thought ossified into scientism and rationalist economic instrumentalism, we have become out of practice in engaging with moral matters in the mainstream public sphere in ways that don't quickly slide into polarization and fundamentalism. Perhaps we, as tourism scholars, can do our part to help turn things around.

References

Aronowitz, S. (2000). *The Knowledge Factory: Dismantling the Corporate University and Creating True Higher Learning*. Boston: Beacon Press.

Aronowitz, S., and Giroux, H. (1991). *Postmodern Education: Politics, Culture and Social Criticism*. Minneapolis, MN: University of Minnesota Press.

Ateljevic, I., Pritchard, A., and Morgan, N. (2007). *The Critical Turn in Tourism Studies: Innovative Research Methodologies*. Amsterdam: Elsevier.

Ayikoru, M., Tribe, J., and Airey, D. (2009). Reading Tourism Education: Neoliberalism Unveiled. *Annals of Tourism Research*, 36: 191–221.

Barnett, R. (1994). *The Limits of Competence: Knowledge, Higher Education and Society*. Buckingham, UK: Open University Press.

Barone, T. (1995). The Purposes of Arts-based Educational Research. *International Journal of Educational Research*, 23(2), 169–180.

Bauman, Z. (2007). *Consuming Life*. Cambridge: Polity Press.

Baumgartner, J., Francia, P., and Morris, J. (2008). A Clash Of Civilizations? The Influence of Religion on Public Opinion of U.S. Foreign Policy in the Middle East. *Political Research Quarterly*, 61(2), 171–179.

Boyd, B. (2009). *On the Origin of Stories: Evolution, Cognition, and Fiction*. Cambridge, MA: Belknap Press.

Caton, K. (2012). Taking the Moral Turn in Tourism Studies. *Annals of Tourism Research*, 39(4), 1906–1928.

Caton, K. (2013). What Does it Mean to be Good in Tourism? In K. Boluk and C. Weeden (eds.), *Managing Ethical Consumption in Tourism*. London: Routledge.

Caton, K. (2014). On the Practical Value of a Liberal Education. In D. Dredge, D. Airey and M. Gross (eds.), *The Routledge Handbook of Tourism and Hospitality Education*. London: Routledge.

Cave, P. (2009). *Humanism*. Oxford: Oneworld Publications.

Dewey, J. (2005). *The Quest for Certainty: A Study of the Relation of Knowledge and Action*. Whitefish, MT: Kessinger Publishing.

Dredge, D., Airey, D., and Gross, M. (eds.) (2014). *The Routledge Handbook of Tourism and Hospitality Education*. London: Routledge.

Eagleton, T. (2007). *The Meaning of Life: A Very Short Introduction*. Oxford: Oxford University Press.

Echtner, C., and Prasad, P. (2003). The Context of Third World Tourism Marketing. *Annals of Tourism Research*, 30(3), 660–682.

Eisner, E. (2008). Art and Knowledge. In J. G. Knowles and A. Cole (eds.), *Handbook of the Arts in Qualitative Research*. Thousand Oaks, CA: Sage.

Fennell, D. (2006). *Tourism Ethics*. Clevedon: Channel View.

Feyerabend, P. (2010). *Against Method*. London: Verso.

Foucault, M. (1998). *Ethics: Subjectivity and Truth*. New York: The New Press.

Giroux, H. (2007). *The University in Chains: Confronting the Military—Industrial—Academic Complex*. Boulder, CO: Paradigm Publishers.

Hall, C. M., and Higham, J. (eds.) (2005). *Tourism, Recreation and Climate Change*. Clevedon: Channel View.

Hancock, J. (2011). *Jen Hancock's Handy Humanism Handbook*. Self-published and available through www.Jen-Hancock.com.

Herrick, J. (2005). *Humanism: An Introduction*. Amherst, NY: Prometheus Books.

Hollinshead, K., Ivanova, M., and Caton, K. (In press). Destinations under Discipline: Foucault and the Transformation of Place Makers. In Y. Reisinger (ed.), *Transformational Tourism: Host Perspectives*. Oxfordshire, UK: CABI.

Inui, Y., Wheeler, D., and Lankford, S. (2006). Rethinking Tourism Education: What Should Schools Teach? *Journal of Hospitality, Leisure, Sport and Tourism Education*, 5(2), 25–35.

Jelen, T. G. (1994). Religion and Foreign Policy Attitudes: Exploring the Effects of Denomination and Doctrine. *American Politics Research*, 22(3), 382–400.

Jeong, S., and Santos, C. (2003). Cultural Politics and Contested Place Identity. *Annals of Tourism Research*, 31(3), 640–656.

Knowles, J. G., and Cole, A. (eds.) (2008). *Handbook of the Arts in Qualitative Research*. Thousand Oaks, CA: Sage.

Law, S. (2011). *Humanism: A Very Short Introduction*. Oxford: Oxford University Press.

Maffesoli, M. (1996). *The Time of the Tribes*. London: Sage.

Mostafanezhad, M. (2013). The Politics of Aesthetics in Volunteer Tourism. *Annals of Tourism Research*, 43, 150–169.

Nussbaum, M. (2010). *Not for Profit: Why Democracy Needs the Humanities*. Princeton, NJ: Princeton University Press.

Pritchard, A., Morgan, N., and Ateljevic, I. (2011). Hopeful Tourism: A New Transformative Perspective. *Annals of Tourism Research*, 38(3), 941–963.

Radest, H. (1969). *Toward Common Ground: The Story of the Ethical Societies in the United States*. New York: Ungar.

Ring, A., Dickinger, A., and Wöber, K. (2009). Designing the Ideal Undergraduate Program in Tourism: Expectations from Industry and Educators. *Journal of Travel Research*, 48, 106–121.

Rorty, R. (1989). *Contingency, Irony, and Solidarity*. Cambridge: Cambridge University Press.

Rorty, R. (1999). *Philosophy and Social Hope*. London: Penguin Books.

Rosales, J. (2012). Cultivating Minds and Hearts. *University Affairs*, August edition, 18–24.

Rydzik, A., Pritchard, A., Morgan, N., and Sedgley, D. (2013). The Potential of Arts-based Transformative Research. *Annals of Tourism Research*, 40(1), 283–305.

Su, X., Wang, H., and Wen, T. (2013). Profit, Responsibility, and the Moral Economy of Tourism. *Annals of Tourism Research*, 43, 231–250.

Tribe, J. (2006). The Truth about Tourism. *Annals of Tourism Research*, 33: 360–381.

Tribe, J. (2009). *Philosophical Issues in Tourism*. Bristol: Channel View Publications.

Tucker, H. (2013). Empathy and Appropriation: Postcolonial Reflections. In *Proceedings of the International Critical Tourism Studies Conference V*, Sarajevo, Bosnia-Herzegovina, June 25–28.

Verducci, S. (2000). A Moral Method? Thoughts on Cultivating Empathy through Method Acting. *Journal of Moral Education*, 29(1), 87–99.

West, C. (2009). *Brother West: Living and Loving Out Loud*. New York: Smiley Books.

Wright, R. (2000). *Nonzero: The Logic of Human Destiny*. New York: Vintage Books.

Chapter 15
Mind the Gap: Opening up Spaces of Multiple Moralities in Tourism Encounters

Hazel Tucker

Introduction

Tourist encounters are considered to be 'closely entwined with the imperial project and colonialism' (Pritchard and Morgan, 2007: 21), in that they 'define and fix both the tourist and the toured "other" in a relationship with each other which stems from colonialism and is always inherently colonial in nature' (Tucker and Akama, 2009: 510). In *Empty Meeting Grounds*, for example, MacCannell (1992: 27) laments that 'The tourist who calls an Indian 'Injun' means to insult, but the well-intended tourist on the same bus is no less insulting'. Even the apparent good intentions of the 'new moral tourisms' (Butcher, 2003), or 'ethical tourism' practices, are critiqued as being yet another branding exercise to attempt to cover over the same relations of domination as the other, more usual 'mass' tourisms. Rather than dismissing that good intention out of hand, however, it would seem worthwhile opening it up a little, in order to look at the possibilities it might hold and the meaning it may have for, what are clearly, the very complex moral encounters of tourism. The possibilities that good intention might hold would arise out of an understanding of tourism encounters as altogether more complex and fractal than a portrayal of them as straightforwardly colonial, and insulting, could allow. There is a need, then, for more in-depth location and interrogation, not only of 'precisely the agents, moments and techniques of the exercise of power in tourism encounters' (Gibson, 2012: 59), but also of the interruptions and destabilizations of that power.

Tourism encounters are moral encounters, and highly complex, not only in an ethical sense, but also in an ontological sense. Recognition of this point necessitates a shifting of the paradigms within which we work and within which we think in order to re-form our questions about 'encounters' so that we more purposefully and more reflectively pose our questions in recognition of 'a supposedly postcolonial, postmodernizing world, and in relation to material conditions and socio-cultural practices that are significantly different from what they were half a century ago' (Venn, 2006: 78). This chapter discusses this paradigm shift as one which moves necessarily away from assumptions of fixed cultural positions in tourism encounters, and towards focusing on the fluidity and mobility of positions and relations between so-called 'tourists' and 'toured'. In turn, this shift encourages awareness of the contradictions and ambiguities with which tourism encounters are filled. The chapter thereby raises the need to further develop nuanced understanding of the relationship between tourist and toured so as to reconsider this relationship as comprising encounters of multiple, and often ambivalent, moralities. To begin, and in order to set the scene further, I will describe one such tourism encounter which occurred during my ethnographic fieldwork in Göreme, in the Cappadocia region of central Turkey.

A Tourism Encounter

Fateme, a Göreme woman, took me outside of the village to see her cave-house and garden in the valley. Her husband had made the cave habitable years ago so that he would have a quiet place to spend his days during his retirement years. When we arrived, there was a bus group of tourists nearby. They were Portuguese tourists and their guide was telling them about the formation of the rock columns and caves in the valley. As we made our way past them to go to Fateme's garden a middle aged couple who had broken away from the main group followed us and tried to engage with Fateme. Using me as a translator, Fateme said that they could come up to look at the house too if they liked. They did and when inside they marvelled at the carpeted rock-hewn dwelling. Fateme and I together answered a few questions that they asked. They took photographs of Fateme, and also of each other with Fateme. After a while, aware that their tour group outside may be heading away, they went to leave. As they went to leave, one of the women in the group, rather awkwardly and clumsily, took out a twenty euro note and placed it into Fateme's hand. Fateme looked embarrassed but took the note. The tourists went on their way to join their group, leaving Fateme and I standing in the doorway of the cave-house. Fateme held the note, looked at me, shrugged, and put the note into her purse.

So how do we conceptualize the giving of the twenty euro note? In one view, it appears insulting, patronizing even, especially as it is likely to be based on an assumption, a most likely erroneous assumption, that Fateme is poor relative to their wealth, and that she is needy relative to their ability to give. Actually, Fateme, or Fateme's family, is really quite wealthy these days. Because of tourism, the value of property in Göreme has shot up in the past decade and, also, one of Fateme's sons has done very well building up a tourism retail business. Indeed, it is possible even taking into account international exchange rates and costs of living, that Fateme is wealthier than many of the people in the Portuguese group. Yet *imagined* stark differences between tourist and local are invoked and enacted: tourist as wealthy, modern, cosmopolitan and independent; and Fateme as poor, traditional, local and dependent. The scenario plays out an unequal, colonial relationship between 'tourist' and 'local' and so, yes, we can read the giving of the twenty euro note as insulting. On the other hand, however, we know that the tourists most likely did not *intend* to be insulting. Therefore, is the well-intended tourist really, as MacCannell had argued, no less insulting than the tourist who means to insult? Perhaps, just as Chabot-Davis (2004: 406) argues that 'scholars cannot afford to give up on empathy's promise of fostering cross-cultural understanding and desires for social justice and equality', critical tourism scholars, likewise, should not give up on the possibilities that good intentions might hold amongst the moral encounters of tourism.

Simultaneously, though, rather than seeing such good intentions as straightforwardly positive and needing to be cultivated so as to reduce 'bad' tourism encounters, we might also ask what contingencies and contradictions good intentions have, and where, why and how do good-intentions fail? Where, why and how do insulting intentions fail? Were there felt ambiguities and doubts working to destabilize the tourists' surety regarding their role and position in the encounter? What are the causes and implications of those doubts, and what are their effects on the intended recipients? Whilst the answers to these questions are never fully determinable, it is only if we try to think these kinds of ambiguities and ambivalences through that we can begin to conceive of tourism encounters as being other than set within a colonial frame. In this chapter, then, I am asking whether, in such moments as the giving of the twenty euro note, there is the possibility of moral ambivalence, the possibility of tourist awareness of their complicity with colonial modes of representation, and whether there is, therefore, the possibility of the interruption of those colonial modes of representation.

Whilst 'analysis of tourism's encounters is now more attentive to how bodies and materials interact in fluid, complicated ways' (Gibson, 2012: 59), there is still more to be done regarding location of tourism's disrupting of colonial relationships. Towards this, postcolonial theory is useful in its consideration of the ambiguities, contradictions and even failures of colonial ideology and pursuits. Bhabha's (1994) notion of ambivalence, for example, developed to challenge the colonial production of binary oppositions, is useful to consider tourism relationships as entanglements of often contradictory and paradoxical processes. Indeed, the notions of ambivalence, contradiction and paradox encourage us to see that intention is never singular, and therefore that 'any reliance on dichotomous postcolonial subject positions [is] problematically simplistic' (Pedwell, 2013: 22). Engaging with postcolonial theory encourages us not only to attend to the processes of domination in tourism, but also 'to consider ways in which tourism provides a space for subverting representations and creating new hybrid spaces of being and becoming' (Keen and Tucker, 2012: 97).

The 'Gap' in Tourism Encounters

Notions of dichotomous subject positions, and ideas of a neat line or 'gap' that defines and describes difference, are pervasive in analyses of tourism and portrayals of tourists and toured or hosts and guests. In his latest book *The Ethics of Sightseeing*, for example, MacCannell begins his appendix piece entitled 'The

Moral Field of Tourism' by arguing that all tourism involves tourists crossing the line, the line crossed being the 'marked or unmarked boundaries between normative differences' (2011: 212). Elsewhere in the book, MacCannell refers to this line as a gap, the gap that separates tourists from the other-as-attraction. Mary Louise Pratt (1992, 2008) has portrayed a similar idea in her writing about tourism 'contact zones'. These contact zones 'are social spaces where disparate cultures meet, clash and grapple with each other, often in highly asymmetrical relations of domination and subordination—such as colonialism and slavery, or their aftermaths as they are lived out across the globe today' (Pratt, 2008: 7).

I too, in my previous ethnographic work looking at tourism relationships in Göreme, Turkey, have portrayed dichotomous subject positions in this way. For example in the chapter entitled 'Close Encounters: Interactions between hosts and guests' in *Living With Tourism: Negotiating Identities in a Turkish Village* (Tucker, 2003), I began, 'Göreme has become a meeting place for a variety of different people whose worlds are far apart from each other' (p. 118). The chapter went on to discuss how the roles of host and guest are played out and, although I did talk about hospitality and the roles of host and guest as being *constitutive* of the 'tourist-host encounter' rather than simply a component of it, I still portrayed the Göreme people and the tourists as two separate and clear-cut subject positions, with the Göreme people as the hosts, and tourists as the guests. Reading this work now, I can see where I was positing a binary divide and emphasizing difference, either explicitly or implicitly. For example, when I wrote about 'hospitality' being an 'integral part' of the Göreme peoples' culture (p. 122), was I implying that hospitality does not have such a place for the tourists? And where I said 'The villagers are extremely sensitive to the issue of respect and if they perceive that the tourists are in any way disrespectful, they will not interact with them' (p. 122), do we read from this that tourists are *not* sensitive to the issue of respect? It is this kind of binary divide, emphasizing clear and fixed difference, which goes hand-in-hand with a view of tourism as always being inherently colonial, and thereby itself perpetuating the view of the tourist and toured 'other' as being locked into a colonial relationship.

Calling the 'Gap' into Question

It is important, then, to destabilize this 'gap' in our analyses of tourism encounters by calling the categories of tourist and toured 'other'; 'host' and 'guest'; insider and outsider into question and by looking at where these categories become noticeably unstable. One possible place to do this is at the intersection of tourism studies and what we might call mobilities studies, where it is possible to see how migrants, 'expats', and other 'long-term tourists' might disrupt and throw open to question our binary categorizations. As Venn (2006: 77) argues, 'forms of worlding are grounded in a plurality of histories and experiences inscribed in temporalities and spacialities that now co-habit'. Indeed, a growing body of literature employs the concept of transnationalism to describe and explore contemporary, novel, migrant 'expat' identities and communities (Urry, 2000; Vertovec, 1999), particularly looking at the ways in which mobile individuals live multiple 'lives' as they retain multiple places, across national borders, that they all call 'home'. Furthermore, 'this increased mobility between places and the associated confusion of insider/ outsider, of who belongs and who does not, indicate a potential point of engagement for the future of postcolonial thinking within tourism' (Keen and Tucker, 2012: 100). 'Long-term tourists', such as many backpackers for whom staying in a place for a while and working in tourism is part of the travel experience, is an example of tourism 'that complicates binary readings of tourism as Third World workers in servitude to rich Westerners (Gibson, 2012: 57; see also Duncan, 2008).

Related to this, Soares (1998) talks about globalization as increasing the opportunities for copying which may be related to a desire to perform one's own fantasies about the 'other'. Soares adds that, therefore, 'mimicry can be a weapon against the political reification of identities' because 'the experience of being something else challenges reified identities and brings the possibility of circulating, shifting, and changing to the forefront of social and cultural life' (1998: 295). It would seem that tourism spaces and encounters are rife with opportunities for such mimicry and 'performing one's own fantasies about the other'. One example of this is where tourists and migrants 'fetishize the idea of 'living like the locals'' (Davidson, 2005: 46). Davidson (2005: 28) studied 'alternative travellers' in India and argued that they 'fetishize the idea of 'living like the locals' in order to overturn the ways of relating to other cultures that have been circumscribed by the West's systematic accumulation of knowledge about the world'. Davidson continues: '[t]hose who participate orientate themselves towards 'new' forms of intercultural understanding … that has the potential to transgress the boundaries of fixed national and Western identities' (ibid.). Whilst it has been widely argued that the motivations and meanings of so-called 'alternative travel' are grounded in just the same ideological concerns with domination as other tourisms, indeed perhaps even more so given that it is a predominantly white middle-class form of tourist consumption, it seems that Davidson is looking here for the possibility that travellers in India might problematize preconceptions about the Western 'Self' and Indian 'Other'' (p. 30). She suggests that one of the ways they do this is through 'integrating themselves within and among local, indigenous communities, learning from them forms of experience and knowledge rejected and repressed by the West' (p. 51).

It is difficult to glean from Davidson's reading of these 'alternative tourists' the extent to which they resist, or conversely the extent to which they inculcate, some of the other key binaries inherent in colonial discourse, such as master/ servant, traditional/modern, centre/periphery, devious-lazy/moral-industrious. Indeed, Davidson does view the 'alternative tourists' in India as 'often genuinely self-reflexive about the nature of their relationships with India's travelled spaces' (2005: 51). She also points to the limitations of their efforts due to the fact that they will always still think with some concepts of home, and so can never fully *become* the other. This resonates again with Soares's (2005) arguments about mimicry, in that whilst performing one's own fantasies about the other can bring 'the possibility of circulating, shifting, and changing to the forefront of social and cultural life' (1998: 295), such attempts to 'live like the other' can never fully succeed and so are always in an ambivalent state of hybrid becoming. With regards to the 'colonized', also, Soares similarly argues that although cultural mimicry might be the only available experience of change, or in other words, 'the only available way of becoming different and distant from one's own identity as dominated' (1998: 295), such mimicry is riddled with paradox and contradiction because, again, it is never possible to fully *become* the other. Undoubtedly, though, it is increasingly important to call the 'gaps' between tourists and toured into question, since 'with the new mobilities occurring, it is crucial to consider how the ways of thinking and being (epistemologies and ontologies) which are the true legacies of colonialism and Western imperialism are being contested through tourism within the new formations of hybrid places' (Keen and Tucker, 2012: 102).

Shame and Reflective Emotion

Another way to look at where the subject positions in tourism encounters become noticeably unstable and called into question is through focusing on emotion. This is because, rather than residing in the individual, emotions act as mediating spaces (Ahmed, 2004, 2010) in encounters. Going back to the notion of intention in tourism encounters that we started with in this chapter, emotions mediate intentions and hence render intentions fluid and unstable. On this, Waitt et al. (2007) have looked at how tourist shame experienced by non-indigenous Australian tourists visiting Uluru can open up a 'moral gateway' towards reconciliation with indigenous Australians. Waitt et al. (2007) identify the ways in which shame 'swings a moral gateway by providing ... a dispositional change, wherein the colonizing group alters behaviours to avoid repeating injustices' (ibid., 260).

> Through experiencing an Anangu (Aboriginal guide's) interpretation of country, Claire expresses a heightened respect for all indigenous Australians through an increased awareness of her own 'whiteness'. This consciousness arose through her body, from feeling shame about being white when participating in the Aboriginal guided tour ... [which] evoked for Claire the possibilities of co-existence in difference' (Waitt et al., 2007: 259–260).

As Gibson has argued, tourism encounters 'elicit emotional responses of guilt, shame and concern—all potentially productive (if complex) responses' (2012: 59).

I also have previously discussed emotion working in productive ways in an article looking at how recognition of shame experienced and expressed by tourists, and researchers, has critical postcolonial potentialities (Tucker, 2009). In the article I developed a reflective account of my own feelings of discomfort and shame during an encounter, not too dissimilar to the one described above involving the Portugese tourists and Fateme, but this time where I attempted to mediate between a German couple and a Göreme woman. My own discomfort and shame during the encounter highlighted the possibility of similar discomfort and shame on the part of the German couple which, in turn, highlights an interest in living ethically and shows that tourist (and researcher) imaginaries, including the self-other binary, can be disrupted. As Tomkins suggests, shame 'is the most reflexive of affects in that the phenomenological distinction between subject and object is lost' (1995: 136). Probyn (2005: 78) also argues that 'shame sets off a nearly involuntary re-evaluation of one's self and one's actions'. This 'nearly involuntary' aspect of shame, together with the point that it is shown in bodily expression, further points to the possibilities which might be opened up by the occurrence of tourist (and researcher) shame. Shame cannot be hidden and it cannot be well controlled. Embodied tourism encounters can throw out surprises, not only to the other, but also to one's self; surprises which manifest in what Mauss (1979) referred to as 'moral discharge' from the body. This 'moral discharge', in such forms as blushing or averting the eyes, is communicative, and it is therefore why colonial tourist imaginaries are, during embodied tourism encounters, always open to 'the potential to be disrupted by the fleshiness of the body' (Waitt et al., 2007: 252) in ways that cannot be fully predicted or determined. As Gibson points out, even within highly 'regulated spaces unpredictable encounters are still possible' so that 'the possibility to interrupt dominance is ever present' (2012: 58–59).

The affect of 'shame' is useful to consider, then, in thinking about the possibility of a critical, reflective, discursive tourist imaginary and tourism encounter. As Probyn argues, '[s]hame illuminates our intense attachment to the world, our desire to be connected with others, and the knowledge that, as merely human, we will sometimes fail in our attempts to maintain those connections' (2005: 14). Juxtaposing the two concepts of 'shame' and 'intention' thus raises new questions about what was occurring during what is revealing itself to be a very 'moral encounter' between the Portuguese tourists and Fateme. Was the giving of the twenty euro note prompted by feelings of shame around privilege and inequality? Was the giving of the twenty euro note intended to alleviate that shame by going some way towards addressing that perceived inequality? Was the giving therefore to 'buy' the expulsion of the feelings of shame? Perhaps even more importantly, was there any doubt on the part of the tourists about their own moral intentions in the giving of the money? Was there any further shame prompted by a reflective awareness that this attempt 'to be connected with others' would most likely be futile?

Conclusions

Such reflective disruptions to intention in tourism encounters relate also to the necessity of reflectivity on the part of us, as researchers, also. We too need to consider the imaginaries underpinning our work, and to reflect on our complicity with, and resistance to, the colonial tourist imaginary. We might ask of MacCannell, for example, where he sees himself in relation to the bus tourists and to the 'Indians', and we can also ask the same of me in relation to the Portuguese tourists and to Fateme. As Bewes (2010: 166) writes, 'Ethnography itself is shameful because it participates in a structure of perception that is inseparable from a certain logic of self-authorization'. In other words, ethnography 'situates the self in relation to the world and to its objects of study' (ibid.), just as tourism does. We therefore need to 'become more aware of [our] own alignment, not only with the (colonizing) tourist, but also with what Hollinshead (2004) refers to as the 'declarative' value of tourism and the 'textual authority' of Tourism Studies' (Tucker, 2009: 447). In our work relating to the moral encounters of tourism we need to always be reflecting, hesitating, and questioning, in regard to the moral encounters of tourism *and* to the moral encounters of research.

Such an approach requires minding the 'gaps' in our analyses and shifting away from binary thinking to a mode of thinking and questioning which always calls fixed categories and subject positions into question. It is only if we do this that we will be able to locate in tourism encounters 'critical spaces for new narratives of becoming' (Venn, 2006: 1). As I have attempted to show in this chapter, also, Bhabha's (1994) notions of ambivalence and mimicry are useful to show that hybrid identities are entanglements of often contradictory and paradoxical processes. Whilst our analyses of contemporary identities and hence contemporary encounters must range from the 'micro-politics of embedded inhabitance and migration, to the macro-politics of transnationalism and global capital' (Ahmed et al., 2003: 2), I have emphasized in this chapter the importance of focusing in particular on the *potentialities* that tourism encounters hold as moral spaces for interrupting, and for destabilizing, normalized relationships and subject positions in tourism.

References

Ahmed, S. (2010). *The Promise of Happiness*. Durham, NC: Duke University Press.

Ahmed, S., Castaneda, C., Fortier, A., and Sheller, M. (2003). Introduction: Uprootings/Regroundings: Questions of Home and Migration. In S. Ahmed, C. Castaneda, A. Fortier, and M. Sheller (eds.), *Uprootings/Regroundings: Questions of Home and Migration*, pp. 1–19. Oxford: Berg Publishers.

Ahmed, S. (2004). *The Cultural Politics of Emotion*. Edinburgh: Edinburgh University Press.

Bewes, T. (2010). Another Perspective on the World: Shame and Subtraction in Louis Malle's *L'Inde Fantom*. In S. Bignall and P. Patton (eds.) *Deleuze and the Postcolonial*, pp. 163–81. Edinburgh: Edinburgh University Press.

Bhabha, H. K. (1994). *The Location of Culture*. London: Routledge.

Butcher, J. (2003). *The Moralization of Tourism: Sun, Sand ... and Saving the World?* London: Routledge.

Chabot-David, K. (2004). Oprah's Book Club and the Politics of Cross-racial Empathy. *International Journal of Cultural Studies*, 7(4), 399–419.

Davidson, K. (2005). Alternative India: Transgressive Spaces. In A. Jaworski and A. Pritchard (eds.), *Discourse: Communication and Tourism*. Clevedon: Channel View.

Duncan, T. (2008). The Internationalisation of Tourism Labour Markets: Working and Playing in a Ski Resort. In C. M. Hall and T. Coles (eds.), *International Business and Tourism: Global Issues, Contemporary Interactions*, pp. 181–194. London: Routledge.

Gibson, C. (2012). Geographies of Tourism: Space Ethics and Encounter. In J. Wilson (ed.), *The Routledge Handbook of Tourism Geographies*, pp. 55–60. London: Routledge.

Hollinshead, K. (2004). Tourism and New Sense: Worldmaking and the Enunciative Value of Tourism. In C. M. Hall and H. Tucker (eds.), *Tourism and Postcolonialsim: Contested Discourses, Identities and Representations*, pp. 25–42. London: Routledge.

Keen, D., and Tucker, H. (2012). Future Spaces of Postcolonialism in Tourism. In J. Wilson (ed.), *The Routledge Handbook of Tourism Geographies*, pp. 97–102. London: Routledge.

MacCannell, D. (1992). *Empty Meeting Grounds: The Tourist Papers*. London: Routledge.

MacCannell, D. (2011). *The Ethics of Sightseeing*. Berkeley: University of California Press.

Mauss, M. (1979). *Sociology and Psychology*. Translated by Ben Brewster. London: Routledge & Kegan Paul.

Pedwell, C. (2013). Affect at the Margins: Alternative Empathies in A Small Place. *Emotion, Space and Society*, 8, 18–26.

Pratt, M. L. (1992). *Imperial Eyes: Studies in Travel Writing and Transculturation*. London: Routledge.

Pratt, M. L. (2008). *Imperial Eyes: Travel Writing and Transculturation*, 2nd edn. London: Routledge.

Pritchard, A. and Morgan, N. (2007). De-centering Tourism's Intellectual Universe, or Traversing the Dialogue between Change and Tradition. In I. Ateljevic, A. Pritchard and N. Morgan (eds.), *The Critical Turn in Tourism Studies: Innovative Research Methodologies*, pp. 11–28. Oxford: Elsevier.

Probyn, E. (2005). *Blush: Faces of Shame*. Minneapolis, MN: University of Minnesota Press.

Soares, L. (1998). Staging the Self by Performing the Other: Global Fantasies and the Migration of the Projective Imagination, *Journal for Cultural Research*, 2(2), 288–304.

Tomkins, S. (1995). *Exploring Affect: The Selected Writings of Silvan S. Tomkins*. Cambridge: Cambridge University Press.

Tucker, H. (2003). *Living with Tourism: Negotiating Identities in a Turkish Village*. London: Routledge.

Tucker, H. (2009). Recognizing Emotion and its Postcolonial Potentialities: Discomfort and Shame in a Tourism Encounter in Turkey. *Tourism Geographies*, 11(4), 444–461.

Tucker, H., and Akama, J. (2009). Tourism as Postcolonialism. In T. Jamal and M. Robinson (eds.), *The Sage Handbook of Tourism Studies*, pp. 504–520, London: Sage.

Urry, J. (2000). *Sociology Beyond Societies: Mobilities for the Twenty-First Century*. London: Routledge.

Venn, C. (2006). *The Postcolonial Challenge: Towards Alternative Worlds*. London: Sage.

Vertovec, S. (1999). Conceiving and Researching Transnationalism. *Ethnic and Racial Studies*, 22(2), 447–462.

Waitt, G., Figueroa, R., and McGee, L. (2007). Fissures in the Rock: Rethinking Pride and Shame in the Moral Terrains of Uluru. *Transactions of the Institute of British Geographers*, 32(2), 248–263.

Chapter 16

What's the 'Use' of Young Budget Travel?

Tara Duncan

Introduction

This chapter examines some of the situated knowledges that exist within young budget travel. Utilizing a mobilities lens, the chapter moves away from an 'economic' valuing of these tourists towards a more nuanced perspective that involves understanding the movement and encounters of young budget travellers. In doing so, it questions current conceptions of such travel which often rely on particular (Western) ways of knowing the world. The chapter asks whether the methodological understandings of this type of travel really engages with the moral encounters that occur between young budget travellers, the many people that they connect with on their travel and perhaps most specifically, the researchers studying them. In doing so, the chapter raises more questions than it answers as it re-thinks the 'why' behind this type of travel in order to recognize the often privileged, power-laden relations inherent within much young budget travel.

Young budget travel, whether seen as backpacking, on an 'OE' (Overseas Experience) or doing a 'gap year', has become increasingly symbolic in contemporary society. From Richards and Wilson's (2004, p. 253) suggestion that the study of backpacking has becomes increasingly important because of the emblematic role that it has assumed in more general debates about tourism and youth culture to Gogia's (2006, pp. 364–365) assertion that '[f]rom academic research to Hollywood films backpackers have become new symbols of über-mobility', young budget travel has continually and progressively been 'discursively constructed as productive and liberating' (Cremin, 2007, p. 527). As Heath (2007) argues, the benefits of taking a year out, such as increasing cross cultural understanding, the building of tolerance (Lyons et al., 2011) as well as the increase in 'soft' skills such communication skills, independence, and a growing maturity, 'are presumed to be considerable' (Heath, 2007, p. 93).

Whilst not defining 'young budget travel' per se, it is worth pointing to a number of factors that influence the direction of this chapter and its subsequent discussions. Firstly, whilst this type of travel is most often associated with those taking time out from education, training or employment (see Jones, 2004; Cremin, 2007; Duncan, 2008), young is somewhat subjective. Restrictions on working holiday visas, for example, may limit the age of certain types of young budget travellers (see

Newlands (2006) for research on such visas). but Neil Carr (1998, p. 313) suggests that the term 'young', when related to tourism, may 'define aspects of a person's social position which are partially caused by age, but not completely determined by it'. This is important to note as there is a growing literature on backpacking and volunteer tourism which includes a wider range of ages and peoples in their studies. Secondly, young budget travel includes a diverse range of activities. These can include any combination of paid or unpaid work, volunteering, travelling, studying, relaxing, leisure time and so on (Heath, 2007). As Allon, Anderson and Bushell (2008, p. 75) state, '[t]he contemporary backpacker ... is also often an employee, a student, a visitor, a seasonal worker, holidaymaker, a semi-permanent resident, and potentially many other roles and identities'. So we need to recognize the nuances to their whole experience in that they may be a volunteer tourist, a 'deviant' backpacker and a worker whilst on their travels and as such reflect upon the ways in which young budget travellers may have numerous moral (or amoral) encounters. Thus in any research encounters with young budget travellers, how do we 'capture' their whole experience?

Finally, much of the rhetoric around such travel primarily considers a cohort of generally white, middle class, western participants. Whilst research into young budget travel does recognize the privileged nature of such travel (see for instance Clarke, 2005; Cremin, 2007), and more significantly, there is a growing breadth of literature that is exploring a much wider cross-section of young budget travellers (see for instance Muzaini, 2006; Ong and du Cros, 2012; Chen, Bao and Huang, 2013), there still seems to be assumptions amongst many (researchers) about who 'does' this type of travel. These factors all suggest that the research encounter is also a moral encounter. The view, therefore, that understanding young budget travel as 'useful', as constructive time out (Cremin, 2007) is somewhat simplistic. As Mostafahenzhad and Hannam point out in the introduction to this volume, the important point is 'that moral concerns can signal the emergence of new notions of space and society which are not neutral' (p. 5) and we need to consider how, methodologically, we recognize this as we move through spaces and encounters with these young budget travellers.

Mobilities

Zeitler (2012, p. 233) suggests that mobility 'is not a neutral term, not even if we frame a technical definition. It will always have moral implications'. If we consider young budget traveller's through the lens of mobilities—starting with Urry's (2007) contention that we are all, in some way, always on the move, then perhaps young budget travellers are, in their own ways, helping to smooth out the world and so working towards greater (global) equity (Skeggs, 2004). Yet, the challenges highlighted within the mobilities paradigm demonstrate the very inequity of this ability to be mobile, as Gogia (2006) illustrates in her example of Canadian nationals travelling to Mexico and vice versa. Cresswell (2010,

p. 20) contends that 'all forms of mobility—they have a physical reality, they are encoded socially and culturally, and they are experienced through practice'. As such, mobility is contingent on the capacity to access the right conditions, technology and networks that can enable movement across borders and cultures (Cresswell, 2010; Cohen, Duncan and Thulemark, 2013).

Despite the tensions highlighted above, being able to move and travel has become normal to many; it is part of our everyday lives (Edensor, 2007; Hannam, 2008). Mobility, therefore is a key component of the world today (Adey, 2010) and one way in which we can engage with the contemporary world (Duncan, 2011). Consequently, the mobility of young budget travellers is 'socially produced' where mobilities are enacted and encountered in and through social contexts (Oakes and Price, 2008). Thus young budget traveller's leisure, working and travelling experiences allow them to explore their own personal and professional possibilities and are bound up in broader social networks associated with the contemporary practices of mobility.

Therefore, whilst we still need to remember that 'some' will always be more equal than 'others' in the ability and freedom to travel and to be able to be, or become, 'global citizens' (Skeggs, 2004; Lyons et al., 2011), the question of how we consider this type of travel and the tensions inherent in our current societal (and academic) understanding becomes methodological. It becomes highly valuable to consider how young budget travellers not only 'make knowledge of the world, but how they physically and socially make the world through the ways they move and mobilize people, objects, information and ideas' (Büscher and Urry, 2009, p. 112).

Why Do We Need Ro Re-Consider Young Budget Travel?

Hence, we must first ask: why should we consider the 'use' of this type of travel? Rather than go into depth on Marxian political economic definitions of use value, I am suggesting that as tourism and travel have become more and more about consumption (Hall, 2012), so the 'use' of travel has been complicated through the contemporaneous, intangible, experiential exchange between producer and consumer (Gibson, 2009). As a result, the 'use' of young budget travel has, as Bianchi (2000, p. 124) suggests 'shift[ed] away from the hippie mythology of drifting, to something much more purposive and calculating'. Therefore, we can see a move towards the commodification of young budget travel. Work such as Kate Simpson's (2004; 2005) on the professionalization of the Gap Year and youth travel, more recent work on how young budget travellers experiences allow them to become 'global citizens' or cosmopolitan (Lyons et al., 2011; Snee, 2013) and Mostafanezhad's (2013) consideration of an aestheticized volunteer tourism experience which allows, in this case, volunteer tourists, to see poverty as authentic and cultural, reflect this growing consumerism of young budget travel.

Young budget travel is still often perceived as 'alternative' consumerism (or perhaps 'post' consumerism). Through taking a gap year they are saying they are travellers rather than (mass) tourists (Richards and Wilson, 2004). Consequently, in talking of their volunteering (and so altruistic) experiences, these young travellers introduce a moralizing element which validates one type of tourism over another, conceivably less ethical type of tourism (Butcher, 2003; Gibson, 2010). In the context of the commodification of budget travel experiences questions emerge around the moral versus the ethical or 'the "is" versus "ought" distinction' (Caton, 2012, p. 1906) which is inherent in this type of travel.

Why do we need to consider the moral encounters of young budget travellers? Firstly, as Noy (2004, p. 82) says the experiences of these tourists 'is perceived to be utmost, personal, and individual' although it 'is actually constructed amidst a tightly cohesive collective practice and is infused with sociocultural themes and tensions'. It is the significance we often place on young budget travel—that it allows young people to become global citizens, to gain a cosmopolitan view of the world which, upon their return from their travels will supposedly enhance their lives and seemingly enrich the lives of those around them—that becomes important. Yet in this very statement, it is their encounters with others that we perhaps tend to ignore. Recent research (see Lyon et al., 2011) specifically into gap year volunteer tourism, has begun to critique how neoliberal discourse sets up the idea of global citizenship and organizations such as the Volunteer Services Organization (VSO) have long argued that there is a need to ensure that "gappers" do not become the "new colonialists" (Ward, 2007). Thus, what is it about the encounters these young budget travellers have that becomes important to ascertain?

If we consider the moral encounters of young budget travel, there is a need, as Caton (2012, p. 1906) advocates, to confront both the 'light hearted pleasure and heavy social consequences' of these experiences. As Tomazos and Butler (2010; 2012) suggest, there is a balancing act to be managed between the hedonistic pursuits of young budget travel and the other altruistic or cultural commitments they have to travel and the work or volunteer experiences underway. This precarious balance is often captured through encounters. Encounters between these young travellers and the locals and communities who they live, work and play with. However, and equally importantly, these encounters are also between these young budget travellers and the researchers who spend their time trying to 'figure out' what motivates these young people (see Tomazos and Butler 2012 for instance).

Gibson (2010, p. 521, italics in original) explains that 'beyond its industrial and labour market structure, at the heart of tourism is *encounter*'. In the introduction to this volume, Mostafanezhad and Hannam suggest that it is through the 'micro-analysis of encounters' that we can 'begin to understand the varied ways that morality mediates the tourism encounter' (p. 6). It is also perhaps necessary to interrogate the moral encounter between researcher and researched and to consider the methodological impacts of this encounter. To continue from the introduction, young budget travellers may well find themselves dealing with 'a range of moral decisions that extend well beyond the potential of their individual experience and cultural knowledge' (p. 6). If this is the case, how can we be sure that the researcher is also not similarly implicated in such moral encounters?

Crick (1985, p. 81) asserts that: '[w]e may dislike the tourist who merely uses other cultures. But anthropology uses the other to create itself. If the tourist has limited interests, so do fieldworkers—they are after a PhD or intent upon publications'. Cohen (2004, p. 58) similarly asserts that a 'researchers' background has doubtlessly coloured their orientation to their research and the interpretation of their findings'. We therefore need to reflect upon the morality of the encounter between young budget traveller and researcher in order to go beyond the motivations, 'use' and individual 'value' that neoliberal agendas place on this type of travel. Instead, our methodological positioning should unpack some of these more situated knowledges and reflexively re-examine our encounters to allow for differing moralities between and within cultures and how these are embedded within spatial, temporal and power relations.

Methodological Reflections

Research into tourism encounters is becoming more attentive to the embodied nature of the construction of knowledge. Yet, it is the engagement with researcher reflexivity which is often still lacking from our research. As Cohen (2013) suggests, tourism has lagged behind the broader social sciences which confronted the reflexive turn a decade or more ago (see also Ashmore, 1989; Lynch, 2000). The myriad ways in which we undertake research—through immersing our embodied selves, through our emotions, our haptic geographies— and how these transect with the research process itself are 'central to strong, rigorous qualitative research and good science' (Dupuis, 1999 cited in Cohen, 2013, p. 336). Yet as Cohen (2013, p. 336) suggests '[p]erhaps this is an ideal, a goal towards which researchers can aim, but will likely not attain'. Immersing ourselves in research and recognizing the role we then play in this research through our interactions with our participants and the community in which we are situated is not necessarily as easy to recognize and reflect on as we think. As Tuan (2001, p. 44) says '[r]eflection may seem, at first blush, a commonplace sort of activity open to all. It does not require, for example, special training and equipment, as scientific experimentation does. Yet it is rare'. A process of reflection/reflexivity remains important. Nonetheless, it also continues to be problematic. It continues to be an area within our research where one 'can be accused of narcissism (Maton, 2003) and self-indulgence' (Cohen, 2013, p. 336); where one might be reproached for 'navel-gazing' (England, 1994) or where our reflexivity is seen almost as 'a confession to salacious indiscretions' (Okely, 1992 cited in England, 1994, p. 82).

In remaining focussed on ourselves as researchers; or rather, in ensuring that we are situated within our research, should we nullify our engagement with not only our research participants but also our encounters with other people, things, ideas and knowledges within and around our research? Perhaps we should also consider non-encounters; the absences which we may not even be aware of—see for instance, the special issue of the journal *Cultural Geographies* on 'absence' (2013). Therefore, it is with 'balance and careful inter-weaving' that we need to 'seek to give voice to others without losing sight of ourselves' (Cohen, 2013, p. 336).

Somehow, it is also occasionally necessary to remind ourselves that young budget traveller's experiences are interactional. Budget travellers' interactions are, 'an affective doing, an interaction doing and a relational doing' (Bell, 2011, p. 149). Thus we need to consider the inter-subjective relationships and not only the outcomes of their experiences (Scott, 2006). In doing this, we can perhaps begin to move away from the 'gazing (back) upon' that seems to happen, especially once young budget travellers move beyond their corporeal travel experiences.

At the methodological and epistemological level we therefore need to think beyond current frameworks. There is value in thinking through how non-representational theory (NRT) or perhaps the 'more-than representational' (Lorimer, 2005) can provide us with fruitful ground to explore. Lorimer (2005: p. 84) suggests that for the more-than representational, it is the 'multifarious, open encounters in the realm of practice that matter most'. Cresswell (2012, p. 97) identifies what he calls the 'heart of NRT' by pointing out its challenge of a number of binaries. These include focussing on,

> the practical and processural fluidity of things (rather than the finished and fixed); on the production of meaning in action (rather than through preestablished systems and structures); on an ontology that is relational (rather than essentialist); on habitual interaction with the world (rather than 'consciousness' of it); on the possibilities of things emerging surprisingly (rather than being predetermined); on a wide definition of Life as humans/with/plus (rather than strictly humanistic); and on all-inclusive materiality where everything produces the 'social' constantly (rather than an already achieved 'social' constructing everything else) (Cresswell, 2012, p. 97).

Conceptions of NRT and the more-than representational illustrate the importance of fluidity, flexibility and an openness within our reflexive methodological positions. Cresswell's (2012, p. 100) thoughts on representation highlight 'how meaning is unstable and unfixable, how power through representation is never complete, and how representation always works with practice and performance'. Utilizing NRT as 'a theory of mobile practices' (Cadman, 2009, p. 458) can begin to clarify that mobility within everyday life, even within the practices of tourism, is not 'simply personal, individual, or local' (Cadman, 2009, p. 459). Rather it is bound up in wider performances where the unexpected and transformative allow for the innate openness and flow in and between individual, community, city, regional and world and where there is an inevitability in the co-creation of the research encounter (Cadman, 2009).

So how does this relate to why we should consider the moral encounters of young budget travellers? Gibson (2010) suggests that tourism research is now more attentive to tourism's encounters, the fluid, complicated interactions and how these highlight the highly mediated nature of such encounters. Büscher and Urry (2009, p. 111), when discussing mobile methods suggest that the use of such methods can create a double transparency which allows researchers 'to study and describe mobility phenomena in the making whilst simultaneously drawing the methods used in their production to their own and their audiences attention'. I argue that the mobilities of young budget travellers are intrinsically bound up with often quite specific (and Western) moral methodological understandings that allow the practice of certain methods which repeatedly continue to capture the neoliberal, consumerist aspects of young budget travel rather than look beyond these to the moral encounters which question, critique and challenge this viewpoint. If our (moral) encounters end up as cultural currency—whether as a journal article or as a line on a curriculum vitae ('look what I did')—how can we see the interactional, transnational and transactional 'value' of such experiences?

It is not just the individual young budget traveller (or even a collective group or cohort of young budget travellers) who mature, grow, develop or gain through and from the transnational opportunities afforded to them by the opportunities to travel. Rather, the relations within and between wider social networks also become more mobile, complex and fluid through such mobile and transnational practices and experiences (Duncan, Scott and Baum, 2012). Such encounters and performances are socially and culturally entwined and so the complexity of these experiences needs foregrounding. As such, our research with these travellers needs to reflect this complexity through a continued and re-evaluated openness to the reflexive, more-than representational encounters that these perspectives call for. Alongside this, the moral and ethical nature of our encounters becomes ever more important to ensure that the political, economic, social and cultural are given equal 'voice' in our findings.

Conclusions

Through examining the moral encounters of young budget travellers, we can begin to carve out spaces that uncomfortably house the contradicting elements of individual fulfilment sought after by neoliberal (western) budget travellers and their recognition of tourism's social consequences (Caton, 2012). However, in order to achieve this we, as researchers also have to inhabit these uncomfortable spaces and utilize morally conscious methodologies in order to gain an insight into the 'why' behind young budget travel.

This tension between the (often overly) decadent enjoyment that can be found in travel and the social, cultural, political and economic consequences of tourism experiences is not novel. Inglis (2000, pp. 20–21), in his book *The*

Delicious History of the Holiday, talks of James Boswell's motivations for going on the Grand Tour:

> But he had come not only with the paternal admonition to get educated but also with the licence of the gentlemanly tourist and he was going to enjoy himself. He was going to eat too much, drink too much, and take as many women to bed as he could. … and after zealous gaming and bouts of remorse, he would view the educative sights of antiquity which would restore a little sacred incense to his enthusiastically profane world (Inglis, 2000, pp. 20–21).

The contemporary young budget traveller, similar to the (male and wealthy) participant of the Grand Tour, is motivated by a 'jumble for desire—desire for the good, the true and the beautiful inextricably mixed with the desire for the forbidden fruits of freedom, ecstasy, excess' (Inglis, 2000, p. 23). Young budget travellers therefore negotiate their hedonistic pursuits and other altruistic, cultural or social commitment (Tomazos and Butler, 2012). As researchers trying to grasp and understand these experiences, performances and encounters, we have to employ moral considerations within our research that go beyond 'just' their experiences to contemplate the interactional, relational and the more-than representational. To understand the 'value' of young budget travel, we have to recognize that every methodological focus will still exclude— 'there is no politically innocent methodology' (Clifford, 1997, p. 19). Thus, it is a reconsideration of the ontology of young budget traveller research rather than simply a more moral methodological approach to young budget traveller encounters that is needed. As researchers, our objective should be to enhance the research encounter with young budget travellers through the recognition and reconciliation of the partial, fleeting, unfinished and sometimes contentious performances we see, experience and are part of. It is necessary for us to recognize that a researcher's viewpoints can be tainted by neoliberal, euro- or western centric positions which can take the 'why' of young budget travel somewhat for granted. Therefore, as researchers, we must take seriously the moral implications of our research questions and methods.

References

Adey, P. (2010). *Mobility*. Routledge, London.

Allon, F., Anderson, K., and Bushell, R. (2008). Mutant Mobilities: Backpacker Tourism in 'Global' Sydney. *Mobilities*, 3(1), 73–94.

Ashmore, M. (1989). *The Reflexive Thesis: Writing the Sociology of Scientific Knowledge*. Chicago: University of Chicago Press.

Bell, D. (2011). Hospitality is Society. *Hospitality & Society*, 1(2), 137–152.

Bianchi, R. V. (2000). Migrant Tourist-workers: Exploring the 'Contact Zones' of Post-industrial Tourism. *Current Issues in Tourism*, 3(2), 107–137.

Büscher, M., and Urry, J. (2009). Mobile Methods and the Empirical. *European Journal of Social Thought*, 12(1), 99–117.

Butcher, J. (2003). *The Moralization of Tourism: Sun, Sand ... and Saving the World?* New York: Routledge.

Cadman, L. (2009). Non-Representational Theory/Non-Representations Geographies. In R. Kitchin and N. Thrift (eds.), *International Encyclopaedia of Human Geography*, http://www.elsevierdirect.com/brochures/hugy/SampleContent/Nonrepresentational-Theory-and-Geographies.pdf. Oxford: Elsevier, pp. 456–463.

Carr, N. (1998). The Young Tourist: A Case of Neglected Research. *Progress in Tourism and Hospitality Research*, 4(4), 307–318.

Caton, K. (2012). Taking the Moral Turn in Tourism Studies. *Annals of Tourism Research*, 39(4), 1906–1928.

Chen, G., Bao, J., and Huang, S. (2013). Segmenting Chinese Backpackers by Travel Motivations. *International Journal of Tourism Research*. DOI 10.1002/jtr.1928.

Clarke, N. (2005). Detailing Transnational Lives of the Middle: British Working Holiday Makers in Australia. *Journal of Ethnic and Migration Studies*, 31(2), 307–322.

Clifford, J. (1997). *Routes: Travel and Translation in the Late Twentieth Century*. Boston: Harvard University Press.

Cohen, E. (2004). Backpacking: Diversity and Change. In G. Richards and J. Wilson (eds.), *The Global Nomad: Backpacker Travel in Theory and Practice*, pp. 43–59. Clevedon: Channel View Publications.

Cohen, S. A. (2013). Reflections on Reflexivity in Leisure and Tourism Studies. *Leisure Studies*, 32(3), 333–337.

Cohen, S. A., Duncan, T. and Thulemark, M. (2013). Lifestlye Mobilities: The Crossroads of Leisure, Travel and Migration. *Mobilities*. DOI: 10.1080/17450101.2013.826481.

Cremin, C. (2007). Living and Really Living: The Gap Year and the Commodification of the Contingent. *Ephemera: Theory and Politics in Organization*, 7(4), 526–542.

Cresswell, T. (2010). Towards a Politics of Mobility. *Environment and Planning D: Society and Space*, 28(1), 17–31.

Cresswell, T. (2012). Review Essay: Nonrepresentational Theory and Me: Notes from an Interested Sceptic. *Environment and Planning D: Society and Space*, 30(1), 96–105.

Crick, M. (1985). 'Tracing' the Anthropological Self: Quizzical Reflections on Field Work, Tourism and the Ludic. *Social Analysis*, 17, 71–92.

Duncan, T. (2008). The Internationalisation of Tourism Labour Markets: Working and Playing in a Ski Resort. In C. M. Hall and T. Coles (eds.), *International Business and Tourism*, pp. 181–194. London: Routledge.

Duncan, T. (2011). The Mobilities Turn and the Geography of Tourism. In J. Wilson (ed.), *The Routledge Handbook of Tourism Geographies*, pp. 113–120. London: Routledge.

Duncan, T., Scott, D., and Baum, T. (2013). The Mobilities of Hospitality Work. *Annals of Tourism Research*, 42, 1–19.

Edensor, T. (2007). Mundane Mobilities, Performances and Spaces of Tourism. *Social and Cultural Geography*, 8(2), 199–215.

England, K. V. L. (1994). Getting Personal, Reflexivity, Positionality, and Feminist Research. *Professional Geographer*, 46(1), 80–89.

Gibson, C. (2009). Geographies of Tourism: Critical Research on Capitalism and Local Livelihoods. *Progress in Human Geography*, 33(4), 527–534.

Gibson, C. (2010). Geographies of Tourism: (Un)ethical Encounters. *Progress in Human Geography*, 34(4), 521–527.

Gogia, N. (2006). Unpacking Corporeal Mobilities: The Global Voyages of Labour and Leisure. *Environment and Planning A*, 38(2), 359–375.

Hall, C. M. (2012). Consumerism, Tourism and Voluntary Simplicity: We All Have to Consume, but Do We Really Have to Travel So Much to be Happy? In T. V. Singh (ed.), *Critical Debates in Tourism*, pp. 61–67. Bristol: Channel View.

Hannam, K. (2008). Tourism Geographies, Tourist Studies and the Turn Towards Mobilities. *Geography Compass*, 2(1), 127–139.

Heath, S. (2007). Widening the Gap: Pre-university Gap Years and the 'Economy of Experience'. *British Journal of Sociology of Educ*ation, 28(1), 89–103.

Inglis, F. (2000). *The Delicious History of the Holiday*. London: Routledge.

Jones, A. (2004). *Review of Gap Year Provision: Research Report 555*. Nottingham: DfES Publications.

Lorimer, H. (2005). Cultural Geography: The Busyness of Being 'More-than-Representational'. *Progress in Human Geography*, 29(1), 83–94.

Lynch, M. (2000). Against Reflexivity as an Academic Virtue and Source of Privileged Knowledge. *Theory, Culture and Society*, 17(3), 26–54.

Lyons, K., Hanley, J., Wearing, S., and Neil, J. (2011). Gap Year Volunteer Tourism: Myths of Global Citizenship? *Annals of Tourism Research*, 39(1), 361–378.

Mostafahenzhad, M. (2013). The Politics of Aesthetics in Volunteer Tourism. *Annals of Tourism Research*, 43, 150–169.

Muzaini, H. (2006). Backpacking Southeast Asia: Strategies of 'Looking Local'. *Annals of Tourism Research*, 33(1), 144–161.

Newlands, K. J. (2006). The Modern Nomad in New Zealand: A Study of The Effects of the Working Holiday Scheme on Free Independent Travelers and their Host Communities. Unpublished Masters Thesis, Auckland University of Technology, New Zealand.

Noy, C. (2004). This Trip Really Changed Me: Backpackers' Narratives of Self-Change. *Annals of Tourism Research*, 31(1), 78–102.

Oaks, T. S., and Price, P. L. (2008). Editors' Introduction: 'The Production of Mobilities'. From *New Formations* 43(2001): 11–25, Tim Cresswell. In T. S. Oaks and P. L. Price (eds.), *The Cultural Geography Reader*, pp. 325–326. London: Routledge.

Ong, C-E. and du Cros, H. (2012). The Post-Mao Gazes: Chinese Backpackers in Macau. *Annals of Tourism Research*, 39(2), 735–754.

Richards, G., and Wilson, J. (2004). Widening Perspectives in Backpacker Research. In G. Richards and J. Wilson (eds.), *The Global Nomad: Backpacker Travel in Theory and Practice*, pp. 253–279. Clevedon: Channel View Publications.

Scott, D. (2006). Socializing the Stranger: Hospitality as a Relational Reality. Unpublished Masters Thesis, University of Otago, Dunedin, New Zealand. Available on-line at http://otago.ourarchive.ac.nz/handle/10523/1283.

Simpson, K. (2004). Doing Development: The Gap Year, Volunteer Tourists and a Popular Practice of Development. *Journal of International Development*, 126(5), 681–692.

Simpson, K. (2005). Dropping Out or Signing Up? The Professionalism of Youth Travel. *Antipode*, 37(3), 447–469.

Skeggs, B. (2004). *Class, Self, Culture*. London: Routledge.

Snee, H. (2013). Framing the Other: Cosmopolitanism and the Representation of Difference in Overseas Gap Year Narratives. *The British Journal of Sociology*, 64(1), 142–162.

Tomazos, K., and Butler, R. (2010). The Volunteer Tourism as 'Hero'. *Current Issues in Tourism*, 13(4), 363–380.

Tomazos, K., and Butler, R. (2012). Volunteer Tourists in the Field: A Question of Balance? *Tourism Management*, 33(1), 177–187.

Tuan, Y-F. (2001). Life as a Field Trip. *The Geographical Review*, 91(1/2), 41–45.

Urry, J. (2007). *Mobilities*. Cambridge: Polity Press.

Ward, L. (2007). You're Better Off Backpacking—VSO Warns about Perils of 'Voluntourism'. *The Guardian*, 14 August. Originally retrieved from http://www.guardian.co.uk/uk/2007/aug/14/students.charitablegiving. (no longer available on-line).

Zeitler, U. (2012). The Ontology of Mobility, Morality and Transport Planning. In S. Bergmann and T. Sager (eds.), *The Ethics of Mobilities: Rethinking Place Exclusion Freedom and Environment*, pp. 233–240. Aldershot: Ashgate.

Chapter 17

To Boldly Go Where No Van Has Gone Before: Auto-Ethnographic Experimentation and Mobile Fieldwork

Sharon Wilson

Introduction

Before I ever imagined studying the phenomena of VW campervan subcultures, I found myself on the internet shopping forum 'Ebay' one evening buying what I called my 'midlife crisis' campervan; a Wesfalia Bay, 1972 model. Perhaps the idea of buying the van evoked a sense of possibility where past freedoms were nostalgically recalled in the fleeting moment between winning the item and doing the bank transfer. I consoled myself via such commodity acquisition 'out of the blue', hoping perhaps that the 'good old days' could somehow be retrieved. The idea that an old classic Volkswagen campervan could enable a return to a world where motility, freedom and being carefree could be achievable again was momentarily articulated through an imagined mobility. As the aforementioned vehicle however was delivered to my door, I began to realize that whatever positive thoughts I had about the holiday ideal at the point of purchase, was in light contrast to the dark reality, which followed. For my dream machine was actually a faulty, rusty, oil hungry, old vehicle which was both difficult to drive and expensive to maintain. It was then I realized that despite an instant attachment to what I would describe as an aesthetically pleasing and thus emotionally seductive form of leisure transport, it was actually more like a 2 star youth hostel on wheels. I panicked about what I was then meant to do with my new mobile home. Where was I to drive? I hadn't thought of how to plan a holiday actually using it, or even considered if I would actually inhabit it at all. The desire to flee the 'horror of home' Baudelaire, cited in (De Botton, 2002, p. 32) was swiftly replaced by frantically taking a paradigm shift to 'there's no place like home'. Paradoxically for some reason I still liked the idea of owning the van as long as it was parked securely on the drive. So in a position where I neither wanted to sell it or keep it, I joined a local VW campervan club in the North East of England and used the support of other owners to help me understand how without any particular logic or rationale I had joined their club. This then became my research vehicle in many senses of the word (see Figure 17.1).

Figure 17.1   Researcher with VW campervan, Harwood Hall, Leeds

As I had bought a VW campervan based on a spurious notion that it would help me escape from the sedentary logic of the everyday, it was a facet of tourist behaviour I thought needed to be understood further. Trying to understand my own romantic motivations about what a vehicle of this kind could achieve allowed for wider conversations about the fantasies and realities of tourists experiences of mobility. Hence by implementing an auto-ethnographic method, my own experiences of driving and camping could be captured by recording personal narratives in the form of storytelling, in tandem with a traditional ethnography where the voices of other VW campervan owners could be traced. Conducting fieldwork involved travelling in a VW campervan to various events in the local area. I visited places such as Biggar in Scotland and Druridge Bay, Northallerton and Leeds in northern England to interview owners about their involvement with travelling cultures. In short, I was interested to understand why owners bought their vans, how they used them and why many owners were emotionally attached to them. As one of them, these questions also turned on a moral issue in terms of how my own subjectivities would tally with pursuing research about the phenomena. From the basic imperative of finding out what these subcultures were about, I developed a research design from a literature review which interfaced with tourism mobilities theory (Sheller and Urry, 2006).

In order to contribute to contemporary debates around the 'moral turn' in tourism studies (Butcher, 2003, Bergman and Sager, 2008, Caton, 2012), this chapter is therefore concerned with both processes and practices of experimental fieldwork as an embodied practice. Firstly because I was a participant observer, in the auto-ethnographic element of the study I took the position of both the researcher and the researched. It became imperative to consider the moral issues which emerged from conducting an ethnography in which the author was both an 'insider/outsider' (Lett, 1990). I also sought to explore how moral encounters are possible if the researcher developed a kinship with the travellers in question. Paradoxically the tension between the desire to proceed with a research plan or halting it out of respect for moral propriety, led me to consider how my ambition to complete the work may have brought me close to the brink of immorality at any point. I was forced thus to consider how my being in a position of possible intimacy with respondents, could be disputed because acquaintances potentially could be objectified for the purposes of a research enquiry. In other words, despite professional detachment as a researcher, moral dilemmas existed where demarcations of confidentiality and privacy with familiars had elastic boundaries. Establishing a connection with research subjects due to being part of the subculture became a passport to access human resources from the owners club on a more intimate level. Yet these relationships were also problematized for moral reasons because data collection could no longer be clandestine. In other words to use a metaphor, the researcher is possibly left sitting on the fence where their moral comfort is found discretionally, somewhere in between the two extremes.

To provide a context for this discussion, the first section contextualizes the research aims, predispositions and potential moral dilemmas. This leads to a conversation about researcher reflexivity and a review of the research strategies employed to overcome the potential hysteria associated with self-managing a duality of roles. Here a social scientist seeking some objectivity is conjoined with a VW campervan owner who was bound by an impulse to use their vehicle for identity formulation and self-expression. As an embodiment of the emotive impulse to use the van to 'get away from it all', juxtaposed with academic imperatives beset by my workload, this meant that my interpretive faculties were at times neither betwixt nor between. In other words I had developed mixed feelings about the vehicle due to its new associations with work, leaving me confused about my relationship with it as a form of leisure apparatus. In lieu of this predicament, my intention was to look at the psychodramas attached to this hybridity of purpose and to provide some insights about how a moral imperative in a context could be implemented. Qualitative research designs are fluid and require the researcher to make choices throughout the process. With this in mind, it was important to question my moral measurements as a researcher who was also a subject.

Moral Methodologies

I often worked alone as I was interested in my own personal travel journey as well as tackling the wider picture of social and cultural diversity at the various VW festivals I visited. Rather than organizing interviews in advance, I wandered around the camping site looking for participants. Mindful of my potential invasiveness, I had to react to situations 'on the hoof'. If potential respondents did not appear hostile to my advances, I would invite them to enter into a conversation about the research. Thus 'going with the flow' was conducive to generating a rich dialogue with participants. Yet whilst I tried to maintain client confidentially and anonymity, alongside keeping a 'research alliance' with them (Grafanaki, 1996), their interventions often occurred without premeditation. This meant I had to make spontaneous decisions about the most appropriate actions to take.

My stance was not dissimilar to Barton (2011) who accepted basic verbal permissions from people who wanted to share their biographies. By her own admission she did not have consent forms to hand, but instead relied on a self-styled moral position where she was the judge of whether compliance of safety regulations and the dignity, rights and the well-being of the human subjects were preserved. *Suffice to say due to a vested interest in completing the research, my own tolerance and elasticity as enquirer and informant was arguably not an ideal benchmark as the bias was subject to immoderation.* That is not to say I was not acting immorally, as I had to be compliant with professional codes of practice and the law. Mindful of these potential issues thus, the aim of this chapter is also to consider to how the resultant social interplays in fieldwork were managed. This in turn should account for how an idiosyncratic approach to fieldwork has arguably led to moral reflection.

Admittedly participant observation and its multi-faceted research techniques are not new. As a multidisciplinary researcher who has engaged in both the Arts and the Social Sciences however, it is worth noting that my hybrid positionality across disciplines did influence the research methods undertaken. An auto-ethnographic approach allowed for the marriage of science and art (Ellis and Bochner, 1996; Richardson, 2000, Atkinson, 2006) and provided a blueprint for which self-centred research could maintain credibility. As I was a practising artist as well as a researcher, I was also aware that I had to deal with my motivation to respond to the aesthetic materialities within the research environment. I questioned whether photography, creative writing and drawing would be relevant to the research as additional ways to construct 'meanings'. However I proceeded to use a number of methodological tools such as video, audio recordings, drawings, photography, and personal diaries to collect knowledge, taking assurances from Barton (2011) who suggested that when dealing with an ethnographic study that almost every element of life becomes data (see Figure 17.2).

As I was exercising a creative approach to auto-ethnography, I was forced to evaluate the moral philosophy I was applying due to using 'the self' as an embodied mediator of knowledge. As I had access to my own experiences, I did not set

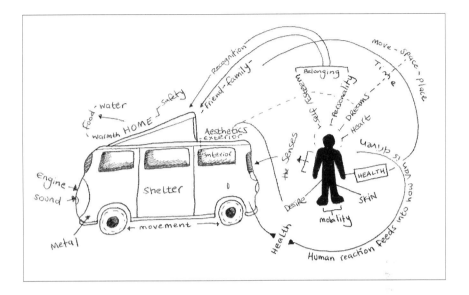

Figure 17.2   Actor network drawing. Source: Author

definitive boundaries upon which I might encounter conflict with the immediate research goals. Thus I worked with some autonomy and regulated my own conduct during self exploration in fieldwork. However this highly individuated process did raise questions about whether I could be trusted to act morally in terms of how I arrived at my own content. How would I know for example if I was or wasn't being moral without objective reasoning as my guide?

Moral Reflexive Practice

This section talks about reflexive practice and on how methodological techniques were applied as instruments in the field. Firstly the mainstay of data was gathered via observations and semi structured interviews by meeting informants in their holiday environments. Whilst this inductive approach had empirical rigor in terms of interview and observational techniques, I also used a mixed-bag of other data collection tools such as audio-visual sampling, drawing, photography and personal diaries. These alternative approaches allowed for flexibility of random sampling with a subject matter that kept evolving. In other words by using an open ended approach during fieldwork, I could 'go-with-the-flow' to see where the research took me. Then depending on emergent factors, I could access a palate of research tools that worked in accordance with how the social phenomena manifested. For example if something at one of the festivals was remarkably visual, it could be captured by lens based media or if a respondent was particularly vocal then a 'vox-pop' method could be used, or personal moments of reflection about the findings could be recorded with a drawing or diary entries where appropriate.

From the basis of experimental fieldwork a substantial volume of material was then organized into different categories. The first data set was derived from an auto-ethnographic approach where I spent time alone in a VW campervan and logged user experience. This strategy meant that my normally 'leisured' experiences of travelling to VW themed festivals also took the form of a fieldtrip. In other words the van also resembled a place of work. Operating with the double agency of observer and observed was problematic for the study, as I was no longer simply a tourist. To widen the scope of the investigation I also spent time with the members of the local Flat 4 Dubs Volkswagen Club as a participant observer. Whilst I had not asked permission to use them as research subjects or to join them in their social activities as a holidaymaker, it appeared to be an unspoken law that being a club member meant that I could 'hang out with the gang'. This allowed me to introduce the idea of them being researched later on. The key challenge due to familiarity with them however was whether I could be comfortable and effective in both roles from a moral point of view. To complete the picture I planned to interview the wider community of VW owners whom I had not met before. This situation lent itself to other experimental approaches by allowing myself to wander the festival sites without the 'burden' of a potentially deterministic plan. I found by roaming freely, I could be reactive to what was going on as opposed to searching for something pre-conceived. Arguably this approach made me methodologically vulnerable, but it was also empowering as I could respond creatively to the circumstances.

One of the limitations of the project was time. Many of the festivals were only 48 hours in duration. Thus the temporary nature of the gatherings meant that unlike nomadic travellers who gathered in groups for longer periods of time, relationships between VW campervan owners were quite transient as most had fixed abodes elsewhere. In other words even the flow of the research process had a 'drive-by' tempo. Data had to be abstracted within a short timescale from brief conversations, semi-structured interviews and observations of the owner's social behaviours. Then a loose structure was accorded to findings by organizing them on spider charts. These visual and textual findings offered a map of networks, showing VW campervan experiences from a range of vantage points. This could only be achieved by being set up to respond to different forms of social stimulus as they emerged. Whilst not entirely indiscriminate, I was open to diverse material manifestations enabling me to follow any subsequent lines of enquiry. For example, whilst I was recording a description of the emotive responses of my time spent in my van by myself, I became distracted by passersby so I turned my attention to them. I found that intermittently stopping one area of enquiry and starting another suited the temporal nature of the event. Semi-structured interviews developed from chance meetings where interruptions and disruptions led to new disclosures.

Caton (2012: 1906) suggests, morality is perhaps a philosophy that humans apply in order to interact with the world and each other. These conceptual ideas are also socially constructed with some variance between cultures due to relations of power, inequality, spatial relations and so on. Morality is perhaps a wider statement of personal beliefs about how things ought to be, as opposed to how they actually are. In other words it is perhaps the blueprint for how myths, fallacies and laws congeal to form 'common sense' practices subject to the jurisdictions of the human imagination. This is unlike the notion of ethics which is a more systematic effort to formulate rules out of out of a series of individual moral experiences (De George, 1992).

In terms this moral debate I would like to deliberate on a few points in relation researcher/respondent proximities. One pertains to the question of whether from an epistemological and ontological standpoint that being an insider of a particular tribe is conducive to producing credible results. As a potential interloper with a motive to glean knowledge about the lives of people with whom I had prior comradeship bonds, could I be biased in relation to informant trust in conjunction with the persuasive tactics of the researcher? Conversely the reverse could happen where by potential informants do not want to get involved in telling their stories due to fear of imagined negative implications or cultural separatism on their part. As a member of the VW collective however I appeared to stand less of a chance of being excluded from the social circle solely because of my researcher role.

As for the treatment of humans as a duty of care, I anticipated that my strategy may differ in terms of how I dealt with people I was not accustomed too. That is not to suggest that I was less conscientious with those I had not befriended, however not knowing them did shape the format of my approach. As I was more relaxed with unfamiliar bodies, I felt able to re-negotiate the border crossings of the so called 'moral' limits in each instance without compromising the research goal. I found I was more likely to dig deeper into people's personal lives if they were strangers, due to having professional distance. I also worked on the basis that if the respondents did not wish to share stories, I could locate others who would. Also as they were not vulnerable adults or children, their willingness to take part I considered approval enough. Admittedly my line of questioning was not in my opinion of an intimate nature, although some people may have perceived my presence as invasive, coercive or ambiguous, whilst feedback suggested that most found being involved in the research, entertaining, made them think and was full of sociability.

In terms of personal safety there was possibly a moral issue around levels of personal risk taken in order to gather primary sources. Admittedly there were no particular dangers to be wary of other than theft from vans left open and some disruptive behaviour due to alcohol consumption by attendees. Those aside, instinctively I felt safe working in the festival environments, although it was a subjective 'feeling' based on prior experience of visiting outdoor events. Perhaps my lack of caution was driven by an enthusiasm for conducting good research, coupled with an unfounded perception that I was safe to connect with people in sometimes an unauthorized fashion. That said, had I been leisure seeker only, I would have socialized in a similar way to how I had whilst conducting the study, but my approach to people would not have been enquiry led. For example I often found myself sitting in people's mobile homes chatting, as well as talking with owners on late evenings when some had been drinking alcohol and smoking cannabis. Also because I was a lone female, I was interpreted as being single and was sometimes propositioned for a date. It was assumed that as a solitary female without my young child and partner in tow, that I was a potential 'love' interest. Admittedly I did not mention anything about myself to respondents upfront as I wanted to appear relaxed and sociable, however taking a slightly 'aloof' approach offering insights to my personal life left space to be misconstrued. Because the festival atmosphere lent itself to different socialities it was clearly a moral issue as to how the researcher could integrate into intimate scenarios, whilst avoiding a defensive stance or putting oneself at risk sexually.

In considering the value judgements associated with 'right' or 'wrong' ways of dealing with the ad-hoc nature of meeting strangers, I used a moral 'common-sense' approach to decide upon which researcher/respondent vignettes could be performed. Due to a reliance on serendipitous encounters however the building of trust in this context had to be enough for people to be open and honest. Hence, even though I was considered as 'one of them', it was a potential barrier as the respondents still did not really know who I was having only met me a few times. Also I did not want to overstay my welcome, thus once I had finished my interviews, switching to socializing with respondents was not easy. I often felt I was an imposition in their space even though they had agreed to let me talk with them. Having an agenda was at times a barrier to forming new friendships with owners. Also because I questioned their behaviour as holidaymakers who were often immersed in their experiences and not always conscious of them, discussions about VW campervan ownership often brought to the fore a critique about how owners used their leisure time. For example, whenever the logic of buying into campervan culture was interrogated, I often witnessed mildly emotional reactions in both a positive and negative directions. Also respondents sometimes used the interview opportunity to confide in the researcher about personal issues that were not always directly related to the research objectives. Conversations evoked displays of sentimentality, regret, nostalgia, annoyance and joy channelled through explanations of mobile home ownership. Their vehicles became catalysts for conversations about such things as relationship tensions, career stress, alternative identities, tax evasion, alcoholism, family loss and love.

The Trouble with Belonging

In this section I will discuss some of the moral difficulties faced due to friendships being formed with the respondent group from owners club, 'Flat

4 Dubs'. As I had socialized with them in the past, I assumed that asking them questions about their holiday experiences with their campervans would be not be problematic. My approach was to spend time within the boundaries of the owner's club territory to glean information. Having privileged access to this social domain meant that conversations with respondents would in theory be easier to facilitate. Being familiar with the group made me feel uncomfortable about inviting them to be research subjects. This anxiety was made worse by the fact that when I arrived on site in my VW campervan, I could not find a parking place close by the group. Instead I was located on the spatial periphery of the gathering and therefore integrating myself with the group was awkward. Having to invite myself into their social circle made me feel instantly marginalized. The plan was to introduce the ideas behind the research and to ask if anyone would like to be part of the study. Rather than addressing the issue of the research with them upfront, I was suddenly overcome by stress which forced me to avoid the subject. It was then that I realized that I was suffering from guilt and found that that acting with them as I had in the past, i.e. enjoying eating, drinking and chatting about VW campervan ownership suddenly proved unusually difficult. I was no longer relaxed with my associates as I had imposed upon myself a work regime which meant that conducting 'authentic' leisure in such circumstances was not as possible. I was no longer an acquaintance of the group, but instead felt like an impostor.

In hindsight I should have considered the moral implications of conducting the fieldwork more covertly. As I knew the respondents informally however, I could not find moral justification to do so. Emotionally I was carrying the weight of the research objectives which impinged on my normative behaviour. Even mentioning that I was doing research and that I needed their help filled me with trepidation. When I eventually explained my intentions to the group later, it was met by a display of mild confusion and some suspicion which was only eased by the fact I was a familiar face. It was a situation where I was neither given consent to observe nor was I ejected from the space, which led to an assumption that permission was granted. I found myself making light of what I was doing in terms of research as I did not want them to think I was undertaking a forensic investigation. With a new awareness that at any point I could be researching them, I feared the group would become distant towards me. Fortunately observational work often meant that it was not obvious that research was taking place. Without the signification of note-taking in a diary or holding a digital voice recorder, the owners could not be certain about whether I was recording information or not. To reduce potential tensions however I would make comments such as, 'I am not researching now, just chilling out guys.' Interestingly when I announced that I was no longer researching, then the campervan owners appeared to relax into usual behaviour. This was when what was observed informally often had more interesting outputs. I could have initiated a conversation about how they felt about my presence but I wanted to avoid 'professionalizing' the camping environment. I considered it to be too officious an approach to start unpacking

Figure 17.3   VW campervan owner at Volksfest, Leeds (2012)

how they may be feeling about a researcher in the camp who used to hang out with them in pursuit of leisure, but now had additional motives. I considered that if I did, that it stood a high chance of alienating the potential respondents further; after all the main use of their communal space was for holidaymaking (see Figure 17.3). Occasionally owners from the Flat4Dubs campervan club would make comments such as:

> 'Oh she will be taking that down in evidence and using it against you.' laughs.
> Or 'I would watch what you say we have the professor of Volkswagen sitting there. Joke. Redcar VW Festival, May 2012'

As Lett (1990) points out, researchers positioned as 'insiders' allows for the voice of the participants to direct the research in an inductive process. At times it was difficult to discern whether I was a representative of the VW campervan owners or not. I was also not sure whether my observations could be entirely authentic, if I was considered to be an outsider. That said I did engage in camping activities and tried to enjoy the company of others. I also assumed that if I persisted long enough then the idea of 'being researched' stood a chance of being forgotten. Whilst I could mentally switch off from observing events and remembering them enough to write them down, I was conscious that a mechanism still ran involuntarily in the background of my thoughts which had the capacity to switch me from leisure maker, into ethnographer should my researcher self be required. One of my concerns was whether my potentially 'immoral' presence in itself was creating an artificial environment in which people conducted a front stage performance, which if I removed should turn into a backstage performance with different script. Without conducting the study as a silent witness, this is something that will remain an anomaly.

Conclusions

This chapter has sought to reveal some of the moral dilemmas inherent in qualitative experimental fieldwork. Due to the auto-ethnographic methods used in the study, the researcher had a duality of purpose as an ethnographer and subject. This arguably embodied position gave rise to debates of an ontological and epistemological nature. To summarize the findings I propose that researcher inter-subjectivities in this context led to some shortcomings on the moral front. By forewarning the VW campervan owners for example that they were potentially research subjects whilst morally considerate, could remove any control from the researcher. Arguably unless the researcher works undercover, potentially a moral mistake in itself, then as gatekeepers of their stories the informants can choose to be guarded. Another consequence of being socially responsible and honest about my research objective was the sense of estrangement. This led possibly to being 'othered' by club members or inadvertently finding myself 'othering' them. In conclusion, with no definitive moral blueprint for experimental fieldwork perhaps the starting point for a moral encounter is perhaps to be honest with oneself and with those being studied and to take it from there.

References

Ahern, K. J. (1999). Ten Tips for Reflexive Bracketing. *Qualitative Health Research*, 9(3), 407–411.

Atkinson, P. (2006). Rescuing Autoethnography. *Journal of Contemporary Ethnography*, 35, 400–404.

Barton, B. (2011). My Auto/Ethnographic Dilemma: Who Owns the Story? *Qualitative Sociology*, 34(3), 431–445.

Bergman, S., and Sager, T. (eds.) (2008). *The Ethics of Mobilities*. Aldershot: Ashgate.

Butcher, J. (2003). *The Moralization of Tourism: Sun, Sand ... and Saving the World?* New York: Routledge.

Caton, K. (2012). Taking the Moral Turn in Tourism Studies. *Annals of Tourism Research*, 39(4), 1906–1928.

De Botton, A. (2002). *The Art of Travel*. New York: Pantheon.

De George, R. T. (1992). *Business Ethics* (3rd edn.). New York: Macmillan.

Ellis, C., and Bochner, A. (eds.) (1996). *Composing Ethnography*. Walnut Creek, CA: Altamira Press.

Grafanaki, S. (1996). How Research can Change the Researcher: The Need for Sensitivity, Flexibility and Ethical Boundaries in Conducting Qualitative Research in Counselling/Psychotherapy. *British Journal of Guidance & Counselling*, 24(3), 329–338.

Lett, J. (1990). Emics and Etics: Notes on the Epistemology of Anthropology. In T. N. Headland, K. L. Pike, and M. Harris (eds.), *Emics and Etics: The Insider/ Outsider Debate*, pp. 127–142. London: Sage.

Richardson, L. (2000). Writing a Method of Enquiry. In N. K. Denzin and Y. S. Lincoln (eds.), *Handbook of Qualitative Research*, pp. 923–948, 2nd edn. London: Sage.

Sheller, M., and Urry, J. (2006). The New Mobilities Paradigm. *Environment and Planning A*, 38(2), 207–226.

CONCLUSION

Chapter 18

Conclusions: The Moral Conduct of Tourism Research

Kevin Hannam and Mary Mostafanezhad

Introduction

In November 2011 the London School of Economics (LSE) in the UK was heavily criticized for a "chapter of failures" in its links with the Gaddafi regime in Libya. A report by former Lord Chief Justice Lord Woolf noted a series of mistakes and errors of judgement had damaged LSE's reputation. The LSE's director, Sir Howard Davies, resigned in March over a £1.5m gift from a foundation led by Colonel Gaddafi's son Saif, a former student (Hughes, 2011). While, this may not seem at first reading as having much to do with tourism studies, there is substantial evidence that the Libyan government under Gaddafi funded tourism research as it sought to diversify from oil to tourism (Moore, 2007). This also raises significant moral issues which did not register with many universities' ethics committees which are primarily concerned with the ethical treatment of vulnerable individuals rather than populations. It also highlights the moral geographies of tourism research where questions of where to conduct research and with whom and in support of which governments can be under-considered. As the chapters in this volume demonstrate, moral encounters in tourism take place within spatial and power relations that render a morality before politics inconceivable (Caton, 2012; see also Butcher, this volume).

In this concluding chapter we highlight three points of departure for considering moral encounters in tourism for researchers. First, issues of the funding (and supervising) of research cannot be disassociated from wider political contexts in terms of regimes of moral governmentality. Second, such funding carries with it risks which Ulrich Beck (2000) has discussed in terms of interrogating the distinctions between knowledge, latent impact and symptomatic consequences. We argue that we need to pay more attention to such risks in tourism research if we are to be able to understand how morality articulates with research practice. Finally, wider issues of economic and environmental security underpin and define the neoliberal capitalist regime that we research tourism practices within and thus we must consider in what ways we challenge or enforce vulnerability and violence onto local economies and environments (see Smith, this volume; Wearing and Wearing, this volume).

The Politics of Funding (and Supervising) Research

Research funding is a key mechanism of change since its reward structure influences the performance and evaluation of research. The structure of research funding has been reformed in most developed countries since the late twentieth century under conditions of neoliberalism in order to make it more entrepreneurially focused. In addition to heightening recognition for scientific merit, such reforms have had the effect of emphasizing the commercial potential as well as the societal relevance of the research supported (Benner and Sandstrom, 2000). Research funding under neoliberalism is, however, rarely neutral as the Libyan case testified. Following McPherson and Schapiro (2010) we might argue that unpacking the moral dilemmas implicit in research funding may not lead to clear, correct answers—but it may enrich understanding and may, in the end, improve decision making.

Research funding for tourism studies, meanwhile, has been frequently complicated because of the underlying commercial imperatives of the tourism industry itself where funding is more likely to support studies that can generalize from quantitative studies (Riley and Love, 2000). Tourism research is also subject to higher education commercial imperatives and has found itself marginalized despite its acknowledged economic and social benefits (Tribe, 2003; Hall, 2004). In Australia and New Zealand tourism research has been given significant prominence and respectability (Bushell et al., 2001), while in China, tourism research has been long associated with planning (Xu et al., 2012). Attempts at harmonizing academic and industry research agendas (see Williams et al., 2012) still need to recognize the moral and ethical challenges implicit in tourism research. Fennell (2013) has recently made an important call for tourism research to recognize the value of the content of tourism research rather than quantitative metrics in order to be recognized as an established field of study.

However, the nascent mobilities paradigm allows us to place travel and tourism research at the core of social and cultural life rather than at the margins (Coles and Hall, 2006; Hannam, 2009). From this perspective, tourism mobilities are viewed as being bound up with both everyday and mundane journeys as well as with more exotic encounters that are the mainstay of much of the analysis in contemporary tourism studies. Tourism is therefore analysed not as an ephemeral aspect of social life that is practised outside normal, everyday life. Rather it is seen as integral to wider processes of economic and political development processes and even constitutive of everyday life (Franklin and Crang, 2001; Franklin, 2003; Coles and Hall, 2006; Edensor, 2007; Hannam and Knox, 2010).

It is not *just* that tourism is a form of mobility like other forms of mobility such as commuting or migration, but that different mobilities inform and are informed by tourism (Sheller and Urry, 2004). In any situation, mobilities involve the movement of people, the movement of material things, the movement of intangible experiences and the use of a range of old and new technologies. In short, proponents of the mobilities paradigm argue that the concept of mobilities is concerned with mapping and understanding both the large-scale movements of people, objects, capital, and information across the world, as well as the more local processes of daily transportation, movement through public space, and the travel of material things within everyday life simultaneously (Hannam et al., 2006). The mobilities paradigm also presents a new critical perspective that may allow the moral concerns illuminated in this volume to take more prominence.

Under neoliberalism, students have increasingly become targeted as consumers of education and pay substantial fees and as such have rising expectations as to what they will receive for these payments. An increased expectation in the value-added by the university includes expectations for broadened social and spatial career mobilities. Students fund universities and, crucially, students travel. As part of their curriculum they frequently go on field trips to overseas destinations. They travel on gap years as backpackers and they travel in search of, and to develop, their identities as volunteers (Mostafanezhad, 2013a and b; Duncan, this volume). Students are thus a very mobile section of society (Duke-Williams, 2009). Be it emigrating to another country for an entire course, a shorter period abroad as a segment of their studies, a gap year travelling or working abroad, studying within a different region within their own country or studying locally within their country of origin and having to tackle the daily mobilities this entails, all add to the growing complexities of student life (Bhandari and Laughlin, 2009; Duke-Williams, 2009; Holdsworth, 2009).

Holdsworth (2009, p. 1852) adds that "[s]tudents are constantly on the move: between halls; from place of residence (which may be halls of residence, privately rented accommodation, or parental home) to campus; as well as from 'home' to university." She goes on to argue that local students' mobility patterns are much more extreme than those who move region or country and that they are often trivialized by policy makers who state that "going to HE [Higher Education] was … the same as going to school or college, all that was different was that they caught a different bus" (Holdsworth, 2009, p. 1860).

To travel as part of education, has been recognized by most cultures around the world and was an integral part of the original Grand Tour. Brodsky-Porges (1981, p. 171) note that the French writer Montaigne in the 1500s argued that students needed "some direct adventuring with the world, a steady and lively interplay with common folk, supplemented and fortified with trips abroad." Moreover, tourism students tend to travel more than most as it is frequently an integral part of their curriculum, on modules or to conduct research for the dissertation. They are also encouraged to take part in wider tours to enrich their experiences so as to become more employable—with some extreme cases such as Arizona State University owning cruise ships to take their students around the world.

But such travel needs funding and is underpinned by moral dilemmas as serious as the Libyan case discussed above. University staff are told by their managers that they need to publish more and they know that if they develop more innovative work by their Masters and PhD students this might bring better results. So they are often faced with a moral question. How innovative should they be? Should students be allowed to take risks in order to obtain more interesting results? The pressures are there. We tell students to go to interesting places to make a good dissertation but do we help them adequately reflect on the moral issues involved? How should we engage with students that want to study poverty tourism or visit places that are deemed dangerous on health grounds or simply uncomfortable to make their studies seem more relevant and exciting to their assessors (see Wilson, this volume)? James Sidaway (1992) has argued, the 'researched' should always be informed of the general purposes and the funding of the investigation and the merits of the research should be put into perspective. Thinking through the issue of the politics of research itself is one (often salutary) way of doing this. As Ulrich Beck (2000) has emphasized, the ambivalences of doing research need to be fore-grounded in order for the risks to be understood.

This brings us back towards the wider moral issues that we are faced with in contemporary society and there are no easy answers as the chapters in this book testify. The concept of environmental security has been one way of describing some of these issues. In the introduction to their edited collection entitled *Safety and Security in Tourism*, Hall et al. (2003) suggest that the concept of security has been transformed from one of collective security to one of common security through the work of the United Nations. They note that tourism is "irrevocably bound up with the concept of security" (Hall et al., 2003, p. 2) but also acknowledge that tourism organizations have had little influence on security agendas. Nevertheless, they persist with a view of tourism as a potentially emancipatory project that may ward off potential future global insecurities like much of the research on responsible and volunteer tourism that has been critically reviewed in this volume.

Conclusions

An examination of the tourism encounters in this volume illuminates the morality of particular tourism spaces and how these spaces are invested in particular structures of race, class, ethnicity, gender, disability, sexuality and other categories of human experience. Thus, in this book, we have worked to integrate critical tourism studies with emerging issues in moral tourism encounters. This integration, we argue, is ripe for further conceptualization as tourism research has yet to fully examine what the implications of morality are for tourism experiences and for tourism research. Hence, just as tourism encounters are moral encounters, we further contend that the research encounter is fundamentally a moral encounter. Like the tourist encounter, the research encounter is a highly moralized territory that requires inspection. Indeed it is worth pointing out how for host community members, the researcher and the tourist might be (or perhaps more accurately, usually are) one and the same. As the opening example demonstrates the funding of research must call into question moral issues. The funding and supervision of tourism research needs to be examined from moral perspectives as much as from ethical perspectives. Like other critical issues of our time such as climate change (see

Lovelock, this volume), it is too easy to drift into a situation where the neoliberal dictates of capitalism mask the underlying reality of moral concerns. Furthermore, in the re-presentation of the peoples that we claim to represent in our stories about tourism encounters, we need to remember that "[e]very focus excludes; there is no politically innocent methodology for intercultural interpretation" (Clifford, 1997, p. 19). We thus conclude that these challenges also open up many opportunities for tourism scholars, practitioners and participants to understand new forms of moral tourism encounters.

References

Beck, U. (2000). Risk Society Revisited: Theory, Politics and Research Programmes. In B. Adam, U. Beck and J. Van Loon (eds.), *Risk Society and Beyond*, pp. 211–229. London: Sage.

Benner, M., and Sandstrom, U. (2000). Institutionalizing the Triple Helix: Research Funding and Norms in the Academic System. *Research Policy*, 29(2), 291–301.

Bhandari, R., and Laughlin, S. (eds.) (2009). *Higher Education on the Move: New Developments in Global Mobility*. New York: Institute for International Education.

Brodsky-Porges, E. (1981). The Grand Tour: Travel as an Educational Device, 1600–1800. *Annals of Tourism Research*, 8(2), 171–186.

Bushell, R., Prosser, G., Faulkner, H., and Jafari, J. (2001). Tourism Research in Australia. *Journal of Travel Research*, 39(3), 323–326.

Caton, K. (2012). Taking the Moral Turn in Tourism Studies. *Annals of Tourism Research*, 39(4), 1906–1928.

Clifford, J. (1997). *Routes: Travel and Translation in the Late Twentieth Century*. Boston: Harvard University Press.

Coles, T., and Hall, C. M. (2006). Editorial: The Geography of Tourism is Dead. Long Live Geographies of Tourism and Mobility. *Current Issues in Tourism*, 9(4–5), 289–292.

Duke-Williams, O. (2009). The Geographies of Student Migration in the UK. *Environment and Planning A*, 41(8), 1826–1848.

Edensor, T. (2007). Mundane Mobilities, Performances and Spaces of Tourism, *Social & Cultural Geography*, 8(2), 201–215.

Fennell, D. (2013). The Ethics of Excellence in Tourism Research. *Journal of Travel Research*, 52(4), 417–425.

Franklin, A. (2003). *Tourism: An Introduction*. London: Sage.

Franklin, A., and Crang, M. (2001). The Trouble with Tourism and Travel Theory? *Tourist Studies*, 1(1), 5–22.

Hall, C. M. (2004). Reflexivity and Tourism Research. In J. Phillimore and L. Goodson (eds.), *Qualitative Research in Tourism: Ontologies, Epistemologies, Methodologies*, pp. 137–155. London: Routledge.

Hall, C. M., Timothy, D., and Duval, D. (2003). Security and Tourism: Towards a New Understanding? In C. M. Hall, D. Timothy and D. Duval (eds.), *Safety and Security in Tourism: Relationships, Management and Marketing*. New York: The Haworth Press.

Hannam, K. (2009). The End of Tourism? Nomadology and the Mobilities Paradigm. In J. Tribe (ed.), *Philosophical Issues in Tourism*. Clevedon: Channel View.

Hannam, K., and Knox, D. (2010). *Understanding Tourism: A Critical Introduction*. London: Sage.

Hannam, K., Sheller, M., and Urry, J. (2006). Mobilities, Immobilities and Moorings. *Mobilities*, 1(1), 1–22.

Holdsworth, C. (2009). 'Going Away to Uni': Mobility, Modernity, and Independence of English Higher Education Students. *Environment and Planning A*, 41(8), 1849–1864.

Hughes, S. (2011). LSE Criticised for Links with Gaddafi Regime in Libya. BBC News Online. Available online: http://www.bbc.co.uk/news/education-15966132 Accessed 16th September 2013.

McPherson, M., and Schapiro, M. (2010). Moral Reasoning and Higher Education Policy. *Forum Futures*. Available online: http://net.educause.edu/ir/library/pdf/ff1006s.pdf Accessed 22nd October 2013.

Moore, M. (2007). Gadaffi's Son Leads Fight to Woo Eco-tourists. *The Telegraph*, 11th September 2007. Available online: http://www.telegraph.co.uk/news/worldnews/1562811/Gadaffis-son-leads-fight-to-woo-eco-tourists.html Accessed 17th September 2013.

Mostafanezhad, M. (2013a). The Geography of Compassion in Volunteer Tourism. *Tourism Geographies*, 15(2), 318–337.

Mostafanezhad, M. (2013b). Locating the Tourist in Volunteer Tourism. *Current Issues in Tourism*, DOI: 10.1080/13683500.2013.793301.

Riley, R., and Love, L. (2000). The State of Qualitative Tourism Research. *Annals of Tourism Research*, 27(1), 164–187.

Sheller, M., and Urry, J. (eds.) (2004). *Tourism Mobilities: Places to Play, Places in Play*. London: Routledge.

Sidaway, J. (1992). In Other Worlds: On the Politics of Research by 'First World' Geographers in the 'Third World'. *Area*, 24(4), 403–408.

Tribe, J. (2003). The RAE-ification of Tourism Research in the UK. *International Journal of Tourism Research*, 5(3), 225–234.

Williams, P., Stewart, K., and Larsen, D. (2012). Toward an Agenda of High-Priority Tourism Research. *Journal of Travel Research*, 51(1), 3–11.

Xu, H., Bao, J., and Su, B. (2012). Planning Sponsored Tourism Research. In C. Hsu and W. Gartner (eds.), *The Routledge Handbook of Tourism Research*, pp. 159–170. London: Routledge.

Index